PENGUIN BOOK

The Practical
AUSTRALIAN
GARDENER

Peter Cundall was born in Manchester in 1927 and came to Australia in 1950. He has been gardening since he was a child, and worked for more than thirty years as a professional landscaper. After being awarded a Churchill Fellowship in 1974, he travelled the world studying landscaping, design and organic methods. He writes gardening columns for several newspapers and magazines, and since 1990 has been the presenter of ABC TV's popular *Gardening Australia* program. Peter Cundall lives on a self-sufficient property in Tasmania with his wife Tina. He has seven sons.

ALSO BY PETER CUNDALL

Pete's Mailbag: Original Tips and Ideas from Australian Gardeners
Peter Cundall's Year-Round Gardening

The Practical
AUSTRALIAN
GARDENER

Seasonal Tasks Using Sensible Organic Methods

Peter Cundall

PENGUIN BOOKS

*To my greatest friend, my wife Tina, for her tranquillity,
tolerance, understanding and support*

PENGUIN BOOKS

Published by the Penguin Group
Penguin Group (Australia)
250 Camberwell Road, Camberwell, Victoria 3124, Australia
(a division of Pearson Australia Group Pty Ltd)
Penguin Group (USA) Inc.
375 Hudson Street, New York, New York 10014, USA
Penguin Group (Canada)
90 Eglinton Avenue East, Suite 700, Toronto, Canada ON M4P 2Y3
(a division of Pearson Penguin Canada Inc.)
Penguin Books Ltd
80 Strand, London WC2R 0RL England
Penguin Ireland
25 St Stephen's Green, Dublin 2, Ireland
(a division of Penguin Books Ltd)
Penguin Books India Pvt Ltd
11 Community Centre, Panchsheel Park, New Delhi – 110 017, India
Penguin Group (NZ)
67 Apollo Drive, Rosedale, North Shore 0632, New Zealand
(a division of Pearson New Zealand Ltd)
Penguin Books (South Africa) (Pty) Ltd
24 Sturdee Avenue, Rosebank, Johannesburg 2196, South Africa

Penguin Books Ltd, Registered Offices: 80 Strand, London, WC2R 0RL, England

First published by McPhee Gribble 1989
Published by Penguin Books Australia Ltd, 1990
This edition published by Penguin Group (Australia), 2007

19 18 17 16 15 14 13 12

Copyright © Peter Cundall 1989
Illustrations © Cathy Larsen 1989
Front cover author photograph courtesy *Gardening Australia*; other front cover photographs courtesy
Getty Images and photolibrary.com; back cover photograph by Allan Moult

The moral right of the author has been asserted

All rights reserved. Without limiting the rights under copyright reserved above, no part of this
publication may be reproduced, stored in or introduced into a retrieval system, or transmitted,
in any form or by any means (electronic, mechanical, photocopying, recording or otherwise), without
the prior written permission of both the copyright owner and the above publisher of this book.

Cover design by Miriam Rosenbloom © Penguin Group (Australia)
Text design by Cathy Larsen © Penguin Group (Australia)
Typeset in Bembo by Meredith Typesetters, Melbourne
Printed and bound in China by Bookbuilders

National Library of Australia
Cataloguing-in-Publication data:

Cundall, Peter 1927– .
The practical Australian gardener: seasonal tasks using sensible organic methods.
Includes index.

ISBN: 978 0 14 011831 5.

1. Gardening – Australia. I. Title.

635.0994

www.penguin.com.au

CONTENTS

How to Use This Book *1*

JANUARY
Guide to Action *3*

First Week
Leaving Houseplants and Gardens Behind *4* ❧ Summer Lawn Care *6*

Second Week
Early Pruning *7* ❧ Citrus – Summer Care *8* ❧ Caring for Tub Plants *8*

Third Week
Summer Pest Control *10*

Last Week
Dry Weather Planting *12* ❧ Organic Growing *13*

FEBRUARY
Guide to Action *15*

First Week
Taking Cuttings *16* ❧ Disease Control *17*

Second Week
Winter and Spring Vegetables *19* ❧ Hot Weather Plant Care *20*

Third Week
Creating a Garden Pool *21* ❧ Landscaping Shady Places *23*

Last Week
Houseplants *25*

MARCH
Guide to Action *27*

First Week
Composting *28* ❧ Irises *30* ❧ Bulbs *31*

Second Week
Harvesting *32* ❧ Lawn Making *33* ❧ Herbs *35*

Third Week
Products from the Sea *37* ❧ Late Vegetables *38* ❧ Feeding the Soil *39*

Last Week
Hedges *40*   More Vegetables for Spring *41* ❧ Garden Design *43*

APRIL

Guide to Action *45*

First Week
Sweetening the Soil with Lime *46* ❧ Pruning the Easy-bleeders *47* ❧
Herbaceous and Perennial Plants *48*

Second Week
Peaches and Nectarines Through the Season *49* ❧
Transplanting Evergreens *50* ❧ Draining the Soil *52*

Third Week
Vegetable Harvesting *52* ❧ Pruning Berryfruit Bushes *53* ❧
Autumn Jobs *55*

Last Week
Choosing the Best Fruit and Nuts *56* ❧ Growing Strawberries *58* ❧
Seeds Under Cover Now – Early Vegetables Later *59*

MAY

Guide to Action *61*

First Week
Which Rose? *62* ❧ Essential Jobs at a Crucial Time *63* ❧
Autumn Pest Control Without Poisons *63*

Second Week
Diagnosis of Plant Disorders *65* ❧
Correcting Mineral Deficiencies in Your Soil *66*

Third Week
Moss in the Garden – How to Eliminate it, or Use It *68* ❧
Which Pruning Tool for What? *69* ❧ Steep Banks *71*

Last Week
Australian Plants Play a Special Role *72* ❧ Selecting the Best
Deciduous Plants *73* ❧ Protecting the Soil with Mulch *75* ❧
Simple Rose Pruning *76*

JUNE

Guide to Action *79*

First Week
Pruning Fruit Trees and Bushes *80* ❧ Reorganizing the
Winter Garden *81* ❧ Wind Damage *83*

Second Week
Fallen Leaves *84* ❧ Ornamental Trees *84*

Third Week
Selecting Fruit Trees *85* ❧ Planting in Containers *86* ❧
Planting Deciduous Trees and Shrubs *88*

Last Week
- The Beautiful Way to Suppress Weeds – Groundcovers 89
- Protection from Possums, Dogs and Cats 90

JULY
Guide to Action 93

First Week
- Winter Jobs 94 • Plants for Winter Colour 95
- How to Raise Seedlings 96

Second Week
- Foliage Plants for a Year-round Display 98
- Growing Onions and Garlic 99 • Creating a Rock Garden 101

Third Week
- What are Companion Plants For? 103
- All About the Acid-lovers 104 • Planting for Privacy 105

Last Week
- Landscaping Before the House is Built 107 • Moving Plants Around 108 • A Scented Garden Throughout the Year 109
- Which Fertilizer is Best? 111

AUGUST
Guide to Action 113

First Week
- Leafcurl in Peach and Nectarine Trees 114 • Jobs in the Orchard 115
- Plant Vegetables! 115 • More on Australian Plants 116

Second Week
- The Dreaded Oxalis Weed Moves In 118 • How to Obtain Massive Yields of Peas 119 • Jobs for the Warmer Weather 120

Third Week
- Towards Self-sufficiency on a Typical Home Site 121
- Growing Juicy Carrots 122 • No-dig Potato Gardening 123
- Gladioli and Dahlias 125

Last Week
- Harlequin Bugs and Scale Insects 125 • Pruning Neglected Lemon Trees 127 • Prune Passionfruits Too 128
- Hard-surface Landscaping – Patios and Paths 128

SEPTEMBER
Guide to Action 131

First Week
- Crop Rotation 133 • Turning Clay into Friable Soil 134
- Spring Lawn Care 136

Second Week
   More on Houseplants *137* ❦ Some Spring Jobs *139* ❦ Magnolias *141*
Third Week
   Choosing the Best Lemon Tree for Your Garden *142* ❦
   Some Citrus Problems *143* ❦ When Trees Become Too Big *144*
Last Week:
   Traditional Potato Planting *145* ❦ Let's Mulch Against a Possible
   Dry Summer *146* ❦ Spring Pruning *147*

OCTOBER
   Guide to Action *149*
First Week
   All About Pumpkins and Winter Squashes *151* ❦ How to Make
   Tomato Plants Yield Earlier and Better *153* ❦ A Vegetable Planting
   Guide for Nutritious Summer Eating *155*
Second Week
   Dividing Dahlia Clumps *156* ❦ Delphiniums, Canterbury Bells
   and Chrysanthemums *158* ❦ Dealing Ruthlessly with Pests *158*
Third Week
   Germinating Difficult Seed *160* ❦ The Joys of Sweetcorn *161* ❦
   Putting New Life into Sandy Soils *162*
Last Week
   Beware of These Toxic Plants *163* ❦ Bush and Climbing Beans *164*

NOVEMBER
   Guide to Action *167*
First Week
   Why Remove Spent Flower Heads? *169* ❦ Watering Techniques *170* ❦
   Landscaping with Stone Walls *171*
Second Week
   A Blaze of Summer Colour with Annuals *173* ❦
   Cunning, Safe Ways of Dealing with Pests *174*
Third Week
   Ornamental Vegetables *175* ❦
   Replacing Part of a Lawn with Flowers *177*
Last Week
   More on Safe Pest and Disease Control *178* ❦ Vertical Gardens and
   Retaining Walls *179* ❦ End-of-the-month Jobs *181*

DECEMBER
   Guide to Action *183*
First Week
   Essential Summer Jobs *185* ❦ Build an Outside Living Area *186* ❦

An Early Morning Stroll in the Garden *188*

Second Week

Easy-care Gardens *189* ❦ Foliar Feeding *190* ❦
Greenhouses *191* ❦ Watch Those Houseplants *192*

Third Week

Growing a Windbreak *193* ❦ Plants Make Unforgettable Gifts *194*

Last Week

Seaside Gardening *196* ❦ Raising Annual Seedlings *197* ❦
Time to Lift Bulbs *198*

Appendix *201*

Bordeaux Mixture ❦ Burgundy Mixture ❦ Lawn Sand ❦
Cross-pollination of Fruit Trees for Full Crops

Index *203*

(Colour plates face pages 70, 118 and 166)

HOW TO USE THIS BOOK

There is no beginning or end to this book. You can open it anywhere you like to start reading, but the best place is the one that corresponds with the time of the year. All you have to do is open it there and you are on your way through a week by week guide to action for the year ahead.

Each month starts with a general list of plants which can be sown or planted and the most important gardening jobs for that time. This is followed by more detailed descriptions of gardening practices. To make things easier for you, some of the more important descriptions, such as recipes and pest or disease control measures, have been repeated, especially where similar tasks have to be carried out through the year.

The information is based on my own experience as a practical gardener and landscaper of more than fifty years. This experience includes mistakes I have made and learned from; experiments I have carried out; successes, failures, accidental discoveries and, above all knowledge gained from other people. Every day of my life I learn something new about gardening.

All the planting, sowing and work schedules in this book have to be flexible. After all, ours is a big country with a wide range of climatic conditions from wet or dry tropical, to the relative cool of southern Australia and New Zealand. However, the timing of sowing or planting in the book would tend to suit people who live in the temperate and cooler regions of Australasia, because that's where most of us live.

Gardening practices are the same everywhere. It is the actual plants growth and the timing of sowing, planting, pruning, spraying and propagating which differs according to the climate. So, wherever you live, be prepared to make some adjustments to what you read, in order to fit the information into your local climatic conditions.

If you want some specific information, I urge you to use the index.

This book is also an attempt to answer in more detail, many questions which I have been regularly asked on the television and radio gardening programmes I have been making with the ABC over the last twenty years, or through the weekly gardening columns I write for various newspapers.

What most home gardeners want are simple, direct and practical solutions to their problems and clear answers to their questions.

What to plant and when? What grows best in different areas and conditions? How can we deal with heavy clay, sandy soil or impoverished land? How can exhausted soil be made fertile? What are the alternatives to harsh chemical fertilizers? How can difficult sites be successfully landscaped? How can our plants be protected against drought, pests, diseases, animals or destructive winds? What's the difference between orthodox and organic gardening? How can gardening be made easy and safe?

These days, more and more people are wanting to know about growing fruit and vegetables without poisons or disruptive chemicals. The trend is towards more intelligent, safer growing methods which improve soil fertility by means of natural fertilizers, compost, companion planting and soil conditioners. A movement towards the conservation of balanced, living soils – our most precious resource. I describe and advocate organic growing techniques not because of their current popularity, but because I believe in them and they work.

Peter Cundall
Rosevears, Tasmania

JANUARY
GUIDE TO ACTION

Ornamental Garden

Lift spring bulbs as foliage goes yellow. Daffodils and jonquils may remain undisturbed, unless overcrowded. Raise mower blades. Prune roses to remove spent blooms, and any leaves showing black spot disease. Spray with Mancozeb if needed. Snap off withered flower trusses from rhododendron and lilac plants. In the flower garden sow or plant: achillea, acrolinium, ageratum, alyssum, antirrhinum, aquilegia, arctotis, aster, balsam, bellis, calendula, Canterbury bells, carnation, celosia, chrysanthemum, cineraria, cleome, cornflower, cosmos, dahlia, delphinium, dianthus, foxglove, freesia, geum, gypsophila, helichrysum, hollyhock, lilium, linaria, lobelia, lupin, lychnis, African marigold, myosotis, nasturtium, nemesia, ornamental kale, pansy, lathyrus, penstemon, petunia, phlox, polyanthus, Iceland poppy, oriental poppy, portulacca, primula, salvia, scabiosa, shasta daisy, statice, stock, sunflower, sweetpea, sweet William, verbena, viola, Virginian stock, wallflower and zinnia.

Vegetable Garden

Clear broad bean and pea trash to prepare soil for winter brassicas. Mulch tomatoes and sweetcorn. Practise deep watering. Apply liquid manure or blood and bone to all parts of vegetable garden and water in. Sow or plant: french and climbing beans, beetroot, broccoli, Brussels sprouts, cabbage, Chinese cabbage, capsicum, carrot, cauliflower, celery, celeriac, cress, cucumber, eggplant, kohlrabi, leek, lettuce, marrow, melon, spring onion, parsley, parsnip, pumpkin, radish, salsify, swede, silverbeet, turnip, sweetcorn and tomato.

Fruit Garden

Pear and cherry slug is now attacking pear, plum, cherry, almond, hawthorn, rowan and even peach trees. Pyrethrum with a dash of Clensel will devastate these pests relatively safely. Codlin moth grubs will continue to hatch unless controlled by an ovicide such as one part of white oil to fifty of water, sprayed on to all parts of the canopies of apples, pears and quinces. Prune raspberry, currant, bramble and gooseberry bushes.

Houseplants

Withdraw vulnerable foliage plants from sunny windows. Mist leaves, especially of ferns, several times daily in hot dry weather. African violets, palms and other lovers of moist, humid conditions can be placed on trays or saucers of wet pebbles. Greenhouses should be damped down with plenty of water, several times daily if necessary, and all ventilators and doors left open on hot days.

JANUARY: FIRST WEEK

Leaving Houseplants and Gardens Behind

The reason houseplants suffer more at this time of the year is that they are often left to try and cope, when people go away for the holiday break. Unlike plants in the garden, houseplants are totally dependent upon us for their basic needs of water and nutrients. Two or three weeks' neglect, at this time of the year, is enough to cause the death or stunting of many houseplants.

It is unnecessary, because a few simple precautions, taken before leaving home, will safeguard plants against dehydration at a time when they are most vulnerable.

Apart from cacti and succulents, which seem to thrive upon mild neglect, move all plants away from the windows, water them thoroughly, allow them to drain then place them in a group in a shaded room. A sheet of plastic doubled over and overlaid with cardboard will protect carpets. If the plants have been carefully watered, they will remain in a moist condition for about a week.

Longer periods of absence demand special precautions. The bathroom is an ideal place to store plants, with the most vulnerable ones in the bath. If the base of the bath is covered with wads of saturated newspapers, the plants can be placed close together on top of this layer. The best way of doing this is to spread the newspapers, place the plants and then partly fill the bath, so the water comes about half-way up the sides of the smallest pots. After half an hour, take out the plug to drain fully. Never be tempted to keep the plug in during your absence. If you have an even slightly dripping tap, you could return to a disaster with water everywhere and a bathful of drowned houseplants.

Sometimes, in hot districts, it pays to surround or pack each container with lots of wet, pulpy newsprint, with generous amounts covering the surface of the potting-soil. This will reduce evaporation while providing a good source of rising humidity.

Afterwards, the great mass of paper can be used outside, either in the vegetable garden or mixed with lawn clippings to rot into a good source of organic matter.

Individual houseplants can be protected against drying-out by enclosing the entire plant and container in a large plastic bag and closing the top after watering. In a shady place, this will help retain moisture for up to three weeks, depending upon temperature. It is fatal to leave such plastic-enclosed plants anywhere the sunlight will strike, even for a few minutes daily. The intense, steamy heat generated can be enough to cook most plants to death.

Large plants, especially climbers, can be virtually impossible to move without damaging them. However, the surface of the potting soil can be covered with wet newsprint after watering, and an additional sheet of slotted plastic laid over the top to seal in the moisture. The entire container can be enclosed in a plastic bag or sheet, to leave the main stem poking through.

One of the most effective means of keeping the roots of a large plant moist over two or three weeks, is a simple syphoning method. A large bucketful of water placed on a chair or table, so that it is a little higher than the top of the container, can be an excellent source of slowly released moisture, if a strip of absorbent material is used to connect the two. A short length of rope or a twisted piece of cotton material, well wetted and sheathed in plastic bags, will slowly transfer the water from the bucket to the potting-soil, taking up to three weeks. The end of the wick within the bucket should be weighed down and the other end slightly buried beneath the soil and covered with plastic sheeting.

In the garden the plants which are at risk include rhododendrons, ericas, camellias, daphnes, azaleas, citruses, pierises, boronias, small or miniature conifers and recently-planted trees or shrubs. All these have shallow roots, or have not yet formed a searching root-stytem. While a deep, heavy watering will sustain them for about ten days, it is not enough for three weeks or more. The answer is lots of water, followed by thick mulching, then more water to saturate the mulch.

> In the flower garden plant: African marigold, ageratum, alyssum, amaranthus, aquilegia, arctotis, aster, aubrietea, balsam, bellis, campanula, carnation, celosia, chrysanthemum, cleome, cosmos, dahlia, delphinium, dianthus, gazania, gaillardia, geranium, gypsophila, helichrysum, larkspur, Livingstone daisy, lobelia, lupin, myosotis, nasturtium, penstemon, petunia, phlox, rudbeckia, salvia, scabiosa, statice, verbena, vinca, wallflower and zinnia.

Any material can be used which will reduce surface evaporation, even if it looks a little messy. Christmas wrapping, flattened cardboard boxes, old bags, newspapers, plastic sheeting or old clothing, can be spread over the root-zones of vulnerable plants, tucked in around the stems, then covered with moist lawn clippings and wilted weeds.

If you can stand the untidy appearance, this treatment will protect such plants for many weeks, provided the initial heavy watering is given.

Young trees, especially deciduous species, can be seriously stunted by competitive weeds and long grass. Each time it rains, or water is applied, the grass-weeds seize it first. The sight of a struggling little tree, surrounded by vigorous grass-weed is a common one to returning holidaymakers. A hard slashing-back of the weeds, leaving them to lie, is a great help. However, if a thick layer of wet straw is spread directly on top of the weeds, without cutting them, it will not only smother them, but their decayed remains will enrich the mulch.

You'll be able to relax and enjoy your holidays away from home much better with the knowledge that your most precious plants will still be in good condition when you return.

Summer Lawn Care

A good, well-fed, bright green lawn will make any garden look good. At this time of the year most lawns, even the neglected ones, have that nice, well-cared for appearance, because the dry, destructive heat of the summer has not arrived yet.

Even so, of all the times in the year, now is the most crucial when it comes to lawn care. The first flush of spring growth is slowing down and much of the plant food in the soil is becoming exhausted. The effect of this starvation won't show until later, and then it will be difficult to make up the loss.

So, the way the lawns are treated now, how they are fed, cut and generally maintained, will determine how good they are going to look in future.

How are lawns best fed?

First, they must be moist. If fertilizers are applied to drying lawns, damage will occur. The grass will be burnt, and the whole lawn will receive a serious setback. Always water the lawn very thoroughly, so that the soil gets a good, deep soaking, preferably the day before fertilizing.

The best fertilizers are the slow-acting ones, because they gradually sink down into the soil over many weeks, and entice the grass roots to follow them down into new areas of growth, deeply enough to resist the drying effects of wind and sun. I have always used blood and bone with added potash to ensure that the lawns remained green and healthy throughout the summer.

Here is a mix, suitable for most lawns in Australia: ten parts of blood and bone, one part of sulphate of potash, and ten parts of ordinary sand. Mix well together in a dry state and broadcast directly over the lawn's surface at the rate of eighty grams (a good generous handful) for every square metre. The sand is merely a means of adding bulk, making the mix easier to handle and distribution more accurate, but it is not essential. Should you use the mix without including the sand, the rate of application is reduced to about forty grams per square (a tight fistful).

As soon as the fertilizers have been applied, the lawn must be watered again in order to wash any residue from the grass leaves and settle it down between them.

Cutting lawns from now onwards must be carried out so that the grass is much longer. The mower blades must be raised so that they are about forty millimetres above the soil level. The depth to which the roots of the grass can delve is determined by the amount of grass leaf exposed to the sun. Short grass means shallow roots, and vulnerability to even short periods without rain. Longer grass still looks short, because it is evenly cut, but has a much deeper root system, and therefore remains greener during the driest conditions.

Watering the lawn must be done carefully from this month. Once the soil has become dry, it is hard for water to penetrate. It tends to run away, over the surface. This is particularly true if the lawn is on a slope. It is important to remember that once irrigation water has started to run like this, the taps must be turned off. Otherwise, the evenness of the lawn will be damaged, and water wasted. Short bursts of watering will really get down below the roots and soak the subsoil, and when this happens, subsequent waterings are able to penetrate.

So don't allow your lawn to dry out now, no matter how green it appears.

The most unsightly problems effecting lawns are the flatweeds. These can evade the blades of the mower by forming ground-hugging leaves. They can compete effectively against the lawn grasses and spoil the general appearance of the turf.

To eliminate these flatweeds, handlifting, using a special short-tine fork, can be a certain and effective way of cleaning up a sparsely infested area. 'Spot' weeding, using a wand impregnated with a selective or total weedkiller, is a very easy way to destroy lawn weeds, and a surprisingly large area can be covered in a short time. I tend to favour the old-fashioned, safe lawn sand, which is nothing more than a mixture of sulphate of ammonia (one part) and sand (two parts) with added sulphate of iron (half of a part). This is a rough mix which is easy to remember and which deals effectively with a wide range of broadleaved weeds. For really heavy infestations of dandelions, plantain, daisies, docks and other persistent weeds, you can use a stronger mix of sulphate of ammonia (two and a half parts), sulphate of iron (half of a part) and sand (three parts).

Don't forget, with these lawn sands, dry mixing is essential, and after broadcasting over the infested lawns, it is not necessary to water it in.

So if you want an attractive lawn all round the year, relatively free from most weeds, now is the time to get weaving.

JANUARY: SECOND WEEK

Early Pruning

Even though many of us are supposed to be on holiday, there are plenty of jobs to be done in the garden. It is a far more intelligent way to get fit, and get rid of the inevitable accumulation of festive lard, than mindlessly jogging through the snoozing suburbs every morning.

One of the first easy jobs is to prune the berryfruit plants. Raspberry, loganberry, youngberry and mammothberry bushes are best pruned now, as berry-picking is completed. It is a simple but essential task. Just cut all canes which bore fruit to the ground and retie the young, vigorous new ones in a loose bundle and secure them to a wire or trellis. Make sure all pruned pieces are taken away and either burned, or dumped on the tip.

Blackcurrants will also benefit from a good pruning now. Cut off, to within a few centimetres of the ground, all old, thick, dark-coloured branches, and retain the light green new ones. This summer pruning is far more valuable than leaving it to be done in the winter. It helps to control diseases, while removing the dragging, dead weight of old, exhausted and non-productive wood.

Mulching around all berryfruit plants with old straw, preferably mixed with plenty of animal manure, then deeply watering the entire bed, will guarantee an outstanding yield next season.

The other pruning jobs concern those trees and shrubs which have started to become a problem because of their sheer size. Summer pruning or lopping prevents the plant storing reserves of food prior to winter. As a result, the frightening eruption of new growth which often occurs in spring, following winter pruning, does not happen.

This is also the best time of the year to kill problem trees such as poplars and willows. These plants can cause some very expensive damage to your own or, worse still, to your neighbour's property. The roots of greedy trees such as these seem to have the ability to block a sewerage system or any drain, from fifty metres away or more. Unfortunately cutting down poplar trees will only make the situation worse, because a forest of deadly, active suckers will spring up in their places. This means poisons need to be used. Roundup and kerosene are less toxic than other tree killers available. Once the tree has been killed, it may be cut down without any further problems.

There are two ways of applying a tree killer. One is to spray it on to the leaves. This can be quite difficult, because of the danger that the spray will drift on to your or your neighbour's plants, causing terrible damage. In addition, it is very hard to squirt a good covering of poison over a large tree.

The safer method is to cut a ring around the trunk of the tree to be killed. The cut should go deeply into the bark, angled downwards so that a circular canal is formed around and into the trunk. This is filled with a mixture of tree-killer poison and water, and kept topped up for a few days. Some people bind a piece of sacking around the tree, over the filled canal, to help reduce evaporation. There are several types of tree-poison available from garden centres, and they work best while the tree is at its most vigorous, which is right now.

The fundamental rule is to make sure that every safety precaution is taken. Protective clothing, including gloves, face mask and long-sleeved shirts, is essential. It is very dangerous to spill any of the mixture on to the bare skin but infinitely worse when the undiluted fluid comes into contact with unprotected areas. Above all, read the instructions on the container, and follow them implicitly. Never make the mistake of adding a bit extra to make the brew a little stronger. You could make it fail.

Citrus – Summer Care

Lemons and other citrus trees need special treatment at this time of the year. Their demands for moisture and food must be satisfied, otherwise the health of these trees will suffer and diseases will strike. Fruit yield too will improve dramatically if the right treatment is given now.

Their most significant need is plenty of water. The roots are now starting to take in more water as the leaves give off vapour in the long, hot days.

So, if you love your lemon tree, give it a New Year present of a deep soaking, especially around the roots. Repeat this every week or so for even better results.

Then feed the tree, using slow-acting fertilizer, such as blood and bone. This fertilizer is best applied at the rate of forty grams per square metre, around the trunk and below the drip line (the outer edges of the branches). Water again to wash it in. Prune off any dead or weak, twiggy growth. Scale problems, which show up as masses of sooty mould on the upper surfaces of the leaves and part of the fruit, can be easily dealt with by spraying the canopy with diluted white oil emulsion.

Black citrus aphids are about and can easily be seen in their hundreds, clustered all over the young, growing tips of the branches. Pyrethrum will kill these pests instantly, without being poisonous to us, but be ready to apply another dose in about ten days, to finish them off.

Newly-planted citrus trees should not be allowed to bear fruit for the first two or three years, so if you have such a plant, be strong willed and cut off all fruits and blossoms, as they form. This will ensure that all the energy will flow into the structure of the tree, creating a good, powerful framework for heavy crops later on.

Caring For Tub Plants

Some plants are particularly vulnerable to drying out and either die, or become so badly checked in their growth, that it can sometimes take several seasons for full recovery to take place.

The plants most in jeopardy are the ones being grown in containers. Tub plants, even out in the open, are only slightly affected by the heaviest rainfall because such a minute amount of water falls within the confines of the container.

Such plants must be watered twice daily during the present warm weather unless they are cacti or succulents. Their response will be excellent, providing the water is allowed to penetrate the rootball.

This, in fact, is the snag. You see, most potting mixes contain a large proportion of peat, not to provide food, but to act as a kind of sponge. This is all very lovely while the mix is still moist, but when drying out occurs, things can get a bit complicated. The entire potting medium shrinks quite markedly when it loses its moisture and becomes surprisingly resistant to absorbing water. If you have ever seen a really dry cow-pat, which will float for weeks on the water in a liquid-manure drum, you will understand what I mean.

When attempts are made to water dried-out tub plants, it is easy to imagine that your efforts are working because within a minute or so water begins to trickle out of the holes at the bottom. But the roots remain dry as the water runs down the outside of the rootball.

So how is the watering to be carried out correctly?

First, don't let drying out occur, then the problem can't arise.

If it does happen, the wetting process must take place fairly slowly. The obvious way to get things normal again is to leave the entire container soaking in water, either in a bigger tub, or even by dropping the lot into the fishpond if you have one. A good soak for an hour or so will do the trick and the main aim from then onwards is to make sure that everything remains moist.

The other types of plants which tend to dry out sneakily around their roots are those in hanging baskets. Usually, a daily watering from a long-spouted can, or even an old teapot, is enough. But once again, when the soil gets too dry, you can finish up with dripping baskets which are dry in their interior. The best way of re-wetting them is to fill a large bucket to the brim with water, unhook the basket and sit the base of it in the top of the bucket. The water will then gradually soak upwards. Take the basket out after an hour and allow it to drain.

The greatest of all errors is to try and apply any fertilizers to plants while the soil around them is dry. Such an assault on the roots by undiluted fertilizers can cause the death of shallow-rooted plants or, at least, serious fertilizer burn. This will cause leaves to drop off, or wither from their tips. However, once adequate water has been supplied, fertilizers, especially in a liquid form for container plants, can be safely used.

It is a good time of the year for foliar feeding. It is only during the last thirty years or so that the enormous benefits of this method of feeding plants has been fully realized. The main substances utilized by plants through their leaves are the trace elements. These are contained in many of the seaweed concentrates now on the market, which are applied in a very diluted form. I usually pour about two tablespoonsful into a large bucket, then spray this mixture directly on to the leaves of various plants. The slight smell of seaweed even seems to help to keep certain insect pests at bay for a day or two.

> Keep all flowering plants 'dead-headed' to make sure the blooms keep coming. Pinch out the growing tips of chrysanthemums. Remove the seed pods of any plant from which no seed is required for later sowing.

The best time of the day to carry out a foliar feeding programme is early in the morning. This allows the plant to absorb the solution fully, and, if the day is a little dull, all the better.

JANUARY: THIRD WEEK

Summer Pest Control

Even a brief glimpse of something creeping, crawling or sliding around the garden is enough to cause some people to don protective clothes, gloves and mask so that, armed with spray equipment, they can kill everything that moves, using the most lethal concoctions they can get their gloves on.

The tragedy is, it is all so unnecessary. The overwhelming majority of insects are either beneficial or part of the normal balance of things. A garden without insects is a lifeless garden.

However, even in the most balanced organic garden, pests can suddenly and inexplicably multiply, causing serious damage to plants. Then something needs to be done and it's possible to control even the most destructive insects and other pests without using poisons.

Aphids are also known as greenfly or plant lice. They suck sap, concentrating upon young growing shoots, and cause distorted leaves and stunting. Their rate of breeding can easily keep pace with the growth of roses, peaches, sweet cherry or any other tree or shrub. Aphids are usually pinhead sized and have plump, squashy bodies. They are black, grey or green and can be covered with a protective wax or fluffy coat.

Sometimes, the first indication of their presence is a sooty mould or a sticky substance on the surface of leaves or an increase in the numbers of ants running over the plant. The mould is another organism, which, like the ants, feeds off the 'honeydew', or droppings of the aphids. A badly infested plant looks a mess.

One of the most effective, safe sprays is pyrethrum, a plant extract. It is a contact killer of aphids and many other insects, while being relatively harmless to humans and animals.

If the spray is squirted directly on to the colonies of aphids, especially in between the folds of infested leaves, most of them will be killed immediately, leaving beneficial insects unharmed.

Ladybirds and their larvae gobble up aphids like licorice allsorts. Unfortunately they don't seem to get started until much of the damage has been done.

Or try making your own anti-aphid weapon: boil three kilograms of rhubarb leaves in three litres of water for half an hour. Strain off the liquid. When cool (and with a little detergent added), it makes an excellent, safe aphid killer, especially on roses.

Ants can be a problem because they often have a special relationship with aphids and scale insects. They can also transport diseases from plant to plant. Once they have found their way inside a house, they rapidly occupy and relentlessly loot every food source which contains sugar. They appear to plunge into a feeding frenzy of such proportions that thousands die a glorious and delicious death in our jams, honeys and syrups.

One of the simplest means of controlling ants is to trace their nests, then place a small container holding one part each of icing sugar and borax mixed with enough water to make a sticky paste. Borax is toxic, so make sure children or animals cannot get at the mixture. It not only kills the ants, but their mates carry their bodies down into the nest as an extra source of food. Eventually the entire nest will be destroyed.

The most relentless of the leaf-munchers are the caterpillars. They also attack fruit and young shoots. Traditionally, derris has been used, but it is of little value on large caterpillars. These days, Dipel is safe and effective. It is a bacterial preparation which affects only caterpillars, first by causing them to stop feeding and finally by killing them.

Slugs and snails are night-feeding gluttons with expensive tastes. They disdainfully ignore even the most luxurious weeds and make a slime-line for every rare seedling, especially those which have taken considerable skill to raise. One snail can comfortably devastate an entire row before it slides away to hide before daybreak. There are several ways to control slugs and snails without using poisons. The midnight crunch method, carried out after dark with gumboots and a torch, satisfies some base, sadistic urge and is extraordinarily successful. If it has been raining that day, twenty minutes tramping around the garden will leave anyone with beady eyes, twitchy feet and several centimetres taller before the gumboots are sluiced.

The cheapest means of plant protection is a thick layer of sawdust around the vulnerable plants. Snails and slugs hate the stuff, mainly because it causes them to run out of juice, especially if the sawdust is fresh and green. Ash has the same effect.

The pear and cherry slug is an unpleasant looking little critter. Covered with a dark-brown, slimy substance, it is hard to see the shape of the grub inside. A little over a centimetre long, it clings to the upper leaf-surfaces on pear, cherry, almond, cherry-plum, hawthorn and rowan trees. It also attacks other stone fruit in a less devastating way. Feeding on the green tissue of leaves, it rapidly skeletonises them, leaving nothing but a fine network of veins. It is the larva of a sawfly and will drastically reduce the vigour of a tree, unless it is dealt with promptly.

The safe way of killing this pest is by using pyrethrum, broken down with water according to directions, but with a good dollop of Clensel included in each bucketful of the mix – roughly about two tablespoons. Sprayed on to the infested trees, this is an immediate contact killer of pear and cherry slug. Two or three sprays at weekly intervals will effectively destroy the main population of this destructive creature.

Borers can cause young trees to lose vigour and, in the case of fruit trees, fail to produce good yields. Peach, nectarine, plum and cherry are now under attack, as are some ornamentals such as silver birch. The evidence is seen, usually at the junction of a main branch, in the form of a mass of clinging, powdery wood-debris, often with a leaf attached. Apart from the wire-poking method of destruction a squirt of methylated spirits will do the trick.

Aphids can strike in the orchard as well as the flower garden. Apple trees often become infested with woolly aphids. These sap-sucking plant lice cover themselves with a whitish, cottonwool-like material and cluster in their thousands on the living bark of the upper branches. If only a small patch of them can be spotted, it is a simple matter to reach down for a handful of soil, to rub briskly into the cluster. Dabbing with methylated spirit-soaked cottonwool will also kill them.

Massive invasions of woolly aphids can be blasted off the tree with a hard jet of water and those which remain will have their protective 'wool' washed off, leaving them prey to birds or other predators. If a poison is preferred, the systemic Rogor will certainly fix them, but special precautions must be taken to protect yourself and anyone else in the vicinity.

The black cherry aphid is a messy pest, causing the foliage on leading shoots to become grossly distorted and form a dark mass of inwardly-cupped leaves. Within

> Beans of all kinds are bearing steadily now and they must be picked continually, even if they cannot be eaten straight away. The pods from climbing beans, such as scarlet runners, can be frozen much more successfully than French beans, because they retain their superior flavour. Golden butter beans are excellent to eat fresh but are lousy for freezing, they tend to go like wet rags.

this grotesque cluster hide thousands of the pinhead-sized aphids, making them difficult to get at. Fortunately, cherry trees are so vigorous they can easily cope with this horde, but fruiting ability is reduced. Even cutting off the infested branch tips is a help and, if this is followed by the pyrethrum-Clensel spray, the rest of them are soon cleaned up. Alternatively, poke the nozzle of the spraying syringe into each cluster and give a good squirt to contact-kill the insects.

JANUARY: LAST WEEK

Dry Weather Planting

There is a curious myth, which still persists, that the only time tree and shrub planting should be carried out is during the winter. The reality is, of course, that in temperate areas of Australia we can plant successfully all the year round.

The exceptions are the large, deciduous trees, roses, some perennials, bulbs and tubers. All these are usually planted in the cooler months. However, modern nursery techniques have been so refined that even these 'tricky' plants can be planted now when they have been grown in containers.

Certain precautions must be taken to guarantee success with summer planting. The most important is the immediate care of plants which have been just purchased. I often wonder how many homes have a collection of plants, slowly withering in their containers, sitting by the back door waiting for someone to find time to plant them. The same plants, had they remained in the care of the nursery, would have continued to grow and develop.

So, either postpone buying plants until you are able to find time to plant them, or give them the same treatment the nursery people are willing to give.

Newly-bought plants must always be placed out of the sun, which includes the most crucial period, in the car on the way back home.

I once saw a car, parked in the sun, with the back seat crammed with a huge selection of fairly expensive plants. Two hours later, almost every plant had completely collapsed in the fierce heat, an almost total loss. I always put plants on the floor or in the boot (providing the leaves don't touch the hot lid), and open the windows, or the boot, just enough to let any overheated air flow out.

Back home, the first act is to water every container, and place them in the shade. At this time of the year, all container plants must be watered twice daily while they wait to be planted out. It is best to wait for a still and overcast day.

The actual planting operations too, need to be carried out in a special way. It is little use digging a hole in dry soil, then planting even a well-watered plant into it.

The surrounding soil acts like blotting paper, and within an hour or so, will have sucked out all moisture from the rootball. The best method is to dig the hole, fill it to the brim with water, let it gradually soak away, then fill it once more. The pile of excavated soil should also be well wetted, although this is much more difficult. If I am putting in a number of plants, I usually dig the holes and fill them with water as I go, so that by the time I have done several, the first lot of water has soaked away.

The more water that penetrates the adjacent, dry soil, the more secure the plant will be. In really dry areas, particularly those with a sandy soil, it pays to leave a shallow, saucer-shaped depression around the base of the plant, to contain extra water. Mulching with stones, straw, newspaper, or even old pieces of lino, will seal in the moisture, and the plants will respond accordingly with massive growth, at this time.

> The best way to get tomatoes with the best flavour, is to select the fruit just as the base turns a distinct pink. If they are then stored inside, away from the windowsill, they will ripen rapidly, with an exquisite flavour. Remember, tomatoes which are ripened on the bush, in hot sun, have much of the flavour destroyed.

Organic Growing

Without question, the best and healthiest form of gardening is the organic method. To grow a wide range of vegetables, fruit, nuts and ornamental plants, without using poisons or harsh, unnatural chemicals, is fast becoming a way of life for an increasing number of people.

Gardening feels natural. It provides the great satisfaction of creating something good, by working the soil. If the tasks become too strenuous, as especially digging can, you may simply stop working for a while, then begin again. Compare this to the ritualized masochism of jogging.

This is probably why people who do plenty of gardening are not only healthier but are also generally relaxed types with a reputation for living to a ripe old age.

Without question, the best and healthiest form of gardening is the organic method. To grow a wide range of vegetables, fruit, nuts and ornamental plants, without using poisons or harsh, unnatural chemicals, is fast becoming a way of life for an increasing number of people.

Organic growing methods mean ensuring the absence of unnatural or toxic substances in the soil and the plants we eat. Many people say that with organically grown produce they suddenly discover their taste buds and for the first time begin to appreciate the flavours of real food.

However, the question always arises, whenever people are first introduced to the ideas of organic growing: 'What about insect pests and diseases on our fruit and vegetables, and how can we get rid of weeds without poisons?'

The answer will not please those who want perfect, unblemished fruit or vegetables. There is nothing wrong with a few spots or insect holes in our produce. It is only bad when the entire crop comes under attack. When there is a massive invasion of pests or diseases, the chances are that the soil has become unbalanced or the plants themselves are under stress, because they are in the wrong place or have been planted too early or late.

Successful organic growing is nothing more than achieving a balance. With soil which has been misused and is hooked on chemicals or unnatural additives, it can take up to a season or more before things come right and nature reasserts itself.

All organic methods use large amounts of organic matter, in various stages of decay. Crop rotation is essential, with the restoring crops, such as legumes, carefully sandwiched between the greedy ones, and companion planting to help keep pests and diseases at bay.

Here are some simple ways to start an organic vegetable garden.

1. Get rid of all poisons and vow not to use any more.

2. Start making compost as a continuous process. This means using up all the so-called waste materials such as weeds, clippings, kitchen scraps or anything else which has once lived, and recycling them into a source of food for plants.

3. Use natural fertilizers such as manures, blood and bone, seaweed and, of course, compost. The aim is to enrich the soil in a balanced way, while constantly increasing the amount of organic matter on and below the surface.

4. It doesn't matter whether your soil is heavy clay or sandy, you can still practise mulch-gardening with enormous success. By mulching the surface through the year, with old straw, wilted weeds, seaweed or even sawdust, and not digging it in, you will encourage a huge population explosion of worms and other soil creatures, moulds, fungi and other micro-organisms. These will rapidly balance the soil, while allowing plants to absorb nutrients as they require them, in the most natural way.

5. Plant seeds or plants directly into the soil by pushing aside the mulch at the place where they are to grow. Leave the mulch pushed back a little to clear the area over the seeds or around the plant.

6. Add manures or other natural fertilizers to the mulch and control weeds by adding more mulching materials directly on top of them. Weeds growing from the bare soil around the plants can be carefully pulled out while they are small.

7. Insect pests can be controlled by using natural means, such as pyrethrum for aphids and similar sapsuckers, and derris or Dipel for caterpillars.

FEBRUARY
GUIDE TO ACTION

Ornamental Garden

Lift old established clumps of spring bulbs which have failed to flower, for division and replanting in the sun. To avoid black spot don't water roses with sprinklers or other methods which wet their leaves, use drip irrigation. Sow or plant achillea, ageratum, alyssum, anemone, antirrhinum, aquilegia, arctotis, aster, calendula, candytuft, Canterbury bells, carnation, celosia, cineraria, cornflower, cosmos, delphinium, dianthus, foxglove, geum, freesia, gypsophila, helichrysum, hollyhock, linaria, lobelia, lupin, African marigold, myosotis, nasturtium, nemesia, ornamental kale, pansy, perennial pea, penstemon, petunia, phlox, polyanthus, Iceland poppy, oriental poppy, primula, pyrethrum, ranunculus, saponaria, scabiosa, shasta daisy, stock, sweetpea, sweet William, verbena, viola, wallflower, and spring bulbs. Take cuttings

Vegetable Garden

Apply liquid fertilizers to tomatoes, capsicums, lettuce, brassicas, sweetcorn, silverbeet and cucumbers. Sow seed of broccoli, carrot, cabbage, cauliflower, sprouts, celery, leek, radish, turnip, swede, endive, beetroot, kale, Chinese cabbage, kohlrabi, lettuce, spring onion, parsley, parsnip and silverbeet. Allow long-keeping onions to die back naturally without bending tops, then lift them out of soil to dry.

Fruit Garden

Water fruit trees consistently to prevent fruit splitting. Remove anti-codlin moth grub bandage and destroy. Heavily mulch berryfruit bushes and vines. Water grapevines deeply. Watch for signs of brown-rot on stonefruit and pick off suspect fruit for destruction. Keep ground clear of fallen fruit. Water citrus, then feed with blood and bone or old manure.

Houseplants

Groom regularly to remove dead or weak growth. Keep the surface of the potting soil clean. Prune off excessive or untidy growth. Apply liquid feed but only after watering. Watch ferns for drying out.

FEBRUARY: FIRST WEEK

Taking Cuttings

If you fancy your chances of increasing your stock of plants, without cost, by striking cuttings, you couldn't pick a better time than right now.

Try striking pieces of azaleas, dwarf rhododendrons, camellias, daphnes, viburnum, hypericum, weigela, spiraea, deutzia, buddleia and a host of other beautiful garden plants.

The key to success lies in the type of wood which is taken from the mother plant. It should be new wood, a growth which has taken place this season. It is easy to choose because it has a different colour (light green) and is softer. It is found at the outer perimeter of the canopy, often just below where the flowers were.

Before you go rushing out to start pulling bits off various plants and shoving them into the ground, pause awhile, because it isn't done this way.

Cuttings are taken either on a dull day, or in the early morning or evening. If they are taken in the sun, they will wilt and that is the end of them before you begin. To keep cuttings firm and moist, always carry a plastic bag with you to hold them.

Cuttings should be short and sturdy. Long, floppy ones don't survive. A length of about ten centimetres is plenty and this growth should be firm enough to stand up on its own without immediately wilting. Remove it from the main plant by gently pulling sideways. It will come away cleanly, with a tiny pointed piece of the older wood attached to its base.

Don't just take one, take several, and before putting them into the plastic bag, carefully cut off most of the lower leaves, leaving just a few at the top of the piece. If these are large, be prepared to cut them in half. This leaf removal is to reduce the amount of water lost through the pores.

Above all, keep the plastic bag of cuttings out of the sun, otherwise your precious collection will be cooked to death within minutes.

One thing you must not do is thrust the cuttings into the open garden. Most, if not all summer cuttings will fail in exposed situations like this. Winter hardwood cuttings, on the other hand, can do well struck in open ground. Cuttings root best not struck into soil. A hungry but moisture-holding mixture of sand and wet peat is perfect, oddly enough, because such a mix contains so little plant food.

The idea is that once the cuttings have been placed in a soil-free medium, and roots emerge, a marvellous thing happens. The roots begin to spread widely in search of food, and this is the time when we 'trick' them and move them into an enriched soil mixture or directly into the open ground.

So use this easily-mixed cutting

medium: half sand, half peat; and have it available in a container, lovely and moist, waiting.

The cuttings are inserted into holes made with a pointed stick (an old ballpoint pen is ideal), as deep as about two-thirds of their length. The medium is then made firm around them. I believe in striking a lot of cuttings of the same kind together in one pot. In a container with a diameter of fifteen centimetres, up to fifteen cuttings can be placed next to each other, so that it looks like a spiny ant-eater.

Carry out all these operations in the shade and water the cuttings afterwards very gently so as not to disturb them. To ensure that they do not dry out, place the container and cuttings into a plastic bag and tie the top. A couple of pieces of bent wire will help to keep the sides of the bag away from the cuttings and the whole thing can be placed in a shady place. Root formation will depend on the plant and can take from a month to twelve weeks. Azaleas take about six weeks.

If you feel a little impatient, especially after a month or so has passed, the cuttings can be carefully knocked out of the pot (never pulled out, otherwise the young roots can be stripped off) and examined for signs of growth. However, small shoots of new growth appearing where the leaves were cut off is a good indication that roots have formed.

The young plants can then be gently separated and either planted into their own little pots or out into the garden.

Disease Control

Each new season seems to bring with it certain plant diseases which are special to that time of the year. Now, with a combination of warm to hot days and dewy nights, fruit and vegetables reaching harvesting stage, and the main flush of flowering plants over, all sorts of disturbing things are happening.

Gardeners become very concerned when all their efforts during the past six months appear to be wasted as disease strikes at this crucial time.

So what can we do?

The first thing is to recognize that plants which are grown correctly in the right position are more resistant to diseases. They are just like we are and react to such things as poor living conditions, overfeeding with the wrong type of food (which is really undernourishment) and other forms of mistreatment, by getting sick.

Many plant diseases are spread by insect pests, often lurking among weeds. A clean garden where weed growth is suppressed often means less disease. Other diseases may be introduced by infected seed. This is a major reason why bought seed, which has been treated, is preferable to seed passed on from someone else's garden. Recently I saw an example of this, when a large batch of tomato plants at a small nursery had to be destroyed because of virus infection. The seed used had been harvested from an area where tomatoes had been grown for many years, the worst place from which to collect seed.

Some diseases are caused through neglect on our part. At this time, in many gardens, tomatoes are starting to develop a kind of black scab at the base of each fruit. This is very common and is called Blossom-end Rot. If you have it in your tomato patch, it is your own fault. It is basically caused by inconsistent watering. That is, allowing the plants to dry out, then watering them heavily. This fluctuation in the water supply causes a condition which makes the plant unable to use certain elements in the soil and the scab results.

The best way to make sure your tomatoes get consistent moisture is to water them deeply now, then mulch them with straw. This will stop the ground from drying out. Remember too, that unlike some plants, tomatoes can be safely mulched heavily, right up to the stem, without any ill effects.

Another disease which is starting to show its ugly face right now is mildew. This will attack cucumbers, melons, marrows and pumpkins, as well as roses, apples, parsnips and some berry fruits such as gooseberries. Growing conditions can influence this disease, especially with cucumbers and roses. If these plants are overshadowed and the atmosphere is too stagnant, mildew can run riot. With some of the woody plants, such as apple or gooseberry, the answer is correct winter pruning. This involves cutting off all the tips of the growing shoots. This is the main harbouring place for mildew during the dormant period.

But there are sprays too, which help to control mildew. For powdery mildew, where the leaves and fruit are covered with a white powdery substance, Benlate or Marathane will do the trick if used early enough and in conjunction with some pruning. Downy mildew often shows itself as blotchy areas on leaves and can affect grapes, onions, and even rhubarb. Treatment is by using a copper spray, such as Bordeaux, just prior to budburst.

Brown-rot of stone fruits is a curse. It strikes just at the time when the fruit is ready to pick. A small area starts to go soft and rotten and soon half the apricot or plum is blighted. This awful disease can sometimes attack apples too, especially if the individual fruit are starting to squeeze and bear against each other as they grow. Benlate has a low toxicity and can be effective in helping to control this disease but real success can only occur if correct garden hygiene is practised. This means the constant removal

---

There is plenty to do now preparing for winter and spring. Daffodils and jonquils can go in now, in sun or light shade. Deep shade means flowers in the first spring season but never again. Lawns can be well watered, fed with a good tight handful of blood and bone for each square metre, then watered again. Stonefruit trees can be pruned as fruit is harvested, especially apricots. Large, vigorous trees which are becoming too dominant are best heavily lopped at this time, rather than waiting until winter. This will effectively control their excess vigour for at least two seasons.

---

of all affected fruit, both from the tree and the ground nearby, and especially any mummified fruit during winter.

A rather strange looking lemon or other citrus often intrigues some people. The fruit becomes curiously misshapen, and, if cut open, is found to be dryish and distorted.

This is the result of the activities of a tiny creature called the citrus bud mite. Fortunately, the tree rarely comes under serious attack, and there is no need to start squirting sprays all over the place. The problem can be spotted early when the blossom becomes swollen and twisted. All you need to do is pinch these flowers off and that's the end of the problem.

My experience has taught me that most sprays are best used rarely but if they have to be used, obey the instructions on the container strictly, then carry out a very thorough job of applying the spray.

FEBRUARY: SECOND WEEK

Winter and Spring Vegetables

It's remarkable how a small amount of timely planting this week can produce a host of highly nutritious vegetables during winter and spring. Apart from the food value, winter-grown vegetables cut food costs at a time when prices are much higher.

So, what can be planted now in the vegetable garden?

The most urgent are the carrots. Seed sown now will germinate halfway through the month and will have reached a good eating size by the beginning of May, when the cooler weather will markedly slow down further growth. An outstanding variety of carrot is Western Red. From the moment of sowing, keep the soil moist and don't let it dry out. This means having a sprinkler handy all the time and using it several times daily if necessary.

Beetroot have a special value during winter, either preserved as pickles, eaten raw with salads or cooked in various ways. Use fresh seed and try Detroit Dark Red or Derwent Globe, both of which develop quickly after sowing in one-centimetre-deep drills, two centimetres apart.

If you are still growing your spring-sown silverbeet, you had better plant another lot now, because the early sown crop will become diseased during winter, mainly with rust. Seeds or plants can go in now and they will respond quickly to weekly waterings with diluted liquid fertilizer, and will have reached a good size within ten weeks.

Spring onions can be sown most of the year in temperate regions of Australia and will grow quickly, provided the soil has been well limed prior to sowing. The method of sowing the seeds is quite simple. Prepare a broad (100 millimetre) drill, about one centimetre deep, and sow the seeds thickly across the entire length and width of it. Cover them with good soil and press it down firmly to make good contact. Be prepared to apply plenty of water, consistently, and when they emerge, like young grass, watch out for competing weeds.

The lettuce seeds to be planted from now onwards are different from the normal, summer-sown lettuce. They are superior in flavour but tend to bolt to seed during very hot weather. Imperial 847 is an outstanding, well-tested variety with a tight, crisp heart. The smaller, loose-hearted butterhead types such as Mignonette, also make delicious eating. Direct seeding is often better than planting seedlings at this time, as they are less likely to bolt to seed. Be particularly generous with the water and aim to keep the plants moving quickly. Once they are checked in their growth, generally through lack of water, they become too bitter to be eaten.

Turnips, harvested from the time they are no larger than a golf ball, can be exceptionally sweet eating. White Globe is a popular, reliable variety and will swell quickly into tender, delicious roots if sown now. It is a bit late in many districts for swedes but, if you don't mind smallish roots, sow some now and you won't be disappointed. The superbly flavoured New Zealand Butter are among the best of all and do not require frosts to sweeten them up.

English spinach is a most valuable winter vegetable but many people here fail with their sowings because of acidic soils. Spinach needs plenty of lime, so be generous and place two good handfuls every square metre and rake it in, preferably a couple of weeks before sowing the seed.

The most valuable of all the radishes for winter is the large, extra-mild China Rose. With its red skin and snowy white flesh, it is good to look at, while holding well in cold soil, without becoming coarse and hot.

The main winter and spring brassicas can be planted out now, preferably as seedlings. This will allow them to develop a good rosette of leaves before the cool weather sets in. Then they will continue to grow strongly through the winter, and can be harvested at a time when they are at their most expensive in the shops.

Here they are in order of importance.

Broccoli. The new dwarf variety, Leprechaun, is small enough to be grown in a container and several will take up little room in a small garden.

Cabbage. The traditional winter varieties are the conical hearted ones, such as Sugarloaf, or wrinkled, dark-green leaf types such as Savoy. A new variety, Eureka, developed in Australia, sounds promising. It produces globe-shaped, well-sized heads which can be left to stand for weeks after maturing.

Cauliflower. Sow or plant six-month, five-month and four-month types to give steady production through the winter. Soak the seeds in seaweed concentrate prior to sowing to help avoid 'whiptail' problems. Alternatively, use a weak solution of sodium molybdate for the first watering after sowing.

Brussels sprouts. These should only be planted as seedlings from now onwards, unless you don't mind eating them well into spring, which means loose sprouts, I suppose.

The main thing with all the brassicas is good, rich soil and, above all, very firm soil around them, so that they don't fall over when they gain weight.

So, you have a busy time ahead of you this week but the joys are awaiting you later on, with good, healthy eating of your own winter-grown vegetables.

Hot Weather Plant Care

We are now entering one of the hottest and driest parts of the year and apart from the increasingly urgent need for keeping the watering systems operating there are plenty of jobs to be done.

In the flower garden, many annual and perennial plants are now blooming magnificently and regular doses of weak liquid fertilizers will provide the extra nourishment they need. Dead-heading, that is, the removal of all blooms as they start to fade, is vital if you want to keep those flowers coming on. For example, many roses have long since withered and already numerous heps, or seedpods, are beginning to form. Cut them off and take a short length of stem, to an outside bud, with each cluster removed. In this way the whole plant can be prepared for the next flowering, during April.

Chrysanthemums should be stopped again at this time, by pinching out the leading shoots. This will cause the plant to branch out, just below that point. Many more flowers as well as sturdier and more wind-resistant plants will develop as a result of this treatment.

If you have been constantly nipping out the growing tips of seedling carnations, you will have neat, dome-shaped buns of silver grey instead of the usual untidy, straggly sprawl which is so common with unpruned carnations. The flowering will be delayed, of course, but when the blooms do arrive, it is a sight never to be forgotten.

Those who have been planting out native Australian plants during the last six months or so, will be amazed by the enormous growth they have made over this relatively short period. The biggest mistake which can be made now, is to try and secure the long, whippy stems by tying them to a stake. Most Australian plants should never be staked, because they are greatly weakened by such treatment. They seem to try and climb the stake, then become top heavy, so that when the inevitable breaking of the stake occurs during the first year or so, the entire plant falls over, usually damaging the roots in the process.

Metal stakes, such as droppers, can be even worse. Eventually they become either unsightly and virtually impossible to remove, or deeply embedded in the main stem of the tree as it grows, causing all sorts of problems later.

The best way to keep fast-growing natives secure is to prune them back by at least a third. This is one piece of advice which will be read, but generally ignored. It is the hardest job in the world to cut back a vigorously-growing plant, because it seems so contrary to every instinct that we have. But, remember, most of our plants are browsed by forest animals when they are growing under natural conditions, and this is nature's

> When collecting seed, use paper bags for storage rather than plastic which can prevent drying while encouraging the growth of harmful moulds and fungi.

way of keeping them strong and sturdy.

Even if you live in a windy area, these plants must not be staked. It is far better to place two or three large rocks as close as possible to the main stems. This will secure them in the ground while helping to keep the roots moist.

In the fruit garden, make sure your stone fruit are fully ripe before harvesting. Don't forget that, unlike apples and pears, they will not sweeten up after picking, so unless they are being harvested for bottling, leave it until they are ripe. Then you will understand why home grown fruit is so superior to the bought product.

FEBRUARY: THIRD WEEK

Creating a Garden Pool

One of the special charms of garden pools is their effect on light, even in the dullest parts of a garden. They can be as small as a metre across and will fit into almost any garden.

There are so many prefabricated, precast pools available these days, anyone can have a go at installing one. You can also make your own, directly in the garden, with concrete. It will last a lifetime if you make it well.

A common error in pool-making is to construct a rounded, bowl-shaped base. A curving bottom is obviously more natural looking but it does create problems. Aquatic plants are not usually grown on the base of a pool but in containers. If the bottom is not flat, only a few containers will sit in the centre and there will be plenty of wasted space towards the pool edges.

So make sure the base is flat and level. If you are using concrete, be generous and make it at least ten centimetres thick and use plenty of steel reinforcing. Badly-made pools can easily crack, which means they will constantly leak. Sealing such leaks is very difficult. I have lost count of the number of useless, empty, cracked garden pools I have come across.

The depth of a garden pool needs to be no more than sixty centimetres. Most aquatic plants are comfortable around this depth.

If you install a prefabricated pool, excavate to the depth needed, plus an extra ten centimetres. Remove all clods, sharp stones or roots. A thick layer of sand over the bottom of the hole will protect the pool's shell and allow easier adjustment of the way it sits. Place the pool into position and wriggle it until it is level. Use a spirit level with a straight piece of wood across the rim of the pool. Then carefully pour more sand or stonedust around the sides to secure the pool. Keep checking the level during this operation. If necessary, gently ram the packing materials to eliminate pockets. Then fill with water.

Heavy-duty black plastic film makes an excellent, long-lasting garden pool. The preparations are the same as for the prefabricated ones. The sand base is essential, because plastic is easily penetrated. Consider also the new butyl rubber linings. Although they are not as readily available as plastic, they are longer lasting and will stretch to cover irregular contours.

Once water has filled these flexible, soft pools, the pressure can be considerable and sharp roots or pointed stones will quickly create leaks.

Even heavy-duty plastic is more reliable if it is doubled. Spread the double sheet into the hole, folding the sides here and there to allow for a snug fit. Make sure there is at least thirty centimetres of overlap around the edges. It helps if some water is poured into the plastic during the initial adjustments. Use plenty of dry sand to pack around the walls as the pool is being filled. If one side is a little too low, pack more sand under the edges to raise it and bring it level. Sand is easier to use than soil and once settled will not compress further.

When the pool is full of water, weigh down the edges of the plastic with large, interesting rocks. If they have plenty of lichen and moss clinging to their surfaces, they will add great character to the surrounds. Flat rocks, laid so that they overhang the pool here and there, will produce a more natural shape while providing shady places for any fish.

Constructing a Garden Pool

Fish need protection from the sun and also from cats and birds. Many fish unexpectedly die for no apparent reason. If they are constantly threatened by cats or kookaburras, they probably die from worry. With a good overhang, fish have somewhere to hide until a protective cover of water lilies or other plants has grown.

A rock garden surround is particularly attractive with a garden pool. Rocks and good soil can be placed around the edges and planted immediately. If a water feature is desired, such as a fountain or waterfalls, remember to do the plumbing first and conceal it with the rocks and plants. Electrical connections must be carried out by an authorized electrician. The danger of electric shock in such situations is very acute and is more likely to be fatal than anywhere else. So don't experiment yourself. Places like this need a special type of conduit and great care with installation.

Plants around a garden pool could include small leafed species and hardy ferns. Large trees are unsuitable, because of leaf problems and shade. Most aquatic plants need lots of light.

Compact, crevice-filling plants always look good around a garden pool because they don't get out of hand and are easily maintained. Here are some which thrive in well-drained, sunny positions: mossy saxifrage, armeria, perennial candytuft, prostrate helichrysum, androsace, dianthus, *Phlox subulata*, prostrate thyme, creeping rosemary, arenaria, *Cyclamen hederifolium*, dwarf irises, stonecrop, and hoop-petticoat daffodils.

> Irises, particularly the common, bearded varieties, can be lifted and divided now. Discard the remains of old rhizomes and retain the healthy, pale-green, swollen part at the base of the leaves. Cut back the leaves so they form a short fan and replant immediately in enriched, well limed soil, keeping the rhizome on the surface, but the roots securely buried in moist soil.

A warning note. Even small garden pools can be very dangerous where there are young children, especially toddlers. They are understandably fascinated by them and will quietly head for the water at any time. If they fall into the water, even if it is shallow, they have great difficulty in getting out.

So, if you want a garden pool but have little children, please forget about it for a few years, unless you are willing to place a heavy, steel mesh over it. That might spoil the appearance.

Landscaping Shady Places

These dark and shady corners of the garden are always a bit of a worry, even to fairly experienced gardeners – what to do, what to plant and how best to landscape these gloomy spots.

They tend to be either ignored or so misplanted they can be an embarrassing corner of an otherwise attractive garden.

Well, I have good news. Even the shadiest area can be landscaped and there is a whole range of outstanding shrubs, small trees and perennial plants which not only grow in these sunless conditions, but insist upon it.

Deep shade may be caused by the close proximity of a building. Or if the shade is caused by a large, dense evergreen, the competition is usually such that only a limited number of plants will grow there, so the landscaping must take other forms, such as paving.

In most cases however, the problem is a combination of too much shade from the house and a large plant or two adding to the gloom.

Start by giving this frustrating area a good clean out. This means not just the rubbish which always accumulates in places like this, but any growth which is unwanted and has become an eyesore. You will be amazed at the amount of room created by this clearance, it may even be possible to install a comfortable garden seat. Remember, places with little sunlight are a marvellous refuge during really hot weather.

The other thing about shady places is the failure of grass to grow very successfully. This is a great advantage, because it allows scope for paving, and reduces maintenance problems.

If the existing soil is any good, cultivate it to a depth of about twenty centimetres. However, if you are going to carry out any major planting operations, be prepared to import good quality topsoil and spread it thickly over the proposed planting area.

Think about using flagstones or pavers for part of the area. These are easy to handle and are available at most garden centres. If you have decided to install a garden seat, a paved area around the seat with a stepping-stone path leading to it will already begin to transform your problem spot.

But the main part of solving problems in areas like this is through the use of those plants which grow happily in the shade. These range from completely prostrate, ground-hugging perennials, to some of the most beautiful trees.

For example, a lovely silver and green variegated ground cover, with pale lemon flowers, is the variegated dead nettle (*Lamiastrum*). This thrives in dense shade and grows vigorously. Another low-growing shade lover is the Christmas rose (*Helleborus*) and the small-leaf variegated ivy will light up a dark corner all the year round.

There are also plants such as lily of the valley and Solomon's seal, which will poke through most ground-covering plants, and with regular watering during the summer, will rapidly populate a sheltered, shady spot.

Among the larger shrubs, azalea, camellias, and the Japanese laurel are obvious choices. One of the most beautiful of all garden shrubs, *Pieris forrestii*, with its pearl-like flowers and bright scarlet new growth, does particularly well out of the sun. The American mountain laurel (*Kalmia latifolia*) with clusters of rich pink, cup-shaped flowers, will grow strongly in semi-shade, but dislikes clay. If your soil is alkaline, try mahonia, berberis or the dependable *Virburnum tinus*.

There is a whole range of Japanese maples, from medium-sized trees, to low growing, weeping forms. The colours are as numerous as the different leaf shapes, and it is understandable why these superb plants are so popular. Big mistakes in landscaping are made when Japanese maples are planted in open, exposed situations. Plant them in the protected, shady places, and they will thank you by flourishing.

Fuchsias will often grow and flower profusely in the shade, provided they are well-watered during hot weather and do not have to compete with larger, greedy plants. A light pruning during July will help keep them in shape, and they can easily be propagated from cuttings at almost any time of the year.

The most popular way to landscape a sunless, gloomy situation is to create a fernery. Larger ferns such as the Soft Treefern (*Dicksonia antarctica*), grow easily, provided they are watered deeply during the first year or so. At planting time they should be completely devoid of fronds, otherwise they will dry out and fail. Other easily obtained native ferns include the Mother Shield fern (*Polystichum proliferum*), which grows about half a metre, and the Fishback fern (*Blechnum nudum*) which will ultimately form a dense colony in any partly-shaded spot.

All the plants suggested are hardy, easily available at nurseries, can be planted at most times during the year and above all, prefer the shade.

When you have completed your landscaping, you will wonder how on earth this new and lovely part of your garden was ever considered a problem.

> One of the important jobs to be carried out this week, is to apply lime or dolomite if needed, to those parts of the vegetable garden which have been cleared.

FEBRUARY: LAST WEEK

Houseplants

There is hardly a home anywhere which doesn't contain at least one houseplant. In fact almost every building in which people live or work has something growing in a pot. This accounts for the enormous interest in trying to obtain the best results from these plants.

At this time of the year, houseplants should be at their best. They will respond strongly to good feeding and watering practices and, if correctly placed, will give you very little to worry about.

However, in order to keep these plants in good shape, certain things must be done during these long hot days. The overwhelming majority must be kept clear of direct sunshine, otherwise they will suffer from sunburn. The exceptions are most cacti and succulents, pelagoniums, hippeastrum varieties, and species of kalanchoe; all of which love plenty of full sun.

A major cause of poor health right now is lack of humidity. Most houseplants need plenty of moisture around their leaves to keep them lush and green. They all appreciate a regular spraying with water, even two or three times daily on really hot days. This is why indoor plants in moist-atmosphere conservatories always look so good.

We can't easily reproduce the temperature and moisture control of a large conservatory, but we can create similar conditions. Some people plunge their pot plants into larger containers filled with moist peat moss. A large bowl or terracotta saucer filled with pebbles or bluemetal, then thoroughly wetted, can be effective as a base for indoor plants. Surfaces like this give off moisture as they slowly dry out. The vapour bathes the leaves of the plants and they thrive on it.

Some superbly beautiful flowering house plants such as the *Saintpaulia* (African violet) can never look their best unless these humid conditions exist. This popular plant originally comes from the mountains of east Africa, but it seems to grow particularly well indoors. It loves our winter sunshine but our summer sun is too strong. The ideal situation for the plant is near a window where it gets plenty of bright light but no direct sun. If all you have obtained from your African violet plants so far are plenty of lovely deep green leaves but no flowers, you can be sure that it is because there has not been enough light.

On the other hand, too much light will cause the leaves to become quite pale and the stalks very short. In severe cases of too much direct sun, the leaves will appear to collapse around the edges of the pot.

Saintpaulias will not bloom if the temperature drops below 15°C. Somewhere between 20°C and 25°C seems to be perfect with our light intensity.

The amount of water needed depends on the plant size and location, but African violets like their water with the chill off, preferably at room temperature. Never splash the leaves. If possible, water from below by using a saucer and after the plant has drawn up enough water, tip out the surplus. If you want to spray the foliage with water to increase humidity, make sure the leaves dry out away from the sun, otherwise leaf-spotting will certainly occur.

Never place African violets into a large pot with too much extra soil. They just won't flower. Pot them into small containers and don't move them into a larger pot until they are really overcrowded.

The most successful African violets I have seen have been grown either on a southern facing windowsill in a kitchen (over the sink) or in a bathroom. The moist atmosphere in these places made the difference.

Oddly enough, although some people have difficulty growing African violets, few complain about getting them to strike from cuttings or leaves. These are the easiest of plants to propagate and it is a good, inexpensive way to increase the number of plants.

Use a medium-sized leaf, with a fairly long stem. Make some holes in the bottoms of some plastic drinking cups, fill the bottom third with small stones or gravel, then fill to just below the rim with a rooting medium. The best medium is fifty per cent moist, granulated peat, fifty per cent sand. Place the bottom quarter of the leaf-stem into the medium and support the rest of the stem and leaf with a little stick. You can place two or three leaf-cuttings in each container.

Then cover the pots with polythene bags and secure with elastic. If the peat and sand mixture has been well moistened there is little need for a further watering, but watch for drying out just the same. Keep the cuttings out of sunlight or deep shade. Within a matter of weeks a root system will form, then shortly afterwards the leaves of the new plantlets will appear at the base of the leafstalk. The new plants can then be potted on into small pots, and the mother leaf cut off at the base. This old leaf and stalk may even be used again.

A similar method of propagation is by using water. In this case, the leafstalk is best suspended from the top so that only the tip is below the surface. You will soon see the fine roots forming. Once this has occurred, take the cutting from the water and plant it out into a small pot containing moist potting mix. The young leaves of the baby plants will soon show themselves, and they may be grown on in the same pot until flowering.

Saintpaulias and related plants such as gloxinias, have quite small roots, and easily rot if they are overwatered or if the soil drainage is poor. The best growing medium should be light enough to allow for good drainage, while containing enough organic matter to retain moisture and plant foods.

A good mixture to prepare yourself is: two parts screened compost, one part moist granulated peat and one part coarse river sand. Add to this, for each bucketful of the potting mix, three tablespoonsful of dolomite limestone, three tablespoonsful of blood and bone, half a tablespoonful of sulphate of potash, and half a tablespoonful of superphosphate.

Feed the plants during spring and summer only, using well-diluted liquid fertilizer, using a small amount of seaweed concentrate added.

Follow the rules, and you will have flowers for most of the year.

MARCH
GUIDE TO ACTION

Ornamental Garden

New lawns can be sown now. Evergreens can be transplanted. Continue dead-heading of all annuals, perennials, flowering trees and shrubs. Take cuttings of many plants. Plant or sow achillea, ageratum, alyssum, anemone, antirrhinum, aquilegia, arctotis, calendula, candytuft, Canterbury bells, carnation, cineraria, cornflower, delphinium, dianthus, foxglove, geum, freesia, gypsophila, hollyhock, linaria, lobelia, lupin, myosotis, nasturtium, nemesia, ornamental kale, pansy, penstemon, polyanthus, Iceland poppy, oriental poppy, primula, ranunculus, scabiosa, shasta daisy, stock, sweetpea, sweet William, viola, wallflower and spring bulbs.

Vegetable Garden

Broad bean seed goes into well-limed soil now. Also sow or plant beet, broccoli, cabbage, carrot, cauliflower, celery, radish, turnip, swede, endive, kale, Chinese cabbage, lettuce and spring onion. Sow ryecorn, tickbeans or annual lupins as a cover crop in vacant beds. Dig, then store potatoes out of the light. String and hang onions for storage under cover in an airy place.

Fruit Garden

Prune fruit trees of weak, misplaced growth as fruit is harvested. Allow stone fruit to ripen fully before picking. Pears and apples are picked as their stalk tips come free when fruit is lifted. Ripen them indoors. Rake away and destroy all fallen fruit, leaves and prunings. Check lemon and other citrus for scale infestation.

Houseplants

Check for mildew, marginal leaf-scorch and unthrifty growth. Keep moist, but check for drying out within rootballs. Mealy bugs can be dabbed with methylated spirit. Re-pot rootbound plants. Bring cyclamen corms into leaf by watering and pot into a fresh potting soil.

MARCH: FIRST WEEK

Composting

I'm a total compost addict and I'm boasting about it. Compost is the most natural, gentle and complete fertilizer of all. Properly made, with a wide mixture of ingredients, it contains more plant foods and minerals than any other fertilizer, in a beautifully balanced form. Compost is the only fertilizer in which it is possible to plant seeds or plants directly, without harming young roots, and produce healthy growth.

This is an ideal time to make compost, because the weather is still warm, and there is a huge variety of organic matter available for conversion.

First of all, what kinds of materials can be used for making compost?

The answer is simple: anything which has once been alive. This means that grass cuttings, weeds, leaves, kitchen scraps, seaweed, old natural-fibre clothing, straw, spoilt hay, dead chooks, and even old newsprint, can all be recycled to produce this marvellous fertilizer and soil conditioner.

A misunderstanding of compost making can be seen in many gardens. People think that by collecting weeds, grass clippings and other garden rubbish and putting them in a pile at the bottom of the garden, they are making compost efficiently. They are not. Collecting garden waste, heaping it up over many months, then allowing it to slowly rot down over many more months, it is true, eventually produces compost. But this method takes far too long.

Compost can be made in about three weeks at this time of the year, and a little longer during cold weather. When compost is correctly made, the heap of organic material becomes very hot, and this heat not only destroys harmful micro-organisms, but also insect pests and even weed seeds.

This is what you must do to make good compost.

1. Collect weeds, clippings, leaves etc. If necessary, bring in old hay or straw or even seaweed.

2. A simple bin to support the material can be made from chickenwire, timber or bales of straw. The dimensions should not be less than a cubic metre. Two such bins, side by side will hold well over one tonne of compost each if necessary.

3. If you cannot build a bin, the heap can be made on the open ground, without supports, but it should occupy an area twice as large as when bins are used. This is to compensate for loss of heat from the exposed sides of the heap.

4. Throw down a layer of the basic materials, about twenty centimetres thick (eight inches). Wet it thoroughly so that it is completely saturated.

5. Spread a thin layer of manure over the surface and wash it in with the hose. Fowl manure, horse manure or even pigeon droppings are excellent, but blood and bone or any other fertilizer with a good nitrogen content will do fine.

6. Add a further layer of the basic materials, topping it up with more manures and keeping everything saturated all the time. Continue with this layering operation until the bin is overful, or the heap is about two-metres tall.

7. The heap will soon start to become hot as the bacteria get to work. By the next day it will be impossible to place your hand inside the pile. If you like, the heap can then be left until it matures – in about two months. If you want the compost in a hurry, the break-down can be hastened.

8. For quick compost, the heap must be turned in order to allow air to circulate through the material, and more water added. This is why having two bins side by side is an advantage. It means that a full bin can be easily turned into the adjoining empty one. The turning process involves forking great masses of the hot mixture and shaking it to fluff it out while tossing it into the new location. Every now and then, sprinkle plenty of water on the new heap as it builds up. If there are streaks of white mould in the straw, it means there is a lack of moisture, so try and compensate by spraying in more. If the heap is too wet, it will be cold and smelly, and the turning operation must be very thoroughly carried out to break up the mass of undecayed material.

This turning is essential for quick results and is best carried out every three days, or even more often.

Within three weeks, the original organic matter will be unrecognizable, and

Compost Bins

will have become dark brown, pleasantly earth-smelling and lovely to handle. In other words, you will have made compost.

Compost must be placed in the planting hole, below the surface, away from the wind and sun. Spreading it over the surface of the soil can waste it, as it just dries out. If it cannot be buried below the surface, it can be spread around plants then covered with a mulch of old straw, hay or wads of newspaper.

Irises

Bearded irises seem to thrive in southern Australia, and some of the best displays I have ever seen have been grown here. The most significant flowering time is late spring but it is now that the important work of dividing and rejuvenating old established clumps takes place.

These beautiful, elegant plants will eventually stop flowering if they remain undivided. Their rhizomes become so congested and numerous that they tend to exhaust the soil of plant foods. A destructive form of competition is set up in which all the plants lose.

To divide bearded irises, carefully lift entire clumps out of the ground. Cut back the foliage to within fifteen centimetres of the rhizome. After the complex system of roots, leaves and rhizomes have been well hosed with water, the parts to be retained will be revealed. These are the thick, fleshy, healthy swellings, directly at the base of each leaf cluster. The remains of older roots are withered and dark coloured. They should be cut off and thrown away.

This will leave the short 'fan' of leaves, with the blunt, bright green rhizome and its roots.

If you want to record the name of the cultivated variety, write it on the leaves, pending a label at planting time.

Bearded irises need good, well-drained soil in full sun. They grow particularly well if the soil has been limed. Dolomite limestone, which contains both calcium and magnesium, is ideal for growing irises, and a dressing of a heaped handful for each square metre of ground will work wonders.

Division of clumps should be carried out every second or third year for continual, good quality blooms.

To plant bearded irises, excavate a shallow hole, big enough to accommodate the rhizome without burying it. It's a good idea to create a low ridge in the centre of the planting hole, on which to rest the rhizome. This will allow the roots to spread downwards on either side of the ridge, while the rest of the rhizome remains in the sun. The roots are then covered with a good layer of soil to provide nourishment while holding the plant securely.

This is why the leaves need to be cut back. Until such time as the new root system develops, the plants tend to be precarious and top heavy, making them vulnerable to even the slightest breeze.

The main aim from now onwards is to help them develop a new vigorous root system before the winter sets in. If this can be achieved, a good flowering will occur. If they remain starved, or insecure in the ground, only a few leaves will grow, and no flowers. So keep the soil moist around newly planted rhizomes until the end of April and sprinkle a good fistful of blood and bone around them every three weeks.

Irises can produce a lovely display when they are planted in a bed of their own but many gardeners prefer to plant them among other, non-competing plants. This helps to avoid a long period of drabness which would occur as soon as flowering is over. Some of the best examples of good mixes I have come across include bearded irises planted in among bush and standard roses. They usually flower together and then, when the irises have finished blooming, the roses will continue to provide good colour. Then the irises build their reserves for their next flowering in early summer.

Other types of iris which can be planted now include the lovely winter-flowering *I. unguicularis*. These will require a season or two to become fully established, because they resent being disturbed. The Californian iris (*I. innominata*) seems to thrive in cold, wet situations and loves acidic soils. When grown from seed, a surprising range of colours is obtained.

> Scale of citrus fruit can be a serious problem right now and is easily identified by the conspicuous, black sooty mould which always comes with the scale insect. White oil emulsion sprayed below the leaves will effectively control it.

Bulbs

This is the most important part of the year for planting spring bulbs, especially daffodils, jonquils, grape hyacinths, Spanish bluebells and a host of other lovely plants. They all provide a brilliant show of colour, with plenty of flowers for cutting, at a time when we feel a special need for them.

All these bulbs are very easy to grow, either in open, grassed areas or as part of a shrub and herbaceous border. The marvellous thing about most of them is their ability to grow and flower in reasonable soil, without the need to add fertilizers, provided the soil can be kept moist during the growing period.

Daffodils and jonquils prefer an open, sunny place, although they will tolerate part shade. However, although a shady place will induce them to produce longer stems and a flower which lasts without fading, too much shade will cause them to eventually cease flowering altogether. This means that old shaded clumps should be dug up now and replanted in full sun. New bulbs can be planted to obtain flowers in deep shade areas. Although these bulbs generally resent too much disturbance, an annual lifting and dividing will cause them to increase their numbers more rapidly than in undisturbed clumps.

So if you want to rapidly double, or even treble your daffodil population, keep lifting and dividing at this time every year.

The rule of thumb for planting is easy to remember. Most bulbs are planted about three times their actual depth into average garden soil. In the case of light, sandy loam, the planting depth should be increased to enable the bulbs to keep in contact with the cool, moist subsoil. It is this which acts as a stimulant and starts the roots moving at this time of the year.

If you want a natural look in the garden, try planting bulbs in drifts, in a grassed area, preferably beneath deciduous trees. All I do in this case is to grab a good handful and toss them casually over the area in which I want to plant. Wherever they land is the spot where they go in. To plant in grassed places like this, simply drive a mattock as hard as possible into the turf, prise it up a little to produce a slot, and drop the bulb in. The wound in the turf is then closed by stamping upon it. The whole area should be immediately given a really deep soaking.

When planting bulbs among other plants in a border, make sure there is no danger of them being overhung and that there is not too much competition from perennials. Do try to avoid planting them in rows – it really looks quite unnatural.

I plant three to five bulbs together in one largish hole. They are kept separate, with a gap of at least five centimetres between bulbs. Before backfilling the planting hole, fill it with water and let it soak away a couple of times, then cover with good topsoil and firm down.

Once the bulbs are out of sight, it is a good idea to mark the spot with a label or a short stick. Last year I planted large numbers in one part of the garden, then later, because I had forgotten to mark the spot, I inadvertently planted a mollis azalea directly over them. The effect was interesting to say the least.

It is easy to plant bulbs in bowls and the result later is quite lovely. A bowl deep enough to accommodate a number of bulbs, and without drainage holes, will do. Place a layer of moistened granulated peat over the bottom of the bowl. Then put the bulbs, crammed closely together, on top of the peat. Fill the bowl with more moist peat so the tips of the bulbs are well covered. Then plunge the lot, bowl, peat and bulbs deep in the soil outside and cover with either peat or sawdust. Later on, when the leaves and flower buds have poked up through the sawdust and flowering is about to occur, lift the bowl, brush it clean and carry it inside to complete its display.

MARCH: SECOND WEEK

Harvesting

All sorts of fruit and vegetables are starting to ripen now and how they are harvested will make all the difference in the world to their quality. It is absolute madness to spend months carefully watering, weeding, pruning and fertilizing vegetables and fruit, only to spoil everything out of impatience or by leaving it too late.

If you pick most varieties of stone fruit too early, before they are properly ripe, you waste all your previous efforts. If plums, peaches and nectarines are not sweet at picking time they won't sweeten up afterwards. That's why too much of this kind of fruit bought from shops tastes so terrible, even though it may feel soft and ripe. Some peaches and nectarines for sale are quite bitter. It is a tragedy and a waste. Don't make this mistake yourself, pick them when they are sweet, then eat them fresh or preserve them.

This is equally true of grapes. Have you ever wondered why the first grapes we buy are always tasteless, whereas the ones we are buying now are delicious? It is because of the impatience of some growers to get their product on the market when the prices are high. In other words, we can be tricked into purchasing an inferior product for a higher price.

Apples and pears are quite different. Most of these will sweeten up beautifully after picking slightly green. You can tell when they may be safely picked – they will come away from the tree easily at the tip of the stalk, when they are gently lifted. If you have to drag them off with an effort, sometimes snapping the stalk, it is too early. So wait a while. When apples and pears have been picked, keep them out of the sun. Store them in a drawer or box, under cover. Don't put them into plastic bags, unless they are well cooled and to be used within a short time, or they will go mouldy.

Some apples, such as Gravenstein or Granny Smith, make good eating when allowed to sweeten up on the tree, but others will go mealy very quickly. Cox's Orange Pippin develop a much more aromatic flavour if they are harvested just prior to ripening, but go off rapidly when they are left to hang.

Pears, almost without exception, ripen better off the tree and stored inside. Nothing is more disappointing than a tree-ripened, mealy, tasteless pear. Pears are among the most health-giving of all fruit. I feel sorry for health conscious people who determinedly munch a bowl of bran every morning (tasting like sawdust, but good for us) when they can achieve the same benefits by eating a couple of pears. Infinitely more delicious, pears have a very high fibre content and contain vitamins A, B, and C as well as significant amounts of iodine.

Tomatoes are starting to become more abundant. These too need to be picked at the right time for the best flavour. As soon as the base of each tomato has started to show a distinct pink flush, even though the rest of the skin is bright green, pick it and store it inside the house. They ripen up, and are better flavoured, out of the sun. Hot sun on ripe tomatoes destroys much of their taste. High temperatures, and low ones, make tomatoes flavourless. That's why those people who wrongly prune away the leaves of their plants to expose the fruits to the sun, are usually disappointed with the final result. It is also the reason why those expensive tomatoes we buy in the off-season have such a lousy flavour. They have ripened under cool conditions. Inside an average home, at this time, the temperature is ideal but don't ruin everything by placing your picked tomatoes on the window sill.

Cucumbers are at their best when they are young, crisp, tender and dark green. Keep picking them continuously, even if meals can't use up the supply. They can always be made into pickle. Once the skin has taken on a conspicuously yellow colour, they are getting a bit past it and are usually quite coarse inside, so chuck them out.

Onions occupy the best part of the garden for longer than most other vegetables. So it pays to get the best value from them at this time, when the long-keepers are due to be harvested. The main thing is to ensure that they will keep well and the way they are harvested will determine this. As soon as the tops start to go pale yellow at their tips, slide a fork beneath each one and lift it out of the ground so that the roots are clear. Shake off any soil, then lay the plants out flat, over the place where they grew. They will gradually dry out and the necks will shrivel and become narrower. Be ready to turn them occasionally, especially after a dewy night or a shower. Then when the tops are fully dried, bring them inside a shed or garage, spread them out and let them dry out further. Sort out any onions with really thick necks or grossly large bulbs and put them to one side. These won't keep, so they must be used up first. The remainder can be stored by spreading them on wire mesh so that there is plenty of air circulating around them, or tied up into ropes.

Making an onion rope is easier to do than try and describe.

You need a metre of strong string, baling twine is ideal, which is doubled, the two ends tied together and looped over a nail. A good, big onion is then secured to the bottom of the string to weigh it down so it is like a pendulum. The dried leaves of the onions are kept on, as each one is thrust through the doubled string, turned around it once, then thrust through again. The next onion is hung in the same manner, but from the opposite side. It is a very simple, quick operation and in no time at all you have an attractive rope of tightly packed but well aerated onions, weighing up to six or seven kilograms.

Then you cut off all the protruding leaves neatly and start on the next rope. This treatment is also good when garlic is dried off in the same way as onions.

Lawn Making

There are many reasons why this is the best time of the year to construct a new lawn or renovate an old one. The main one is the approaching cooler, moister weather and the enormous advantages this will give to newly sown grass seed.

Once the seed has been sown and watered a few times, the weather virtually takes over the job, so that by springtime an excellent sward will have developed. Winter and spring rains will encourage the new roots to delve deeper and spread into areas which remain moist well into the summer.

The basic difference between spring and autumn sown lawns is that the spring ones need constant watering through the summer. Even then the results, after several months, can be patchy and shallow-rooted.

At this time of the year there is still enough warmth in the soil to ensure a fairly rapid germination of seed. This means that the grass can compete effectively with the inevitable weeds which also pop up. Soil is more easily worked at this time of year, being dry and, after cultivation, loose. This makes levelling operations much easier.

When preparing an area for a new lawn, it isn't necessary to cultivate to a great depth. Usually, about ten centimetres will be sufficient, unless there is considerable unevenness to be eliminated. Deep cultivation can create all sorts of problems, particularly hollows which appear after the lawn has been laid, as the loose subsoil settles here and there.

Once the initial cultivation has taken place, carefully rake the surface, levelling any depressed spots or slight mounds. This raking, which is best carried out while the soil is quite dry, will also disturb any weed growth which may be trying to re-establish itself.

Ideally, fertilizers should be applied about three weeks before the seed is sown, but this is not always possible. People tend to go straight into the business of cultivating and sowing without a break and there is no real harm done.

The best fertilizers include blood and bone, which is slow acting. This relatively slow availability means the roots chase the nutrients downwards as they are released, taking them into moister areas. If virgin soil is being made into a lawn, it pays to rake in a tiny fistful of fertilizer for each square metre, actually as the seed is being raked into the surface. I always add about ten per cent by bulk

---

> Trees can be safely pruned now, especially those which tend to bleed easily such as walnuts, silver birch and maples. Fruit trees which have borne can have misplaced and in-growing branches removed.

---

of sulphate of potash to blood and bone, making an excellent, balanced fertilizer for most soils. In other words, if you are about to construct a lawn, apply a mixture of blood and bone with potash (500 grams of potash for each five kilograms of blood and bone) at the rate of forty grams per square metre of newly cultivated soil. Then, a week or so later, when the seed is sown into the prepared, even surface, include half a matchboxful of superphosphate per square metre.

Don't make the mistake of concentrating on a superfine seed for average lawns. This only creates extra work later when coarser grasses keep germinating conspicuously in the fine turf. Unless you are prepared to put up with this, it is better to have a mixture containing some coarse grass. A good mix for most conditions is one part each of Browntop, Chewings fescue and perennial ryegrass.

This can be sown at the rate of thirty to forty grams per square metre, as evenly as possible, and raked gently into the surface. If you insist upon a fine lawn, cut out the ryegrass altogether.

At this stage the area should be watered evenly and consistently so that it can be saturated without washing away the soil. With very dry soil this means a series of gradual waterings, stopping often to allow a good soaking-down to occur and, above all, making sure that washaways do not begin.

Most seed will germinate within three weeks and then the irrigation may be slowed down a little, but watch out for dry spots.

Herbs

Every garden should have a small section dedicated to the growing of different types of herbs. Herbs can be used for adding important flavours to food, as a type of medicine, for applying externally to relieve aches and pains, for making soothing drinks, and for growing among other plants to help control diseases and insect pests.

Herbs differ from most other plants because of the strong volatile oils and other substances contained within them. Many herbs use these pungent flavours to survive because grazing animals are able to eat relatively small amounts of the stems and leaves.

The enormous advantage of growing herbs is not so much the saving in money, or even the convenience of being able to pick them fresh from the doorstep. The good thing about growing your own is that you can be sure they are free of pesticides and herbicides. Far too many of the herbs we purchase in a dried form from shops have been imported from parts of the world where pollution is a serious problem and where indiscriminate use of toxic substances is allowed to go unchecked.

To plant a herb garden is fairly easy. The main planning task is to locate it in the best place for both convenience and growing conditions. Ideally, this should be as near as possible to the kitchen, because the majority of herbs here are used in cooking.

Most herbs need a lot of sunshine to fully develop their characteristic flavours.

The other thing most herbs require is a very well drained place in the garden. If there is any doubt about the free drainage of an area or if the soil is mainly heavy clay, it could be a mistake to plant in those conditions. Usually, it is much better to import fresh soil to add to the existing clay, so that the surface of the herb garden is much higher than the surrounding garden.

Large rocks can be used to create what appears to be a natural, rocky outcrop, and a soil mixture added. This will produce a kind of rock garden, but one for growing herbs rather than alpine plants. The main soil mixture should have mixed in with it a large amount of granulated peat (about one third, by bulk) and a few barrowloads of coarse bluemetal screenings. These will keep the texture of the soil open and free draining. Dolomite limestone, spread at the rate of two double handfuls for each square metre will, if worked well into the soil mix, provide an important source of calcium and magnesium.

Fertilizers, apart from sulphate of potash and an initial dressing of bone meal or superphosphate, are best used very lightly in herb gardens. Too much, and the flavour of the herbs will fade as their lushness increases. The aim, when growing herbs, is to force them to grow in fairly impoverished soil. These hungry conditions allow for the development of extremely strongly-flavoured herbs. Some exceptions to this rule include varieties of mint, most of which seem to thrive in damp situations.

Many herbs complete their flowering during the one season, and these can be dried for storage. Dried herbs are invariably three times stronger than fresh green ones.

The easiest way to dry herbs is to cut them off just above the ground, tie them in bundles, and then wrap a sheet of newspaper around each bundle. This will keep the drying herbs free from dust. They should never be dried in the sun, as this causes an immediate loss of important, volatile oils.

The simplest method of ensuring that the herbs dry evenly and slowly, is to hang the bundles from the ceiling of a garage or attic, where there is a good flow of dry air. Later, when the leaves and stems have become dry and brittle, the herbs can be crushed and stored in airtight containers, rejecting only the hard, woody material.

Here is a list of some of the most common herbs, their growing conditions, and uses.

Balm *(Melissa officinalis)*. This is a low-growing perennial plant, with a sharp, lemony scent and flavour. It will grow in sun or part shade. The leaves are used as a flavouring for seasoning and can be cooked with vegetables to enhance their flavour. Lemon balm tea has been appreciated for many centuries, and is used as a soothing drink to help dispel flatulence.

Basil *(Ocimum basilicum)*. This highly regarded annual is grown mainly in summer, forming a bush about half a metre tall. Often eaten with tomatoes, it is a major ingredient in many Italian dishes.

Chives *(Allium schoenoprasum)*. Probably the oldest of all cultivated herbs, the delicately onion-flavoured chives will grow in any sunny position. Often planted among roses to help dispel greenfly, they make an attractive plant when in flower. Used for flavouring salads, omelets, sandwiches, fish, poultry, and soups, their main advantage is when onions may be considered too strong.

Comfrey *(Symphytum officinale)*. This remarkable herb has an outstanding reputation as a healer. Its nickname 'Knitbone' speaks for itself. It is mainly used as a poultice on damaged muscles and external wounds. A recent fashion for eating large quantities has now been frowned upon, because of adverse effects.

Marjoram *(Origanum majorana)*. Mixed with sage, thyme and other herbs, this sharply-flavoured plant makes up the common 'mixed herbs' used in cooking. It grows strongly on the edge of the herb garden, and its growth is improved by regular division and replanting.

Mints *(Mentha* spp.). Most of us know the common English mint, or spearmint, of which there are many varieties. This is one herb which can be used generously in a wide number of savoury and sweet dishes. Peppermint is grown mainly for making a special tea, which will relieve indigestion. There are many other mints, most of which will grow strongly under average conditions.

Parsley *(Petroselinum crispum)*. Here is one of the great herbs, being very rich in minerals and vitamins. Like the peppermints, parsley can be used in large amounts in most dishes. Plants can be used as ornamentals to provide bright green borders in the flower garden, and can be planted out all the year round.

Sage *(Salvia officinalis)*. This is a superbly pungent herb, which loves a sunny, well-drained spot. It can be grown easily from seed, and even very old clumps can be cut back hard and then divided into separate healthy plants for replanting. Apart from the magnificent flavour it gives to a huge range of dishes, it has the ability to aid the digestion of fatty foods.

Tarragon *(Artemisia dracunculus)*. French tarragon is considered by many of the great chefs of the world to be the queen of all the herbs. However, this plant is propagated from divisions during spring, and not from seed. The seeds we see in shops are those of the Russian tarragon, and this is almost worthless as a culinary herb.

Thyme *(Thymus vulgaris)*. Another ancient herb, and a lover of dryish soil, thriving in the sun. A good handful of limestone around the plants every now and then helps to keep the flavour sharp, and the leaves beautifully aromatic.

MARCH: THIRD WEEK

Products from the Sea

Our greatest source of good soil fertility is the sea. The greatest of all soil conditioners is seaweed.

How is seaweed best used in the garden, and does it need any special treatment to get rid of the salt?

The amazing thing about seaweed is its ability to reject salt. It does this so effectively that even though it grows in very salty water, it contains little salt. So it can be used directly on the garden, without washing. Even taken straight from the water, it is salt free.

Seaweed is best used either as a mulch spread over the soil or as part of a compost heap. It must never be dug into the ground, as this would cause serious problems of imbalance, mainly in the form of a massive nitrogen deficiency. Also the seaweed would lie in the soil, without properly decaying, for very long periods.

Spread thickly over the surface, around and between plants, seaweed breaks down with great speed, and soon disappears naturally into the soil.

It is even better if the seaweed can be mixed with a little manure, old straw or even grass clippings, because then it becomes a weed supressor too.

Are there any problems caused by using lots of seaweed?

Yes. However, the problems are actually caused by other materials such as beach sand, crushed shells or dead marine creatures, all of which are mixed up with seaweed when it is collected.

This type of material is alkaline and acts upon the soil in the same way as lime. This is fine for most plants, especially in the vegetable garden, but when heavy dressings of seaweed are applied around acid-loving plants such as rhododendrons, azaleas, camellias, ericas, and a whole host of Australian inland native plants, some of them become quite pale and lose vigour.

So go easy with the seaweed on plants such as these.

The vegetable and fruit garden are the natural places to use seaweed because so many of the important minerals contained in it are absorbed by the plants and fruit, and we get a bit when we eat them.

Spread seaweed in a layer about ten centimetres (four inches) deep. Sometimes a generous sprinkling of blood and bone or fowl manure, over the surface of the soil or the mulch, will help it break down even more rapidly.

What about making compost with seaweed?

This is the best compost of all, especially with a good mixture of pulled weeds, straw or any other waste organic matter. With the addition of a few shovelsful of manure and constant turning while watering, the compost produced is suitable for all plants, including the acid lovers.

What other products from the sea can be used for the garden?

Apart from fish waste, which makes superb manure, there are some surprising products. One is sea-sand. Not many people realize that our beach sands have a high degree of alkalinity and that they can often be used in place of lime. In heavy, acid soils, large amounts of this sand can be mixed into the top twenty centimetres with very good results. Heavy, sour, unproductive soils can be rapidly converted into good vegetable or flower gardens, which are easily worked. However, remember that sea-sand contains very little plant food and minerals, apart from calcium, so these will need to be added.

One other substance obtainable from the sea, which can be used in the garden, is seawater itself. This is because it contains, in suspension, an extraordinary number of different elements, apart from salt. Naturally, seawater must be used with very great care, and heavily diluted, otherwise plants will be killed by it. Some people even use it as a weed killer on paths and other hard surfaces, without adding fresh water. This is a practice to be handled with care because, should any surplus run off onto an adjoining garden area, considerable damage will be done to plants growing there.

A desertspoonful of seawater added to a full bucket of fresh water, and definitely no more, will make a useful foliar feed for spraying onto vegetables and fruit trees. Make the mistake of adding a bit more than this and certain damage will occur.

So, one answer to problems of diminishing soil fertility lies in the sea, or on the beaches, provided we don't overdo it. And in some states, removal of seaweed from beaches is illegal. So check with your local department of agriculture first.

Late Vegetables

Many people will be scratching their heads at this time, wondering which vegetables can be successfully planted.

Well, there is a surprising range, although it is easy to make mistakes. Some will start to grow while the soil remains warm but will fail later as the really cool weather strikes.

For example, cabbages, caulies and broccoli sown outside, directly into the soil, will remain half-developed through the winter, and many will be unable to cope with the inevitable late winter, early spring rains, because they are too small.

So, if you must plant brassicas, sow the seed under cover and allow the seedlings to develop into well-sized rosettes before placing out, perhaps during July. Otherwise, plant well-grown, sturdy seedlings out now, and feed them with diluted liquid fertilizers to help them grow quickly.

English spinach is a particularly useful winter vegetable which has not been grown as much as it should in Australia. One of the reasons has been its tendency to bolt to seed, or a failure to grow to any good size.

The secret of growing good spinach here is to use plenty of lime. Some fairly acid soils, untreated, mean a certain failure with these lime-loving plants. A good double handful every square metre may sound too much, but you will be astonished by the response. If using limestone or dolomite, use twice as much. Ideally calcium should be applied several weeks before planting time, so plant your spinach seeds into previously well-limed soil, or lime now, rake it in, water well, then plant into this soil, without nitrogenous fertilizers or manures. Never try to plant seedlings of spinach, or even transplant overcrowded seedlings to new places. They will bolt to seed. Like carrots and even beetroot at this time, direct seeding should be the method of planting.

The main vegetable to be planted from now onwards are the broad beans. These too are lime-lovers, so be generous, especially if the soil is old pasture, or virgin soil.

The main benefit from an early planting of broad beans is the winter-hardening process which takes place. One of the great pests of this vegetable are the black aphids which attack during mid-spring and later. Plants which have been toughened by cold weather are unattractive to these insects and are usually left alone. It is always the spring-sown crops which are vulnerable.

The varieties of broad bean types give good scope for a wide range of growing conditions. In windy areas, the low-

> In the flower garden, the various spring bulbs are now being planted. Tulips and hyacinths can go in now, and if the soil is good, don't bother using fertilizers. Some people have been chilling their tulip bulbs for a few weeks in the refrigerator before planting them out. This will help them produce long stemmed, healthy blooms. They need the cold to be able to do this.

growing Coles Dwarf Prolific should be planted. These are short, sturdy plants which bear a generous crop of tasty beans. On the other hand, the much taller Aquadulce, or Leviathan Long Pod, are excellent for average gardens. They are best planted in double rows, 150 millimetres between seeds, each row a metre apart. The double planting helps to reduce wind damage.

Apart from a need for calcium, broad beans are also hungry for potassium and phosphorus. A complete fertilizer containing both these essential elements will be needed in most soils. I have always preferred blood and bone with about ten per cent added sulphate of potash, and have obtained excellent yields year after year. However, on virgin soil this is not enough and a tight fistful of superphosphate should be applied to each metre of ten-centimetre-deep drill, and the seed planted directly into this.

Other vegetables which can be sown or planted now are parsley, winter lettuce (Black Velvet, Imperial D, Winterlake, or Mignonette), radish, silverbeet (plants) and turnips. If you want to take a chance with late sown carrots, have a go, but they may be small and pale coloured when they are harvested.

Feeding the Soil

The importance of organic matter in the soil cannot be overestimated. It plays a role of enormous significance, not simply by helping to control sharp fluctuations in soil temperature, but acting as a kind of sponge and helping the soil hold moisture.

Organic mattter also acts as a kind of larder for various minerals and other plant foods, allowing the plants to absorb their requirements in a gentle way.

So, the question is: which is the best way to incorporate this important ingredient into our garden soils?

The simplest and easiest way is to spread half-decayed plant matter such as lawn clippings, wilted weeds, leaves, old straw and spoilt hay over the surface, as a mulch, and let the worms and other soil creatures do the job of gradually taking it down. It is staggering to see the speed with which earthworms deal with a layer of organic matter. One week the surface is strewn with a thick, healthy layer and a week or so later, bare patches start to appear. Before long the whole surface needs to be replenished.

The interesting thing about the role of worms is that the more organic materials are available on the surface, the more the worms will multiply in the soil. Gardens without worms are invariably gardens with little organic matter in the soil.

Digging plant wastes into the soil can be a bit tricky. If the material happens to be a little bit woody or coarse, the effect of the soil's micro organisms trying to break it down can actually produce a serious deficiency of nitrogen. The worst cases I have ever seen occurred when people incorrectly dug sawdust or seaweed into the ground. The effect of this subsequent nitrogen deficiency was unthrifty growth of plants, with a poor, pale leaf colour.

This is the ideal time of the year to enrich the soil in a special way. Green manure crops can go in now as seed, so that later on the resultant growth can be cultivated into the soil. Digging in this raw organic matter will not cause nitrogen deficiency problems because, being green and lush, it contains good quantities of this element, plus many more.

It must seem odd to many people, to actually grow something to a certain stage and then dig it in. The secret is that this process is carried out before the 'winter-tares', as they are called, have started to form their seed and become a bit woody.

The traditional seeds for people to sow at this time, for green manure, have been Algerian oats and tickbeans. These provide good quantities of excellent organic matter and plenty of nitrogen, especially from the legume. Blue lupins too are used as a good source of nitrogen.

The other advantage of these winter crops is that they occupy and grow strongly in cool, wet soil. They keep the soil active and sweet, while the density of the planting also helps to supress weed growth.

Recently I have changed the type of plant I use for green manure. Instead of Algerian oats, I have been experimenting with ryecorn. The variety King II grows with extraordinary vigour, producing much more green matter than the Algerian oats.

The best results of all were when a combination of tickbeans and King II ryecorn were sown together at this time last year. They developed into a thick mass of healthy green growth, even in a fairly wet, cold area, and they were turned into the soil during the first week in September. At that time, the rapidly-warming soil ensured a quick decaying process and I had tomatoes growing rapidly in the enriched healthy soil about five weeks later.

MARCH: LAST WEEK

Hedges

People are still planting hedges around their gardens, but over the last decade there has been a significant change in the type of plants used.

At one time, the most popular hedge in south-eastern Australia was Lambert's cypress *(Cupressus lambertiana)* and there are still thousands everywhere. There were two major problems with this bright-green attractive hedge: the cost of clipping, which should be carried out twice yearly to be effective, and the serious problem of fire danger. These hedges burn with intense heat, presenting a menace to adjacent buildings, and once they are burned, there is no recovery.

Another problem with *lambertiana* hedges occurs when attempts are made to cut them back hard, into the older wood. Regrowth rarely takes place, and hundreds of disfigured hedges around Australia bear witness to unskilled efforts at hedgecutting.

The trend today is to plant shrubs which will grow into easily maintained, compact forms that need very little clipping.

There are hundreds of shrubs which can be used as hedges, some producing masses of colourful flowers. They come in all sizes, and their main characteristic is a close, dense foliage and the ability to respond to an occasional pruning.

Australian native plants are particularly well-suited for growing into hedges, because of their ability to withstand the fairly dry summers we have. Here are some of these plants, ranging from quite small plants to large screening plants.

Melaleuca diosmifolia. This neat bush grows about half a metre, producing plenty of attractive mauve brushes during summer. It seems to thrive in cold, saturated conditions, and can stand heavy clay. A light clipping for the first few years will make a compact hedge which can be quite an eye-catcher.

Calocephalus brownii (cushion bush). This silvery dome needs full sun and very well drained soil. It is a marvellous seaside plant. Growing to about one metre, and with a spread of the same, it produces an extra bonus of hundreds of tiny yellow-green flowers. A hedge of cushion plants, with some occasional but necessary clipping, makes an unforgettable sight. No clay and an open, sandy soil provide perfect conditions.

Eriostemon myoporoides (wax plant). This is a superb, tight, frost-hardy plant, which grows to one and a half metres. It is a startling, beautiful sight in full bloom, with hundreds of white, star-like flowers in late spring. Very easy to grow in most situations.

Correa baeuerlenii (Chef's Hat correa). This lovely shrub is a fascinating sight with masses of dark green, glistening leaves among which nestle dozens of unusual green bells, looking for all the world like a miniature chef's hat. Here it grows to about one and a half metres, can be freely clipped after flowering, and is ideal as a medium hedge plant.

Grevillea 'Golden Sparkle'. This is one grevillea which grows well in a clay soil, and can even withstand some shade. It has bright, variegated leaves and masses of dull red spider flowers. As a hedge it can offer great character to the edge of any garden. Grows to over a metre and spreads about the same.

Hakea laurina (pin-cushion plant). This popular large shrub will grow to over two metres. Its round red flowers with interesting white protruding spikey styles make this one of the great shrubs in any native landscape. Grown as a hedge, the pincushion plant, with regular pruning after flowering, is extraordinarily beautiful. Good drainage essential.

These are but a few of the many plants useful as hedges. All of those mentioned should be easy to obtain from native plant nurseries. The planting distance depends upon the size, but on average, about a metre or more between plants is close enough, except for the really small ones. These are planted much closer together.

> Evergreen trees and shrubs can be transplanted successfully at this time of the year if the summer heat has passed its peak. The still-warm soil allows for that little extra root growth before winter brings it to an end. Citrus trees, azaleas, rhododendrons, camellias, and a whole range of similar plants can be moved now to a new position, but don't forget to keep the rootballs intact.

More Vegetables for Spring

Later on this year, particularly during spring, many people will be paying high prices for a whole range of vegetables.

With a little planning now, and some judicious planting, you can be walking smugly past these expensive vegetables in the shops, because you have a well-stocked garden of your own.

Here are some of the vegetables which can be planted out within the next week or so, to be ready for eating from August onwards.

Broad Beans. Plant them now and they will be up and moving within a fortnight. They will continue to grow slowly until the really cold weather, then they remain without moving for a month. About August they take off again to start bearing from the end of September. This winter chilling is important because it toughens the foliage, making it unattractive to insect pests. Broad beans planted in spring will still mature at the same time, but inevitably get attacked by black aphids. Make sure the soil has been well limed and add a side dressing of potash at the rate of forty grams for each two metres of row at the end of July. Varieties to try are: Coles Dwarf (excellent for windy areas), Leviathan Longpod, and if you are a gourmet broad bean eater, Green Windsor.

Cabbage. Plants are more reliable than seed this late in the season and most nurseries will have seedlings available of good varieties. These, too, like a well-limed soil, preferably from a previous crop of lime-lovers, such as onions. They need plenty of well-decayed manure working into the soil, but never at the same time as the lime. However, if you are using dolomite or ground limestone, the manure can safely be applied at the same time. Good varieties for planting now are: Superette, Oxheart, and Diadem. A good tasty winter cabbage is the diminutive Sugarloaf.

Cauliflower. These are grown, if possible, in the same bed as all the other members of the cabbage tribe for easier rotation. Plant now the most reliable type, Paleleaf. To prevent 'whiptail' of the leaves, spray with a heavily diluted mixture of Sodium Molybdate. (About a thimbleful to a bucket of water, with seaweed concentrate added, is an excellent foliar feed for seedling cauliflowers.)

Lettuce. Seeds of Imperial D, Winterlake and the small, sweet Mignonette varieties can be sown now. They all do best in a sandy soil, because the drainage is so good, and the soil will not become dead-cold during winter. If yours is a clay soil, be prepared to transplant onto low ridges to allow for good drainage. In really cold districts, place a plastic bag over the growing plant to protect it from cold winds. Lettuces love plenty of water but it must be moving through the soil for best results.

Onions. These are very hardy plants indeed, that's why so many varieties are sown during the winter months. Right now you can sow the seeds of Odourless and White Spanish types. With some of the long-keepers, a too-early sowing will cause them to bolt to seed, so wait until later before planting these. Spring onions can be sown successfully all the year round, and these can be simply broadcast into a broad drill, and sown quite thickly. But don't forget, onions just will not grow without plenty of lime in the soil!

Peas. Selected varieties can be planted now in warmer areas. William Massey is only a short-growing plant which will mature quicker than most others. Peas are traditionally planted in the winter-spring period, and the general aim is to achieve blossom and fruit pod-set after the frosts have finished. Early districts can produce good yields of peas, provided there are no frosts, the drainage is good, and there is plenty of organic matter in the soil. They are also lime-lovers, so avoid sour soil.

Radishes. Can be grown all the year round in most districts. Good types to try are Long Scarlet, White Icicle, French Breakfast and Red Prince. They are all valuable during winter, and will mature with great speed.

Silverbeet. Will succeed from seed only in warm areas now, but seedlings can often grow and be at a picking stage within a couple of months in any well drained part of the garden.

Spinach. This is a winter vegetable which, like onions, will remain stunted if the soil is too acid. But sow the prickly seed now.

In cooler districts it is either too late or too early for most of the other vegetables.

Later I'll tell you how to get the best results from planting long-keeping onions, as well as high yields from peas, so prepare now by liming those parts of the vegetable garden where they are to be grown.

Garden Design

Autumn is always a good time to carry out landscaping operations. The weather is cool enough to enable most of us to work hard without getting too overheated, while the soil is still warm enough to allow for the transplanting of a huge range of evergreens more safely than at most other times of the year.

The prospect of winter rains, giving most new plantings a chance to settle in, is also a major reason why it is such a good time to reorganize a garden or begin from scratch.

An enormous amount of rubbish is written and said about the actual task of designing a garden. There appears to be a growing trend these days to try and mystify or obscure this most creative art. There is even a new kind of jargon which seems to be aimed at intimidating people into believing that landscaping is something so extraordinarily complex and difficult, that only a tight group of self-styled experts can do the job properly.

When faced with this kind of thing, it is easy to forget that the greatest gardens in the world have been created by plant lovers who have been willing to experiment with trees, shrubs and other plants, learning as they went.

In other words, the real satisfaction from landscaping comes from solving simple site problems, working out rough plans and guiding the developing garden into the kind of place we are aiming at all the time.

In essence, good garden design is nothing more than a compromise between what is wanted, and what the site will give. Every site is different, even with adjoining, identically-shaped pieces of land. By understanding the special char-

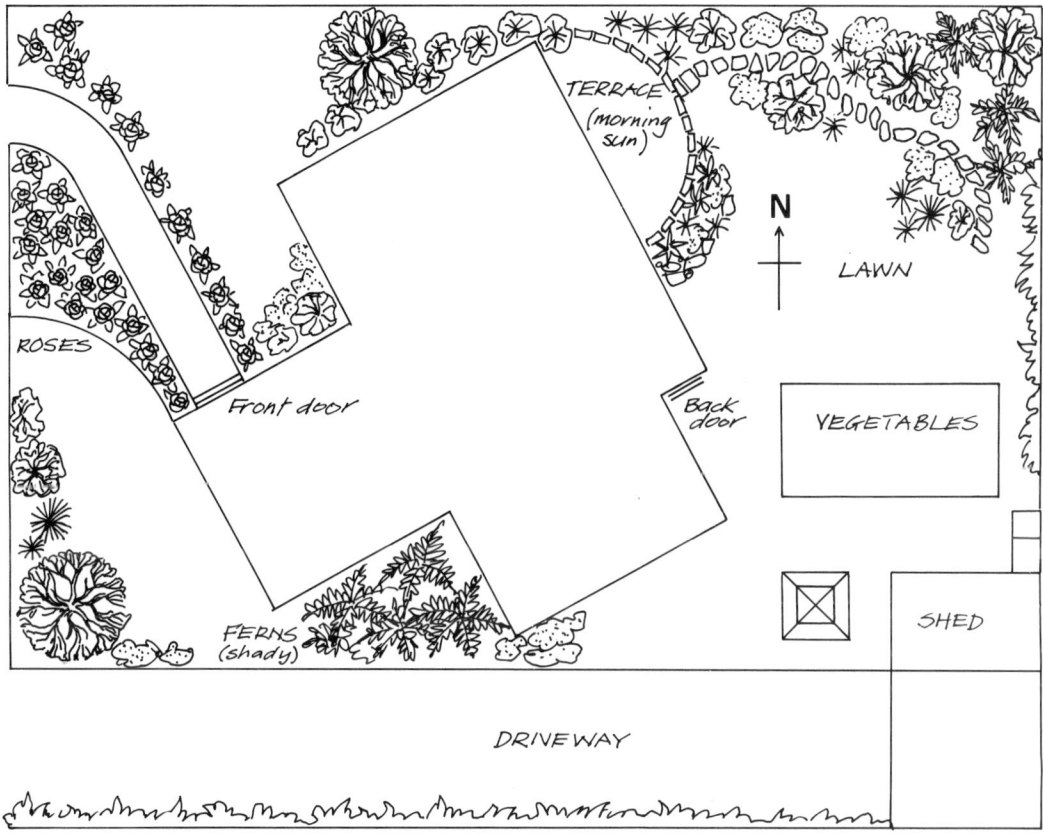

Sketch Plan of a Site Drawn to Scale

acteristics of your own site, it is possible to create a successful and attractive garden, provided you don't go beyond what the site offers.

Here are some of the things which must be taken into consideration before making any purchases, or any plans.

1. The quality of the soil, whether it is clay, sandy, or a mixture, will determine which plants will succeed. Sometimes, with newly-built homes, good soil can be ruined by the indiscriminate excavating of useless subsoil, and spreading it everywhere. Importing fresh, good quality topsoil can often be better than a lifetime of trying to make non-productive deposits grow good plants. But try to salvage the original topsoil, which may simply have been compacted by building machinery. It could first be mechanically cultivated and then spread with organic material. Beware of new weed species if you must import topsoil.

2. A site with a persistent wind blowing through it will never succeed with normal plants. If the wind is from the sea, the salt content will play havoc with some of the most cherished shrubs and trees. The answer is to plant a first line of defence, using special wind resistant plants to disperse the wind. Alternatively, plant a garden containing only those trees and shrubs which can withstand harsh, exposed conditions.

3. Badly-drained soil will always produce stunted, diseased and miserable plants, unless only those plants which thrive in such conditions are used. A good, subsoil drainage system is relatively cheap and easy to install these days. Provided it is deep enough, most problems of wet feet will be avoided.

4. The shadows thrown by existing trees or buildings at crucial times of the day will decide where most plants can be located. It is wise to sketch in, on a rough plan, where the sunny and shady places are, especially during the first part of the day. Plants do have preferences: roses love the sun, azaleas and camellias like afternoon shade, and all plants thrive in places which suit them.

Other factors such as views, privacy, overhead wires and underground pipes also help to determine the location and type of plants in a garden which has been thoughtfully designed.

APRIL
GUIDE TO ACTION

Ornamental Garden

Lift and divide overcrowded lily of the valley plants. Plant spring bulbs. Take rose cuttings. Prune easy-bleed trees, such as birch, maple and walnut. Lay or sow lawns. In the flower garden plant: achillea, alyssum, anemone, antirrhinum, aquilegia, arctotis, calendula, candytuft, Canterbury bells, carnation, cineraria, cornflower, delphinium, dianthus, foxglove, geum, freesia, gypsophila, hollyhock, lupin, myosotis, nemesia, ornamental kale, penstemon, polyanthus, Iceland poppy, oriental poppy, hellebore, primula, ranunculus, scabiosa, shasta daisy, stock, sweetpea, sweet William, viola, violet and wallflower.

Vegetable Garden

Make compost. Rough dig vacant beds, lime if needed and sow cover crops for digging-in later. Well-sized brassica seedlings must be planted out in cool districts to succeed now. Sow broad beans, Chinese cabbage, spinach, turnip, winter lettuce and, in warm areas, brassicas. Spring onion seed can be sown thickly in wide drills, one centimetre deep. Leeks go in as thick, well-developed plants. Make liquid manure for dribbling around leafy vegetables. Watch out for caterpillars on young brassicas and, if necessary, safe spray with Dipel. Apply lime to beds which will be used for onions or peas later on. Cut asparagus ferns to the ground as they fade.

Fruit Garden

Spray peach and nectarine trees, as leaves are cast, with Bordeaux for controlling leafcurl. Prune all stone fruit trees as fruit is harvested. Apply limestone or dolomite around stone fruits and those apple trees which have been showing signs of 'bitter pit' in the fruit. Prune berry fruit by removing all old canes of raspberry and bramble bushes. Loosely tie together the new canes for next year's crops. Prune blackcurrant bushes by cutting out all old, dark-coloured branches to leave younger ones. Clean up strawberry beds, cut off all large leaves and plant out new runners if plants are two years old or less. Remove codlin moth grub bandage traps and burn. Mulch all fruit trees and berry fruit plants.

Houseplants

Place gloxinias on side to slightly dry out. Reduce watering of houseplants as temperature falls. Re-pot rootbound plants. Spray for two-spotted mite and scale with pyrethrum or Clensel. If a toxic spray is considered, do the job outside.

APRIL: FIRST WEEK

Sweetening the Soil with Lime

Soils which are left cleared until spring can remain in a cold and saturated condition all that time. As a result they become sour and, in slow draining areas, difficult to cultivate. Many forms of essential soil bacteria disappear. All this means a poor start to each growing season, because such soils never achieve their full potential.

It's an ideal time right now to do something about it. Autumn is perfect for soil-sweetening operations, and it is easy and cheap to do.

Calcium, in the form of lime, limestone or dolomite should be applied now to the surface of the soil in most parts of the garden. Only those areas where certain ornamentals which dislike lime, such as rhododendrons, azaleas, ericas, camellias, and most Australian native plants, should not be limed.

The most important parts of the garden for liming are the vegetable garden and the herbaceous borders, where this element is essential. Fruit trees, especially stone fruits, should also be given an annual serve.

How much is needed, and how is it best applied?

It depends on the form of calcium used, as well as the acidity of your soil. A simple soil-testing kit can be bought, which will show you the alkaline-acid balance of the soil. I just use observation, noting which plants, especially weeds, seem to thrive. For example, sorrel grows so strongly in acid soil that it can become a serious problem. When there is a lot of this weed around and other plants are becoming crowded out by it, you can be sure that the soil needs lime.

Dolomite is a form of limestone which contains magnesium as well as calcium. This is the most valuable way to reduce acidity because of the extra mineral available. Because of the slow availability of dolomite, it is safe to use with fertilizers and also remains in the soil longer. However, to obtain the same effects as lime, almost twice as much dolomite must be used. With soil which has had no lime for many years, or virgin soil, the amount of dolomite required in typically acidic soils would be about two good handsful for every square metre. It is of some consolation to know that if you overdo this heavy application very little damage will be done.

Crushed limestone is dark greyish coloured, like dolomite, and the only basic difference is that limestone doesn't contain any worthwhile amounts of magnesium. Otherwise it acts in the same way and, like dolomite, will become slowly available over several years. Limestone is the cheapest way of placing plenty of calcium into the soil, costing much less than dolomite or lime.

Lime is the active one. It is snow white, and so fine that it feels silky. It becomes available very quickly and is the sort of calcium I would apply now to onion beds which are to be sown in July. It can also be used with the direct sowing of broad beans, or peas (in protected areas), which are going in now. The effects of using lime on acidic soils can be quite dramatic. Not long ago I spread two bags in an area about the size of half a tennis court. The cabbages, caulies, broccoli, sprouts, carrots, beetroot and particularly onions which grew profusely in that area had to be seen to be believed. Lime is not a fertilizer, it is a means by which certain essential elements in the soil can be 'unlocked', so that they may become absorbed into the plants.

If there is a problem about the overuse of lime and other forms of calcium, it is caused by the speed with which soil so treated will break down organic matter, and use up fertilizers. In other words, to continually apply lime, without subsequently increasing the amount of fertilizers, will eventually impoverish the soil.

> The ornamental garden will be starting to look a bit tired now, so ruthlessly get among all perennial and herbaceous plants, removing all dead flowers and wood. Clean up any weedy areas, if possible before they begin to throw out seed, and throw everything on to the compost storage pile.
>
> Some plants will have already died down. Paeony roses, especially the herbaceous ones, can be lifted and divided now. They will have become unproductive if they are overhung by more dominant plants. They must have full sun and perfect drainage. The divisions of old clumps will probably sulk for a year or so and refuse to bloom.

Pruning the Easy-bleeders

Most plants may be safely pruned at any time of the year. The main factor which determines the timing of cutting back ornamentals is their flowering period.

In other words, the ideal time for almost all trees and shrubs which are grown especially for their blooms is during flowering, or just after. This will allow the plant to develop new flowering wood in order to produce blooms again the following season. Most of these plants have their main flowering time during spring and early summer, and this is why it is such a mistake to prune these plants during winter, when it seems to be the natural time of the year.

What happens, too often, is that such winter-pruned plants are never seen at their best, and few people who carry out such incorrect winter pruning regularly, ever become aware of the potential of their flowering trees and shrubs.

However, in the case of fruit trees and berry fruit, pruning operations may be safely carried out during summer and winter, although the winter is usually preferred because it is much easier to see where to make any cuts. Tradition also plays a significant role. Just the same, over-vigorous trees are much more likely to be curbed if they are cut back while they are in full leaf. This prevents the tree from storing extra reserves of food within its trunk and roots during the dormant season, and consequently reduces the vigour of the new growth in spring.

Trees which are more likely to become

infected with diseases are best pruned while they are actually growing, because the pruning wounds begin to heal immediately, thus sealing any point of potential infection. Apricot trees are a good example of this, and summer or autumn pruning is always to be preferred.

However, there are some trees which resent pruning both during the late dormant period, and in spring or summer. These are the ones which tend to bleed easily, and careless lopping or pruning can often produce weeks of miserable weeping from the wounds. This must seriously weaken the plants as well as leaving them open to infections.

The main trees in this group are the maples, birches and walnuts. All of them present problems of excessive growth after a few years, and they tend to dominate a small garden.

Now is the best time to prune such plants in order to avoid bleeding. It is not necessary to carry out this job every year, or even anytime, except to remove misplaced or dead wood. But when they start to encroach upon areas occupied by plants which cannot stand the competition, or block views, then it is time they were curbed.

Silver birch trees have a characteristic shape which can easily be destroyed by incorrect lopping methods. Sometimes ruthless cutting back cannot be avoided, especially when the trees are grown beneath power lines and need to be dealt with every year. Even then the tree will gradually assert a good shape, although a bit more round in the crown. Normally, correct pruning means reducing the height without spoiling the shape, and this is done by selecting an upward-growing branch, well below the top of the tree, and removing all growth above it. Side branches can then be reduced and cut back, and the result is a smaller tree with roughly the same shape.

Walnut trees can grow much more quickly than people realize, and within a short time can occupy a large part of an average-sized garden. Pruning now, by reducing the height and spread of the crown, will reduce yield, but if all cuts are made at a junction of a branch, some well into the centre, the vigour will be lessened and the height reduced.

Maples should be pruned or lopped basically in the same way as silver birches, and the best time to carry out this treatment is right now, provided that such pruning is really necessary.

Herbaceous and Perennial Plants

Nothing is quite so astonishingly beautiful as a herbaceous and perennial garden in full bloom during summer and autumn. Cool and frosty winters are supremely valuable when it comes to growing these hardy plants, because they are forced to die down and rest during the cold months.

Gardens composed of such hardy plants as delphiniums, foxgloves, lupins, paeonies, achillea, astilbe, carnations, border pinks, Canterbury bells, gypsophila, irises, perennial aster and Japanese wind flowers, as well as dozens of other delights, are reminiscent of old cottages but are suitable for even the most modern homes.

To create such a garden is surprisingly easy, and now is the perfect time to make a start. The site must be a sunny one and any reasonably good garden soil will do, so long as the drainage is good. If the existing soil is heavy clay, it may pay to import some good quality topsoil, and spread it over the surface to a depth of about twenty centimetres. Alternatively, the heavy soil can be lightened by digging in plenty of organic matter or well-decayed old leaves.

The first job is to cultivate the area carefully, preferably with a mattock or heavy hoe, trying to avoid bringing up any of the subsoil. The surface can be left rough and lumpy, and a thick whitening of lime applied over the surface. This is left to lie there and, during the next month or so, the action of the frost and rain will break up any clods and work the lime into the ground naturally.

Most of the plants referred to detest acid soils, and a major soil problem is lack of calcium, so the lime is very important for success.

Many of the herbaceous and perennial plants can be purchased or divided now. Paeonies will have almost completely died down and may be divided into pieces, each with at least two buds attached to each piece of root. The root system can be massive in old clumps, with long, fleshy, brittle taproots going down as far as sixty centimetres or more. It is virtually impossible to lift such roots without breaking them, but the plants rapidly develop new ones within the first season after replanting. However, they generally fail to bloom for the first year while the new roots are being formed.

Other perennials, such as asters, can be gently tugged apart and planted in a waiting bed until early spring when their permanent positions have been prepared.

Lupins can be planted now. If you wish to save costs, save seed. Lupin seed is hard skinned and in order to effect good, even germination, it is best treated by rubbing it gently between two pieces of sandpaper to scratch the hard surface without penetrating it. Planted now, such seed will germinate rapidly and the individual plants can be pricked-out into small pots or plastic drinking-cups with holes in their bases.

There is a big selection of perennials now coming on to the market. They are good value because they can be divided up every year and you will soon get your money's worth.

Tiny seedling delphiniums, available in punnets from nurseries, will grow quickly as soon as the days become longer. They will flower almost non-stop, with some magnificent shades of blue and purple, right through the summer. The expensive alternative is to pay two or three dollars for well-grown crowns during the winter. Once, at this time, I bought seedling delphiniums, carnations, pinks, hollyhocks, Canterbury bells and gypsophila (baby's breath), and potted them into separate containers. By spring, they had all developed strong root systems and never looked back after planting out into the garden.

Perennials such as blazing star (*Liatris*) and canna lilies can be planted. Cannas make a magnificent display with their tall spikes of bright orange, scarlet or vermillion flowers. If you have any old clumps in the garden, which haven't been divided for many years, it will pay to do the job now. Simply wash off the soil from the roots as soon as the clump has been lifted, and pull them apart so that there are two or three points of new growth per division. These plants seem to thrive in the open sun, and all they require is a good, deep soaking at intervals during summer.

Finally, remember to divide up your tuberoses, because if you don't, that will be the end of any flowering.

APRIL: SECOND WEEK

Peaches and Nectarines Through the Season

We can grow beautiful peaches and nectarines in Australia and it is possible, by carefully selecting suitable types, to be able to eat a whole range of them from just before Christmas until half-way through April. The secret of success in growing these fruits is to understand their food and water needs and to be extremely accurate and resolute when dealing with their main disease problems, such as leafcurl and brown-rot.

Now is the time for one of the most important sprays for controlling leafcurl. The substance to use is the good old Bordeaux mixture, which has a very low toxicity rating. In fact, if you decide to mix your own, it is even more effective than the prepared stuff. A simple, easily made recipe can be found on page 201 (Appendix).

Remember Bordeaux is never used on plants or trees when they are in leaf, only when they have just dropped their leaves, or just before the leaves appear in early spring. If you want to really make it stick, add about four tablespoonsful of white oil emulsion, pre-mixed in a little water.

Bordeaux mixture is one of the old, traditional fungicides, and in spite of all the millions of dollars spent on research, it is still one of the best.

If you want to, you can prune your peach and nectarine trees before spraying, but the most urgent task right now is spraying for leafcurl control.

Later, the trees can be sprayed again with a winter wash, to kill any insects, or their eggs, which are in crevices in the bark.

Mulching with straw or old hay during winter and summer will make an enormous difference to the final weight and size of the subsequent crop. During summer, plenty of manure spread on the mulch, and a weekly deep watering over and around the roots, will work wonders.

As for the varieties, one of the earliest is Starking Delicious, with sweet yellow flesh, or Cardinal (another clingstone) with firm fruit. Anzac is a great early favourite, dripping with juice. Mid-January to about the end of February will be the main cropping time for such delights as Red Haven, Blackburn Elberta and the extraordinary J.H. Hale, which produces massive-sized sweet, aromatic, mottled red, yellow-fleshed chunks of sheer heaven – this is one variety which needs to be cross pollinated with another peach.

Among the late or very late, the well-known so-called bottler, Golden Queen, is outstanding for eating fresh, providing it is left to hang on the tree until its firm flesh begins to soften a little. Tatura Sunset is another very late clingstone, which is bigger and juicier than Golden Queen.

The nectarines are Nectered (early), Goldmine (mid-season) and Masterpiece (late). See page 201 (Appendix) for more information on cross-pollination.

If the nursery does not have these varieties in stock, the chances are that they will have already selected a good range of well-tested peaches and nectarines. There are some remarkable sized types now coming on to the market, and the trend these days is to strive for disease resistance, regular, even yields, and delicious flavour.

Transplanting Evergreens

When we have this present situation of cooling weather, but still-warm soil, it is ideal for planting and transplanting a whole range of evergreen trees and shrubs. Ahead are the moist winter months, and this period of semi-dormancy will play a special role in consolidating good conditions for new plantings.

Almost every garden contains plants which could benefit by a move to a new position. These plants may have been correctly located in the first place but have since become dominated by other, more aggressive, trees and shrubs.

If a plant is in the wrong place, according to its own special needs, it will not thrive and often remains stunted and disease-ridden. This can apply to plants which have been mistakenly planted in full, open sun, when they prefer a shady spot.

The most common example of misplanting can often be seen on front lawns. There is nothing quite so sad as the sight of a miserable-looking rhododendron, or a pale, bleached camellia, sitting exposed and lonely in the full blaze of the sun.

The effects of transplanting such unhappy specimens to a position where they receive some afternoon protection are amazing. They are easy to move right now, and it doesn't really matter how long they have been growing in their current spot. Last year I moved a rhododendron which had hardly grown for nearly thirty years, because it was wrongly placed, and within six months it had doubled its size, and this year will bloom for the first time in decades.

So, if you have any such 'problem' plants, this is how to shift them.

First, dig up the new planting area. Excavate a planting hole big enough to hold the approximate size of the rootball, and fill with water. Allow the water to soak away, then, if the area is fairly dry, fill with water again. Also, wet the excavated soil thoroughly. Then leave to soak, overnight if possible. Deeply water the plant to be moved to make sure that the rootball will remain intact during the transplanting operation. Dig out the plant with as much root as possible. With rhododendrons, azaleas, camellias and many conifers, try to include all roots which are within a circle about one third of the way out from the main stem to the edge of the foliage. I usually slide the spade into the soil as deeply and vertically as possible, all the way around the plant first, and with most plants, this is usually enough to loosen the rootball.

Then, the whole lot can be lifted cleanly out of the ground, ready to be moved to the new spot. If there has been any serious root damage, it should be easy to see, so be prepared to remove an equivalent amount of the foliage and branches to balance things.

Don't leave the plant out of the ground, exposed to the drying sun and wind, for more than a few minutes, otherwise it will receive a set-back. Plant straight away in to the prepared site. (If the plant has to be left out of the ground, cover with wet bags and tuck them well in around the roots.)

> Lawns sown now will develop rapidly, but some of the finer grasses will be slower to germinate. Apply fertilizers a week or so before sowing the grass seed. Once sown, keep the seed moist until well after germination.

Unless the plant is quite small, don't haul it around by its stem. Place it carefully on to a bag or plastic sheet and carry or drag it to the new place.

Adjust the new planting hole to ensure a loose fit, but make sure that the top of the rootball is level with the surrounding soil surface. If the plant is even slightly unsteady or straggly, secure it to a wooden stake, driven into the base of the hole first.

Backfill, without adding fertilizers, although a few shovelsful of well-made compost will work wonders. Tread the soil firmly to eliminate any air pockets, and water during the backfilling operation to help consolidate the soil around the roots.

Most citrus fruits can be successfully transplanted now, by the same methods, but with large trees, some root damage will occur, so be ready to start pruning-back or removing branches.

Other plants which can be easily and successfully transplanted at this time are many conifers including cypresses, *chamaecyparis, thuja* and junipers, lily of the valley shrub and *Kalmia latifolia*.

Magnolias such as the deciduous *M. soulangiana* are best transplanted just as their leaves start to fall. Although they are dormant during winter, try to retain the soil around the roots of these plants.

All other deciduous trees can only be successfully moved in winter, and this is particularly true of roses. So if you have a few misplaced problems among these plants, wait awhile.

Draining the Soil

Now is a good time to do something about preventing the soil from becoming too cold during winter, especially in the vegetable garden.

When the soil becomes saturated during the winter, it becomes almost dormant. Cold, wet soil, especially during the months of June, July and August, is virtually non-productive. Part of the reason is poor drainage. This, without doubt, is a major cause of most plant problems. Installing a good, deeply laid, subsoil drainage system will have the most amazing effects on plant health and growth. Normally, such a drain need only be laid into the clay. This may be only twenty centimetres, or less, below the surface. This will take away surplus water from the top portion of the soil, and even if it rains continually, the fact that the water is always moving through the soil, because of the drains, makes such wet conditions harmless.

But, if you are energetic, it is worth considering laying a deep drainage system in districts which are fairly wet during the winter.

About five years ago, I decided to take this step in a very wet part of my own garden. During summer it was hard and very dry, but in winter, especially after about a week's rain, is was so wet, that if it had been cultivated earlier, it was impossible to walk over. I used to sink down in the liquid mud until it was well over the tops of my gumboots. I recall digging a few shallow holes for a later planting of fruit trees, only to find they remained completely filled with water for months.

I dug drains almost two metres deep and spread a thin layer of medium bluemetal over the base of the trench to provide an even fall. Then I laid a plastic drainage pipe along the entire length. Finally, I covered the pipe with more bluemetal, tossed in every stone and brickbat I could find, covered this mixture with some black plastic, and backfilled the remaining thirty or forty centimetres with the best of the top soil. From then onwards water flowed from the drainage pipe outlet day and night, whether it rained or not, except in summer.

The most remarkable effect of this continuous draining away was a dramatic improvement in the soil over the next few years. Because the plants, including weeds, which grew during the winter were able to send their roots down much further, the soil was more or less kept 'working' all the year round. It never had a chance to become cold and stagnant. Not only was the texture and quality of the soil greatly improved, but during the hottest part of the summer, it stopped getting so dry and hard. This was because the essential moulds, fungi and bacteria within the soil were able to extend their area of activity.

The additional value placed upon this small piece of land as a result of the extra-deep drains, is difficult to calculate. Now, even during the coldest, wettest winter, this part of my vegetable garden is producing a wide range of high quality vegetables, whereas a few years ago they would have just sat there without moving.

APRIL: THIRD WEEK

Vegetable Harvesting

Pumpkins will keep for a very long time if they are harvested carefully. The main thing to remember is to try to keep them on the vine as long as possible, while avoiding damage from frosts. I cover mine each night, with an old bag or a forkful of straw over each fruit. When the frost starts to blacken the leaves they can be safely harvested, but should you forget to cover each individual pumpkin, and frost strikes them, they will only last for a few weeks.

If you feel you dare not take the risk, by all means harvest them now. I leave up to half a metre of vine still attached, and take special care not to snap off the main stalk, which is very brittle. Never make the fatal blunder of trying to carry even a light pumpkin by this tempting 'handle'. It will surely snap, and you will either have to eat this one first, or, if there are too many similarly mutilated, give the base of the stalk this special treatment to prevent rotting.

Pour in some melted candlewax so that the broken end is covered, but wipe any dirt away first. Then start to harden the pumpkins off with the others.

If newly harvested pumpkins are left out in the open every day in a sunny place, and carefully covered each night, the skin will set very hard and most slight wounds will seal up. After a week or so of this treatment, the fruit can be stored under cover, with the vine still attached.

Some pumpkins will keep for more than a year by this method.

Carrots and beetroot can be left in the ground through the winter of course, and if they were planted about January or February, they should have reached a good size now, without being woody or coarse. Carrots retain their tenderness and sweetness until about the beginning of August, and then they start to form a harder core as they prepare to go to seed. Beetroot will become much larger through the winter, and will tend to become more starchy and less sweet. This condition is easy to spot by cutting open the beetroot and looking at the rings inside. They should be barely visible; but if they stand out clearly with conspicuous white divisions, starchiness has set in.

When carrots or beetroot are pulled the tops must be screwed off immediately. If this is not done the leaves will suck the bottoms dry, and you will quickly find you have wrinkled, soft and unpalatable roots.

Pruning Berryfruit Bushes

Berryfruit plants grow so easily in southern Australia that we tend to take them for granted, and even neglect them. Yet the enormous difference to both quality fruit, and yield, which is added by reasonable maintenance, has to be seen to be believed.

Black and redcurrants, for example. How many of us can honestly say they have already been pruned, as they should be, immediately after the fruit has been harvested? Many of us still wait until winter before carrying out this essential job, partly out of habit, and mostly because we have other jobs to do during summer which seem to be more urgent.

If these plants haven't been pruned yet; by removing all old, dark-coloured branches to the ground, and leaving the young vigorous canes (in the case of blackcurrants), or pruning back the previous season's growth by about a third, and shortening the small side branches (as in the case of redcurrants); go ahead and do the job now. Early pruning would have let the plant guide its energy and plant foods directly into the limbs which are to carry next year's fruit, and not waste them on wood to be cut out later.

Brambles should receive the same treatment. Their pruning is limited to the removal of all canes which have borne fruit this recent season, and the careful tying of new canes to one side in a loose bundle. The brambles include some of the most delicious of all berryfruit. Loganberries are reputed to be an accidental cross between raspberry and blackberry plants, and will bear a surprisingly large amount of fruit in a small area, especially when they are encouraged to climb up a lattice, or on two or three horizontal wires.

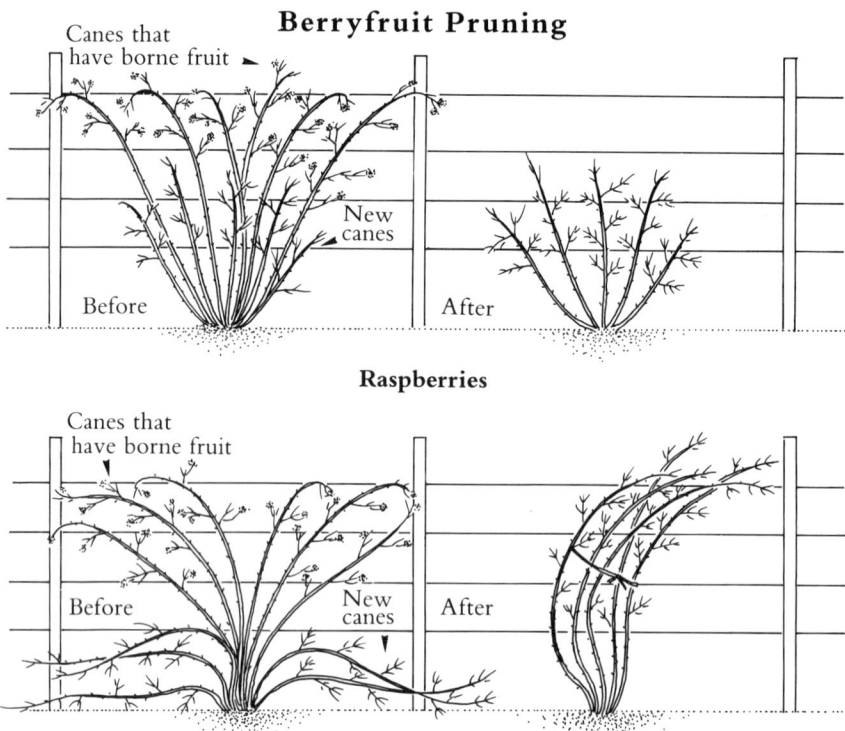

Berryfruit Pruning

Raspberries

Brambles (e.g. loganberries)

Boysenberries have a dull, dark purple colour, and when fully ripe make delicious eating. They are treated the same way as the other brambles and, although the crop may seem lighter, the weight of the quite large berries makes up for their lack of numbers.

The shiny black-purple youngberry has a rich, mouth-watering flavour but like all brambles, they must be allowed to become fully ripe.

All the brambles will grow easily along a fence and, because most of their growth is vertical, they seldom spread into the garden, provided they are kept tied back.

Feeding most berryfruit is a simple task, and now is a good time to begin laying down a larder for the plants to feed off from spring onwards. A thick forty centimetre layer of old, spoilt hay, straw or a mixture of both, with plenty of old animal manure mixed into the surface, is the perfect autumn dressing for berryfruit bushes. This mulch can be tucked in, right up to the bases of the bushes and it will not only suppress weeds but retain water in the soil. By the time spring arrives, much of the mulch will have partly decayed, but will still be lying on the surface. The plants feed off this during the rest of the season.

Raspberry bushes are pruned by cutting out every cane which was produced last season. Most of them are dead anyway. If you have some of the autumn-bearing varieties in your garden, such as Lloyd George, it is a good idea to cut about ten per cent of the bushes right down to the ground now, leaving nothing but a few stumps sticking up. These plants will not bear at all during December-January, but they will bear quite heavily next April. The remainder of the bushes, which are pruned normally, will bear a good, regular crop at the usual time, but are best prevented from bearing in autumn by constantly pulling off their flowers during March.

Any suckers from raspberry bushes should be dug out now, and the pruned bushes tied loosely together with twine. If any of the canes have grown very big, these too can be pruned, by cutting them back to remove the 'hook' which always develops at the top of the most vigorous canes. Remember, however, not to cut back good raspberry canes too hard, because the lower they are cut, the lighter the yield of berries.

> It is still not too late to plant bulbs such as hyacinths or tulips. In fact many experienced gardeners deliberately wait until now to plant them as they need really cool ground conditions to grow.

Autumn Jobs

In the vegetable garden, earlier sowings of broad beans should be well up. This is a good time to give them a side dressing with one substance they seem to need more than most other plants – potash. Sulphate of potash is the best form at this time of the year and about twenty grams for each metre of row should do the trick. There is still plenty of time to continue sowing the seeds, although as the weather becomes really cold, and the chill penetrates into the soil, they will be slow to germinate.

These pre-winter sowings are important because, although spring-sown broad beans will come into bearing at the same time, the danger of insect attack is more likely with the softer, later ones.

If you haven't started to prepare your onion beds for the June-July sowing of long-keepers, do it now. These plants should be started in a weed-free environment, so start to control them now. The main job in the preparation of onion beds at this time is to use plenty of lime, and in virgin, highly-acidic soils, be really generous. A couple of heaped handfuls for every square metre may be needed on really acid soils, and if the grey-coloured ground limestone or dolomite is used, double the amount applied.

In the ornamental garden, hydrangeas will require pruning as soon as the blooms begin to look a bit weathered. They are easy to prune, and once you have grasped the knack, you will be amazed at the size and number of flower heads which develop every year. Simply remove, to the ground, all thick, old branches. If there are young, green branches growing from the bottoms of these old limbs, it is better to retain these. Once the older wood has been cut out, it should leave plenty of young canes – usually about a dozen or so. These new canes need only be pruned back lightly, cutting to a pair of plump buds. If the young wood is reduced too much, you will find that there are no plump buds left, only tiny, dark coloured ones.

When hydrangeas are pruned back too hard, there will be plenty of vigorous new growth, but hardly any blooms. With really old plants, especially those which have been neglected for a number of years, it will be hard to find much new growth. In this case, it is better to cut every second main branch almost to the ground, and leave the rest to produce some blooms. However, next year at this time, there should be plenty of new wood, so it is just a matter of removing the rest of the old stuff.

In other parts of the flower garden, the main job is pruning off the withered remains of last summer's perennials. However, make sure that the location of these plants which die down during the winter is carefully marked with a suitably labelled stick. Planting out annual and perennial plants this month can still be carried out to a surprising extent, considering the cooler conditions. Bulbs such as tulips and hyacinths are available, and will make steady growth from now on. Anemone, ranunculus, freesia, nerine and belladonna lily bulbs and corms will, if carefully planted, produce a stunning display next spring and summer. Seedlings of carnation, border pinks, wallflowers, nemesia, viola, sweet William and stock can all be safely bedded out now, and the rewards will come later.

Liliums do best in the same acid soil loved by rhododendrons and azaleas. This is why I always grow these bulbs in any space I can find among these plants. With good, well-drained soil, fertilizers need not be applied when putting in liliums, except perhaps for well-made compost.

Dahlia plants will be looking a bit frost-bitten in some districts, and it is a good time to lift them for winter storage. Cut back the foliage to leave about fifteen centimetres (six inches) of stalk remaining. Then lift the entire clump of tubers out of the ground with a fork and shake off some of the soil. They must be stored out of the frost, preferably inside a shed, and the name or description of each flower carefully marked on a label which is attached to the clump. They can be divided in spring, but don't allow them to become dried out in the meantime.

APRIL: LAST WEEK

Choosing the Best Fruit and Nuts

It's lovely to be able to go out into your own garden and pick fruit from your own trees. Home-grown fruit is particularly delicious because we can wait until it has ripened to perfection before we eat it.

Our climate is so varied we can grow an enormous range of fruits, including peaches, nectarines, sweet cherries, Japanese and European plums, apricots, apples, pears, citrus, especially lemons, quinces, grapes, passionfruit, figs, mulberry, Chinese gooseberry and persimmon.

In addition, there are the berryfruits, such as raspberries, blueberries, brambleberries, strawberries, gooseberries and currants.

Among the valuable nut trees we can produce excellent yields of almonds, walnuts, hazelnuts and sweet chestnuts.

It is an amazing list, and there are few places on earth where such a big variety of fruits, nuts and berries can be grown successfully.

The key to success is in the type of plant chosen. Some varieties grow better here than others, and many of the fruit trees need to be cross-pollinated with another plant of the same species before it will set fruit.

Now is the time to place your orders for fruit trees, so that they can be planted out during winter.

Apricots, peaches and nectarines usually don't need to be cross-pollinated with another variety. Here are some good types which do well.

Apricots. Moorpark, Tilton, Trevatt.

Peaches. Anzac, Brigg's Red May, Starking Delicious and Golden Queen.

Nectarines. Goldmine and New Boy.

Sweet cherries. These must be pollinated with another variety, otherwise there will be no fruit. Early Rivers, Moss Early, and Ron's Seedling will pollinate each other, as will Lambert, Black Boy, Florence and William's Favourite.

The sour cherries are self-fertilizing, but bigger yields can be obtained if another variety is nearby.

European and Japanese plums will not cross-pollinate each other, so you must have a pair of each for best results. The European plums are perfect for eating and bottling, with an outstanding flavour. Greengage, Golden Drop and Prune D'Agen are great mates, and remember they can be several gardens away and still cross-pollinate successfully.

Japanese plums are earlier and juicier, but will not dry very well. Try Santa Rosa (sweet yellow flesh), with Satsuma

(Blood Plum) and you will get excellent results.

Apples will bear reasonably well without another variety, but if there are other varieties blooming at the same time nearby, a bigger crop is ensured. Gravenstein is the exception which needs a mate or two, and Cox's Orange Pippin, Delicious (Golden or Red), Sturmer and Granny Smith will provide good company and superb eating throughout summer and most of winter.

Pears will not bear unless they have a partner, which is why so many multi-grafted plants are available. Good eaters and bottlers are Williams, Packham's Triumph, Doyenne du Comice, and Winter Cole or Winter Nelis for late bearing.

Quinces can grow like weeds, and it is a common sight to see completely neglected trees, bearing a huge crop of bright yellow fruit. The common variety available is Smyrna, which is basically self-pollinating. See page 201 (Appendix) for more information on cross-pollination.

More people are growing nut trees these days and the popular choice seems to be hazelnuts. The awful problem is that many keen growers have planted dozens of seedlings and these nameless plants are virtually useless. They are often non-productive, or if they bear at all, produce small, worthless nuts. There are exceptions of course, but not many.

If you want to grow decent-sized hazelnuts, spend a bit extra and buy named varieties. Strong growers which bear good crops of tasty, meaty nuts are White American, Cosford and Kentish Cob.

Many walnuts offered for sale are only seedlings. This means that they are more likely to become infected by blight, produce smallish, hard-shelled nuts, and often take up to fifteen years before starting to produce. They are difficult to propagate from grafts and this is why the good, named varieties such as Franquette, Wilson's Wonder and Freshford Gem are so expensive.

> Sow green manure crops in all parts of the vegetable garden which are not being used for a few months. Collect all plant debris, weeds, leaves and the discarded remains of vegetable crops for use as compost. Rough dig the ground where possible, to allow winter frosts to penetrate and break up heavy soil.

Sometimes the seedlings of these named varieties are offered for sale and turn out to be completely different from the parent. It pays to get the best, grafted varieties which come into bearing quickly and are more disease resistant.

Almonds grow strongly, flower profusely, and bear well in most districts. But you must have two of them, each of a different variety, which will bloom at the same time. I can never really agree with some people who plant flowering almonds, it seems such a waste of space when the fruit of these trees cannot be eaten. The nuts from ornamental almonds are poisonous.

Good varieties of almonds which bear well, are Johnstons Prolific and Chellaston. The first light harvests are within three years.

Sweet chestnuts have been greatly ignored for some reason. This could be because of disappointment in the quality of the nuts. Again, the cause has been the use of seedlings rather than named varieties. There are named types now coming on to the market, which bear bigger crops of meatier nuts. These include Aprilgold, Emerald Gem and George Sands.

By deciding what you want to grow now, and ordering early, you will have a much bigger and better choice of fruit and nuts.

Growing Strawberries

Strawberries are not only delicious to eat, they are also very easy to grow, and there is nothing quite as satisfying as to be able to pick and eat your own berries.

Strawberries will grow and thrive in a wide range of conditions, including pots, hanging baskets and window boxes. Just as long as they are watered often during the summer, and get plenty of sunshine.

Now is the time to plant them.

First, buy certified, virus-free plants. Don't take runners from old, existing clumps, because the chances are that they will be diseased. Certified plants are grown under very strict supervision so that their runners are free of diseases and insect pests. Ten plants will take up very little room, yet, if looked after, will provide as many strawberries as you and your family can eat. As soon as the new plants are purchased, unpack them, wash the roots, pull off any battered or discoloured leaves and place them in a waiting bed with the roots covered with moist soil.

Then, prepare the soil of the strawberry bed. Dig carefully, trying not to bring up any subsoil. Remove all perennial weeds, especially twitch-grass. Young plants must not receive any competition, otherwise they will not grow strongly or produce much fruit. Strawberry plants prefer a slightly acid soil, so if yours is reasonably good garden soil, you will not need to use lime. However, the plants are shallow-rooted and can dry out easily, so the addition of plenty of organic matter to the soil will be of crucial importance.

For some reason or another, lots of pine needles, worked into the top 200 millimetres of soil, with plenty of really old animal manure, will produce remarkable and delicious yields. It is probably the fairly acidic nature of the pine debris which does the trick. If you are very fortunate, you can get a load of that lovely mixture which occurs under pine trees where animals have been sheltering. A couple of bucketsful of this for every square metre will work wonders. Naturally, if the strawberry bed is prepared and fertilized well ahead of planting, it is much better for the plants because the soil will be lovely and mellow.

Good drainage is essential. Don't plant directly into a flat surface, where water may lie during wet periods, but create ridges up to 200 millimetres (eight inches) higher than the adjacent soil. A ridge four metres long should accommodate ten plants.

To plant the strawberry runners, make two grooves seventy-five millimetres (three inches) apart on either side of the top of the ridge. Then, divide the root system into two parts, and straddle the ridge with them. Wriggle in the crown a little and bury the roots into the two grooves. I always place a generous handful of compost into the grooves first, to give the plants a good start. Finish the planting by watering with a diluted seaweed extract to provide trace elements and consolidate the roots.

If you wish to help reduce weed competition, black plastic film is extremely effective. Sheets of it can be stretched over the planted strip tightly enough to produce distinct bulges where the strawberry plants are. Then, with a pair of scissors, or a sharp, pointed knife, cut a slit where the plant beneath presses, making sure that you don't damage the crown. Pull the top part of the plant through the slit, and bury the edges of the plastic to stop the wind from causing problems.

But I'm still a bit old-fashioned and I like to use straw as a mulch and a weed suppressor. It also keeps the berries clean by keeping them out of contact with the soil. Slugs happen to love these conditions, so be ready to carry out a 'search and squash' operation periodically.

If your existing strawberry plants are still producing flowers and a few immature fruit, you can extend the season by placing a plastic bag over each plant, propping it up with a couple of bent pieces of wire, and burying the base in the soil.

You will be pleasantly surprised by the amount of fruit you will obtain at a time when usually very little is available. A weekly application of well-diluted liquid fertilizer will make all the difference to the yield. But, if you can't be bothered doing this, it is better if all the green berries and the flowers are completely removed.

Some of the most popular varieties of strawberry are:

Red Gauntlet. A large, angular, bright red strawberry with a medium flavour. A steady cropper of considerable vigour.

Cambridge Vigour. These have a better flavour and come into bearing fairly early. Very vigorous, so go easy on the fertilizers.

Tioga. I personally think this to be the best flavoured of the three. It grows particularly well in cool districts, producing plenty of dull red, conical fruit, with a sweet red flesh. Many commercial growers are concentrating on this variety because of high yields, high quality fruit, and a longer-lasting plant.

If you have very little room in the garden for strawberry plants, they can be planted and grown successfully in containers. The biggest problem with this method is that they are always drying-out during the summer. Once the medium in the pot has dried out, even a little, it is hard to get it wet again, and the plants suffer. This is why many people become disappointed with the results of container planting. For best results, and yields which will be the envy of your friends, water daily with up to half a litre per plant in summer and add a weak liquid fertilizer every week.

The potting mixture should contain up to fifty per cent granulated peat. This means that, during warm weather, if you miss out and forget to water one day, the whole mass of the medium can shrink. Then it will be a really serious problem trying to get things wet again.

Don't forget, if your existing plants are more than three years old, chuck them out and replace them. You won't regret it.

Seeds Under Cover Now – Early Vegetables Later

Even though very few seeds can be sown in cool districts at this time, apart from broad beans, especially in the open garden, there are a number of protected sowings which can be made.

If you tried to sow the seeds of any members of the cabbage tribe outside now, many could be lost due to cold. However, seeds of cauliflower, broccoli and spring and summer cabbage can be sown in small containers this week and allowed to grow under cover for a month or two.

Any container, even margarine cartons, can be used, provided there are plenty of drainage holes at the bottom. The soil medium doesn't have to be anything special, although the incorporation of a good proportion of granulated peat and coarse sand into some good garden soil will virtually ensure success.

Placed upon a windowsill and kept moist, brassica seeds will germinate within two weeks and grow quickly. If the light is only coming from one side, the containers should be turned every day. Once the second pair of leaves has appeared, the young seedlings can be carefully pricked out into larger containers, so that there is about three centimetres between each plant. This essential spacing prevents the disease problems associated with overcrowded conditions.

The good thing about this early sowing of brassica seeds is that it allows us an extra couple of months for sturdy plants to develop. These can be planted out at the end of July. From then onwards, with the gradually lengthening days and extra warmth, the heads will be ready to eat at a time when these vegetables are in short supply and expensive.

Meanwhile, in the established vegetable garden, certain protective measures will be needed from now on. Cauliflower curds will need to be covered on frosty nights to stop discoloration. A leaf or two, broken off from the outside of the plant, is enough to do the trick.

Incidentally, the white cabbage butterfly caterpillar is still active, in spite of the cold weather. A great deal of damage can be done because many of us assume that the problem has disappeared for the winter. Derris dust is the safest means of controlling the small grubs, and Dipel, the safe biological spray, will stop them skeletonizing the leaves by making them sick for a few days before they die.

Sprouts will be inclined to topple over in wet soils. This is always a problem with these top-heavy plants and they must be planted into well-firmed soil. When picking the sprouts, start from the bottom and work up. Pull off the large decaying leaves as the crop is gradually harvested.

Young brassicas will only respond to liquid fertilizers at this time of the year. These can be applied in the form of weak compost 'tea', or heavily diluted manure water.

Young lettuce plants can be virtually standing still now, and the only way to get them to move is to encase each separate plant in a plastic bag. This will stimulate growth to a remarkable degree. If the drainage is properly attended to, good, well-hearted lettuces can be secured when most people are paying high prices for them in the shops.

M A Y
GUIDE TO ACTION

Ornamental Garden

Continue sowing lawns. Plant spring bulbs including nerines, belladonnas, tulips, hyacinths, freesias, ranunculi, anemone and liliums. Autumn colour plants can be selected for suitable shades at nurseries now. Transplant evergreens, clear withered annuals and lime beds as required. Prune and tidy herbaceous borders and mulch with old straw. Prune hydrangeas, buddleias and other late-flowering shrubs and take cuttings if needed. Other flowering plants to go in this month are achillea, alyssum, aquilegia, arctotis, calendula, candytuft, Canterbury bells, carnation, delphinium, dianthus, foxglove, geum, gypsophila, lupin, myosotis, ornamental kale, pansy, penstemon, polyanthus, Iceland poppy, oriental poppy, shasta daisy, stock, sweet William and herbaceous paeonies. All container grown trees and shrubs will settle in rapidly this month. Order roses and deciduous trees.

Vegetable Garden

Harvest pumpkins before frost strikes. Leave plenty of vine attached and put out in the sun for a couple of weeks to harden off. Cover at night with bags or straw. Frost strike will ruin them. Sow broad beans and apply forty grams of sulphate of potash per metre of row to those which have already emerged. Tomatoes in cool districts will be ripening slowly and vulnerable to frost. Pull entire plants from the ground and hang upside down in a protected place. The green fruit will continue to ripen. In warmer districts brassicas, lettuce, peas, Chinese cabbage, leek, turnip and shallots can still go in.

Fruit Garden

Spray peach and nectarine trees at leaf-fall with Bordeaux mixture to help control leafcurl. Cut asparagus foliage to the ground and mulch bed with seaweed. Prune fruit trees which have cast their leaves and remove prunings. Apply dolomite lime around stone fruit trees. Order new fruit trees and prepare planting sites. Complete pruning of berry-fruits then mulch heavily.

Houseplants

Start to reduce watering. Spray scale pests with white oil solution. Clear away old leaves and other debris from surface of potting soil. Use weak liquid fertilizers for flowering plants.

MAY: FIRST WEEK

Which Rose?

Over the next few weeks, the nurseries and garden centres will be filled with displays of rose plants. While roses can be planted at other times of the year, from containers, winter planting is more reliable. This is because the roots are bare and you can see their condition and extent when planting holes are dug. Sometimes, container grown roses, particularly the vigorous ones, develop a spiral root system, which can seriously retard the development of the plant.

By making decisions now, you can place an order and be fairly sure of getting what you want.

Here are some of the kinds of roses which will be coming on to the market soon.

Hybrid tea. These are the popular bush or standard roses, which are most commonly stocked by nurseries. Their main characteristic is the large, double, scented flowers on fairly long stems. Generally there is one bloom at the end of each new stem growth.

Floribunda. The main difference between these and hybrid tea roses is in the number of flowers produced. Floribunda roses tend to produce their blooms in clusters, and modern cultivars have flowers which are just as big as the hybrid teas. The number of scented varieties is much smaller but rose breeders are rapidly overcoming this problem.

Miniatures. These are delightful plants which grow only to a fraction of the height of the other roses. Their leaves and flowers are small, but they are beautiful. Miniature roses are ideal for planting along the edges of garden beds or paths, where they rarely spread outside their own little area. They are about the only type of rose which looks good in part of a rock garden. Their small stature helps them to blend in marvellously with other rock plants and the rocks themselves.

Shrub roses. These include the lovely old-fashioned roses, the species roses, Gallicas, Damask, Bourbon, Moss, Rugosa, China, Centifolia and hybrid musks. Their names alone conjure up delightful images and scents. They are grown for their beautiful foliage and colourful fruit, as well as their flowers. Shrub roses will thrive under cool conditions, especially in frosty districts. They don't need much pruning, apart from the normal removal of weak or dead wood at any time of the year.

Prepare the ground now for later planting of the roses you have ordered. Dig well, breaking up any clods, removing perennial weeds, and fertilizing with old manure and blood and bone. Roses must be planted in the open sun for best results.

Essential Jobs at a Crucial Time

Many plants can also be pruned right now, especially those which have flowered recently. One year I pruned one of my hypericums ruthlessly at this time, and the result was beyond my wildest expectations. The large-flowering *Hypericum* (Rowallan Hybrid), can be spectacular, and this one simply refused to stop blooming all summer, being constantly covered with hundreds of clear yellow blooms like giant buttercups. All that is needed right now is the removal of all small twiggy growth, and any old main branches, cutting them as low as possible.

Hydrangeas can also be pruned now, unless the old flower heads are required. Few shrubs are more badly pruned than these, mainly because people tend to ignore them for a few years, then virtually cut them to the ground. The key to success is in the young canes, most of which come up from the base of the bush. If these are left on, and all the older wood removed right to the base of the plant, an enormous amount of diseased and insect infested material is taken away and the plant must benefit. However, the next important stage in pruning hydrangeas is the cutting-back of young growth. It must be done correctly, otherwise few flowers will appear, although there will be plenty of leaves.

The flower buds of hydrangeas are plump and bright green. They form in pairs down the young stems. They are smallish at the top, then gradually become larger down the branch until about the third pair down. Then they diminish in size until they change colour near the bottom, going almost black, as well as being quite small. The buds to prune to are the fat, green ones. If the branch is cut back too hard, to the small black buds, there will be few flowers the following season.

It is a good time to deal with hydrangea scale once pruning has been completed. This looks as though someone has scattered lots of tiny pieces of cottonwool all over the stems and the undersides of the leaves. Scale pest also attacks varieties of American dogwood, especially *Cornus florida*. A spraying with white oil emulsion will suffocate these insects, but two or three applications at weekly intervals may be needed to complete the job. White oil is not considered to be a dangerous spray.

While this scale pest is being exterminated, it is a good idea to give your lemon or other citrus trees a squirt too. These trees are particularly vulnerable now. People never really see the scale lying along the underside of the leaves, only the black, sooty mould covering the fruit, leaves and branches, with hundred of excited ants chasing up and down. After a spraying operation, the black mould gradually disperses as it is washed off by rain. The ants also disappear when the scale is of no further value to them.

All prunings can be burned green, provided they are given a start. The ash from most of them is a particularly valuable source of potash. However, it will lose its strength rapidly unless it is scraped up and placed under cover. One shower of rain upon a heap of exposed ash will render it worthless.

Autumn Pest Control Without Poisons

In some ways it is like early spring now. The temperature is about the same, although it is much drier, and there are many spring jobs which can also be carried out now.

Many insect pests are vulnerable at this time because they are about to settle down for a winter rest. Disease control is also very effective. If pests and diseases can be dealt with before winter, there are less of them to get started later on.

One pest which tends to be forgotten is the white cabbage butterfly caterpillar.

> Lawns may have been stimulated into fresh growth as a result of cooler, moister conditions, but they will soon settle down into a state of semi-dormancy for the winter. Just the same, the value of mowing them at this time cannot be overstated. The mower will pick up many leaves which, if left to decay on the lawn, will cause unsightly dead patches. If the lawn has not been renovated for some years, now is a good time to do the job. Scratch the surface with a stiff-tined grass-rake to bring up the matted dead grass lying over the surface. Do this before mowing because the mower will pick up some of the loosened dead material.

The eggs have been laid on a massive scale over the last few weeks and many untended brassicas are now under a devastating attack. Caterpillars can withstand hard frosts and some of our most important winter and spring crops can be seriously weakened unless measures are taken to control the invaders.

The spray marketed as Dipel is excellent because it only affects caterpillars. It stops them feeding and after a few days, they either die or are picked off by birds. The old-fashioned derris is of use only with small, immature caterpillars and will not kill the big ones. Another simple, cheap and safe way of caterpillar control, is to spray the attacked plants with weak salty water. It is easy to test whether the mix is strong enough because it can be tested on living caterpillars, starting with a dilution of two tablespoons of salt to a bucketful of water. Spray directly on to the pests, and if the correct strength has been mixed, they will roll off and eventually die on the ground.

Aphids are not as active now as at other times of the year. However, those which are destroyed now are important because they could be the start of next season's infestation. Roses which are still producing some new growth will be under attack and a quick squirt with pyrethrum will stop the aphids dead in their tracks.

Grass grubs, or 'corbies', knock hell out of some grassed areas in May. In many cases there will be no grass left, just a dead wig of loose grey, rootless grasstops. One way of dealing with any insect or pest below the surface of the ground is to use the type of poison which will not break down easily, or quickly. I prefer the cheap, safe way. Ordinary household detergent, broken down with water at the rate of one part in fifty will help control 'corbies'. When watered on to an infested lawn area, it trickles down the holes made by these pests. This brings them out on to the surface instantly. They can be hand-picked and dropped into a bucket containing some salty water. One elderly couple told me that they picked up two bucketfuls of 'corbies' in about an hour and completely cleared the lawn of these pests. The actual strength of the mix can be tested first but don't make the mistake of overdoing the detergent.

Incidentally, 'corbies' are like large, ugly, grey caterpillars and are not to be confused with cockchafer grubs which are usually curled like the letter 'C' when dug out of the ground. The detergent treatment seems to work with them too, but it is difficult to say how effectively because they don't jump to the surface when treated.

Blackcurrant bushes are subject to attack from borers. The effects of their activities can be easily seen in the older, dark coloured branches. Most home gardeners can control these pests by cutting out the old wood in each bush. If the bush has not been pruned for a few years, the young wood will be growing in the upper parts of the bush, with just the odd young branch coming up from the base.

In this case, cut out most of the old wood to the ground. This will encourage the development of plenty of young, healthy canes which are free from borer attack. Next year the rest of the old wood can be cut out. This way the shock to the plant is reduced and a reasonable crop of currants can be harvested. However, the borer will never stop boring away, but regular pruning will make the bush much less vulnerable.

The most common of all diseases of peaches and nectarines is leafcurl. The normal method of control is spraying with a fungicide such as Bordeaux mixture in late winter. However, the same spray, freshly mixed, applied around this time of the year, just as the leaves are falling, can help to make the later spray even more effective. But don't mix this spray with other sprays, and avoid applying it when the leaves are on the tree.

MAY: SECOND WEEK

Diagnosis of Plant Disorders

When a plant is sick, the first signs are in the leaves. They change colour, curl, appear scorched or fall. Fortunately it is usually possible to diagnose the problem early, by recognizing certain symptoms.

When the tips and outer edges of leaves appear burnt, the most common cause, especially with houseplants, is overwatering. The potting soil becomes saturated and these stagnant, airless conditions encourage bacteria to attack the roots. The plant tries to compensate for a reduced root system by dying back. The plant must not be watered until the soil is drier and recovery is taking place. Sometimes, leaf die-back is caused by extra-dry conditions, so it pays to check the potting soil by feeling well below the surface.

In the garden, marginal leaf-scorch is less of a problem, but will occur when rhododendrons are situated in poorly-drained spots. The treatment is to transplant to a better place, or raise the plants, even if they have to be replanted into a low mound to ensure free drainage. This can be done anytime but now is particularly suitable. Never plant rhododendrons too deeply and when transplanting them always bury the roots to the previous soil level.

When a plant unexpectedly begins to drop its leaves, things look bad. There are many reasons for this happening, the most common being a sudden change in environment, temperature, light, careless use of harsh chemical fertilizers and sprays, or indiscriminate applications of fresh, raw animal manures, especially poultry droppings. All bird manures are 'hot' and, unless allowed to mature, can cause dramatic defoliation of shallow-rooted plants such as citruses, camellias, daphne and azaleas.

Poor, weak, growth during times when it should be strong is a cause for concern. A major reason is underfeeding or impoverished soil. This can be gently corrected. However, most plants will remain stunted if they are planted into heavy clay. Clay soils are rich, but the nutrients they contain are hard to obtain. Organic matter spread over, or worked into the soil is the best way of overcoming this problem, preferably before planting. Never dig a planting hole filled with organic matter, in a bed of clay. It will act like a well and drown the plant.

Spots on leaves are unsightly. Attacks by sucking insects, water-marks or fertilizer burns are typical causes. Thrips are tiny insects which produce whitish spots and streaks. Contact sprays such as pyrethrum are safe to use but several applications are needed to do the trick. Rogor is a poison which gets into the system of the plant. It is effective, but needs careful handling.

Brown spots on the foliage of houseplants such as African violets and gloxinias, can be caused by beads of water lying on the leaves in the sun. The water magnifies the sun's rays, and the result is unsightly areas of scalded tissue. Correct watering at the bases of these plants will avoid this problem.

Wilting is an obvious sign of distress, usually caused by lack of water. However, too much water will produce the same result. Strong sunlight and a dry atmosphere around plants which prefer humid conditions will cause leaves to collapse. African violets, incorrectly placed in a sunny window, will protest by drooping their leaves stiffly over the rims of their containers. A bright, southern window is the best place for these lovely plants.

When a plant which is supposed to flower fails to do so, it can be disappointing. Too much fertilizer causing excessive growth at the expense of flowers is the usual cause. In the vegetable garden overfeeding will cause tomato plants to bear too late, while broccoli plants will be all leaf and little else.

Lack of light will also prevent flowering. Bulbs which have gradually become overshadowed will eventually cease to bloom. Herbaceous paeonies, once established, will continue to flower regularly for decades, but when they become overhung with dense evergreens, they only produce leaves. Flowering houseplants need more light than those grown for their foliage. As soon as they are brought into brighter conditions, recalcitrant potplants begin to form flowers.

When a plant lacks certain minerals, the way the leaves respond can be a clear indication of the type of deficiency occurring.

When phosphorus is unavailable, the leaves have a purplish look, growth is poor and the foliage generally has a curiously upright appearance. Magnesium deficiency shows up as yellow leaf-patches with occasional bright colours. When iron is in short supply, the leaf veins show bright green while the rest of the leaf becomes pale yellow, with young, new growth almost white. See page 190 for some other indications of mineral deficiency.

Foliar feeding with well-diluted complete liquid fertilizers and added seaweed concentrate is the quick way to overcome many nutritional deficiency problems. However, the use of well-made compost, animal manures and, with sandy soils, clay which has been broken-down with water, is the most reliable way to restore the balance.

Correcting Mineral Deficiencies in Your Soil

In many ways, plants and people have a lot in common. If they are overfed, they become fat, soft and occasionally unproductive. Overweight plants have too much lush foliage. This is fine for those houseplants grown for their large, beautiful leaves, but even with these there can be problems. Insect pests have a special appetite for soft, carbohydrate-rich plant material and diseases spread rapidly in these luxuriant conditions. So there must be a limit to the supply of fast food.

The key element is nitrogen. It is the great plant builder and is essential for healthy growth of most plants. If there is a deficiency, the appearance of the plants tell the story. Their leaves are small and pale. A general lack of vigour is obvious and few new shoots are produced. Deciduous trees drop their leaves prematurely and the few fruits they carry are small, highly-coloured, have a concentrated sweet taste, are woody and store well.

Sources of nitrogen include animal manures, blood and bone, hoof and horn meal, steamed bone flour and well-made compost. Chemical sources, which are far more concentrated, include urea and ammonium sulphate.

When nitrogen-rich fertilizers are added to the soil, the response from plants can be dramatic. Leaves appear, rapidly taking on a dark green, healthy appearance. The best way to supply nitrogen to garden soil is by using plenty of bulky animal manures. The large amount of organic matter acts as a combinaion of buffer and storage reservoir, allowing the plants to utilize the nitrogen and other elements safely, as they are needed. In the vegetable garden, a constant supply of nitrogen can be made available by supplementing fertilizers with cover crops of legumes such as annual lupins and tickbeans. These plants use certain organisms to fix nitrogen into soils which are deficient. In a well-planned rotation system, legumes such as peas or beans can play a restoring role if they are grown between greedy crops during the cycle.

Houseplants, which often show signs of nitrogen deficiency, can be gently rejuvenated by weak liquid fertilizers, or slow-release granules.

In soils which are impoverished, free-draining and subjected to high rainfalls, plants will show many symptoms of mineral deficiency.

The potting-soil in containers is also easily leached of many soluble minerals. Potassium, one of the major plant nutrients, is needed in relatively large quantities, but is often in short supply in clay-free soils. Plants in these conditions are often squat and abnormal looking. I once saw silverbeet, the leaves of which were much broader than they were long, each with a broad, sharply-tapering midrib. They were trying to grow in a district where most of the potash had been leached out by almost constant rain. These conditions are duplicated in the potting-soil of many house and container plants. Other signs of potash shortage are marginal leaf-scorch and early fruit drop. Sulphate of potash is one of the best ways of supplying this element. It

> Keep the water applied to chrysanthemums and other perennials which are still developing blooms. A weak liquid fertilizer around those about to bloom, after watering, will make an enormous difference to the quality and size of the flowers. As soon as dahlias start to show the effects of frosts, cut them back ready for lifting.

looks like fine white sugar and can be applied directly to the soil at the rate of a tight fistful for every square metre. Better still, try mixing it with blood and bone to make up about ten percent of the total bulk. This produces a good, well-balanced, all-purpose general fertilizer, suitable for all parts of the garden. Other sources of potash include ash of bark, twigs or hedge-clippings, but this must be scraped up and stored out of the rain or placed directly around plants. Wood ash from combustion stoves or woodfires is of little value in this regard.

The ancient soils of Australia seem to have a general shortage of phosphorus, but most of our native plants have come to terms with this and are able to keep growing. However, most of the plants we grow in our homes and gardens come from parts of the world where phosphorus is more readily available. A deficiency shows up when plants have little vigour, the shoots are thin and curiously upright and the leaves are a dull purple-green. Fruits are small, oddly-coloured and have a poor taste. The most common method of adding phosphorus to the soil is by using superphosphate. Only very small amounts are needed and, because it can be rapidly locked-up in deficient soils, it is best used in a thin band next to seeds when they are sown. Blood and bone is a good source, with bone-meal being even better.

When the leaves, particularly the older ones, of some plants gradually start to develop unseasonal striking colours, then start to drop, there is a chance that magnesium is in short supply. Acid, sandy soils which are leached as a result of a high rainfall can be seriously deficient in this mineral.

An easy way to overcome magnesium deficiency is to make a thin gruel with clay and water and dribble this around plants growing in sandy, leached soils. This will also strengthen the soil, giving it an ability to absorb and retain nutrients. In acid soils, dolomite limestone, which contains both calcium and magnesium, can be applied generously. A large double handful for each square metre may seem a lot, but unlike garden lime it is not caustic and can be used with blood and bone. Epsom salts is another form of magnesium. It can be sprinkled around deficient plants at the rate of a teaspoonful per square metre and watered in. An even quicker way of treating suffering plants is to spray the leaves with a solution of a heaped teaspoonful of epsom salts dissolved in a bucket of water. Several applications may be needed with seriously deficient trees.

Calcium deficiency is common in acid, virgin soils and is needed more in the vegetable garden than the ornamental area. If you cannot grow onions, garlic, peas, beans, celery, spinach or asparagus successfully, the chances are your soil needs liming. Soil testing kits are cheap, especially those which measure the pH, or acid-alkaline balance. A quick test is the best way to start understanding your soil and improving it.

MAY: THIRD WEEK

Moss in the Garden – How to Eliminate it, or Use it

There are many reasons why moss becomes established in the garden. The most common is poor drainage, usually manifested in lawns by large, unsightly patches. Excessive moisture lying close to the surface, which remains there for weeks or months, creates ideal conditions for the growth of spongy, saturated mosses, usually in company with daisies.

The answer to this type of drainage problem and weed infestation, is to change those conditions by installing a simple drainage system. Weedkillers or selective herbicides will not be needed if water is allowed to drain away steadily all the time. Plastic, subsoil drainage pipes are readily and cheaply available in various sizes and lengths. With bluemetal screenings packed under and around the pipes a drainage system can be constructed that will last for many years.

Moss also establishes itself in places which are fairly well drained. It can often be seen in places where the soil has become impoverished, particularly near large, greedy trees. The soil has become too poor to grow grass, so moss occupies the vacancy. The answer is to apply blood and bone over the infested area, topdress it with enriched soil and re-sow a more aggressive lawn grass.

Moss in the open lawn, or around certain shrubs, can be dealt with according to location. A great deal of moss in lawns results from incorrect grass cutting methods and feeding with highly nitrogenous chemical fertilizers resulting in acid soil. If the grass is constantly cut too short, so that the ground is virtually scraped, moss will soon make its presence felt. These problems can be overcome with surprising ease by raising the blades of the mower by at least three centimetres. And this is a good time to apply enough lime to thoroughly whiten the surface of the lawn. This will sweeten the soil enough to make it unattractive to mosses.

Moss which grows around acid-loving plants such as rhododendrons, azaleas and camellias cannot be dealt with by using lime. Instead, it can either be tolerated (it doesn't look too bad in these situations), or smothered by adding a good thick layer of pea-straw or spoilt hay. If this mulch is sprinkled with blood and bone in spring, it will become a valuable feeding mulch and the plants will benefit enormously.

In deep shade areas, moss can add to the beauty of the planting, especially where lots of ferns are involved. A combination of tree-ferns, smaller fish-backs and shade-loving rainforest plants, with a few old logs or weathered rocks covered with a soft-green blanket of moss, is beautiful.

Different types of moss can be added to the soil between rocks in alpine gardens. Mosses tend to mould themselves over harsh surfaces, including sharp edges, and have a softening effect.

Many people are furnishing their gardens with species of *scleranthus*, which will thrive in exposed, cold and windy situations. These are the intriguing cushion plants which form humped, bright-green mounds or carpets. They can be easily propagated by pulling off a small piece and inserting it into moist soil where it quickly takes root and begins to spread.

Moss or liverworts can sometimes be a problem with houseplants. They can exist on the surface of the potting soil even when the rootball down below has started to dry out. They can form a thick, water-repellant crust which makes watering difficult. Potted ferns which have developed a well-established layer of moss are almost certainly rootbound and need repotting. Liverworts have a flattish growth which develops into colonies around the base of cool greenhouse plants. They are removed by carefully scraping them from the soil with a flat knife. A thin layer of bluemetal screenings spread in their place will prevent reinfestation.

Which Pruning Tool for What?

If you want to make a proper job of winter pruning, make sure you have the right equipment. The number of awkward and occasionally brutal pruning cuts which are being carried out right now, using scissors, carpenters' saws, axes or even pliers must be frightening. The remarkable thing is the survival rate. Plants can be much tougher than we imagine.

Protective clothes, especially gloves, are most important. Once your hands are injured it can make even simple tasks difficult. It pays to take great care of them. The best type of gloves are those which are flexible enough to enable the fingers to be used easily. Thick, stiff, heavy leather gloves can be worse than useless because you just get sick of trying to handle things while wearing them. You will end up taking them off.

I've never seen a cheap pair of secateurs which were any good. Usually they are poor cutters, difficult to handle, heavy, break easily and can even snip out pieces of your hand if they are not held in a special way. My own choice is for brands made by Sandvik, Wilkinson Sword or Felco. The advantages of sophisticated designs are that they are easy to work with, last a long time and cause less damage to the plants being pruned.

Incidentally, secateurs rarely need sharpening. My own favourite pair has been in almost constant use since the late 1950s and, apart from the odd drop of oil every now and then, has had no maintenance. Unskilled sharpening of secateur blades can destroy the finely-shaped curve of the cutting blade which is designed to work with the narrow lever-type blade opposite.

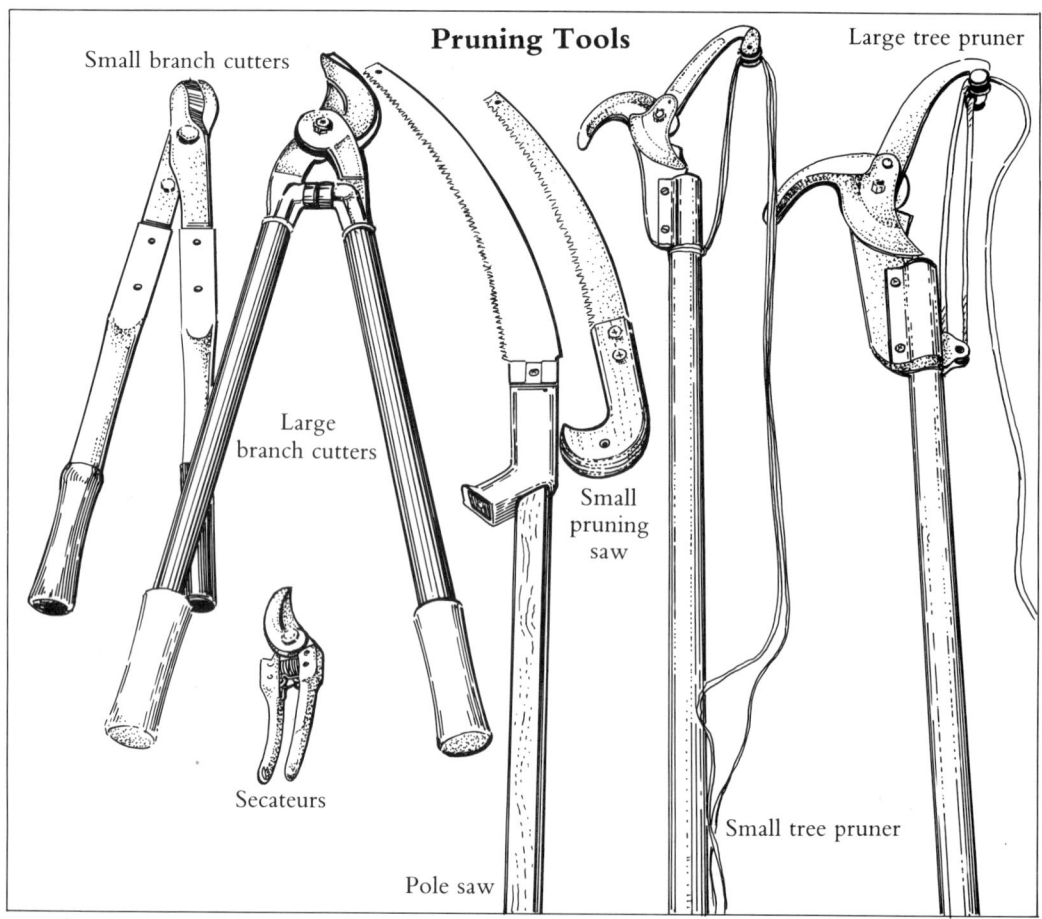

Pruning Tools — Small branch cutters, Large branch cutters, Secateurs, Pole saw, Small pruning saw, Small tree pruner, Large tree pruner

The difference between a pruning saw and a carpenter's saw is vast. Trying to cut a branch from a tree with a carpenter's saw is a difficult experience. It sticks, becomes clogged with sap, is difficult to insert close to main branches or in narrow forks, is highly flexible and painfully slow to cut with. Good pruning saws, especially those made in Sweden, are a pleasure to use. They are short, firm, have large sharp teeth which are set to make wide cuts and the blades are tapered to fit easily into difficult places. Cutting rapidly through even large branches is child's play with the right tools.

Some pruning saws can also be attached to a long piece of wood and made into a pole-saw. They can be used to reach up into a tree to remove limbs, avoiding the tedious use of a ladder.

Long-handled branch cutters can also be used effectively from the ground to carry out pruning of large trees. They are nothing more than a specially adapted pair of secateurs fastened to the end of a pole, with a length of thin nylon rope attached to an operating lever at the top. The best of these are made by Sanvik, and are used by professionals all over the world.

In addition to these pruning tools, various types and sizes of bow-saws are excellent for quick cutting of easily accessible limbs, but their awkward shape prevents their use in highly congested trees.

The effects of lopping dead or weak, spindly growth from a tree can be enormously liberating to a plant. The sight of an expertly pruned tree, shorn of all the weight of unnecessary growth, is a satisfying sight.

Crown Prince pumpkin. Excellent keeper. Here is one of a previous year's crop with new season's pumpkins.

Potato onions. Grown only from divisions. Now scarce.

Elberta peaches. Organically grown and pest free.

Strawberries thrive in slightly acid, enriched soil with a straw mulch to keep berries clean.

Jerusalem artichokes. A type of tuberous sunflower.

Carrots. From left to right: Western Red, Early Horn, Zeno.

Greenfeast peas. A heavy cropper.

Steep Banks

Some landscaping problems and situations can be quite a headache for people who are starting a garden from scratch.

Landscaping problems can include steep sites, windy, exposed situations, salty, coastal districts, areas prone to frost and heavy clay soils.

The good thing about all these difficult sites is the challenges they offer, and the outstanding gardens which can result from working with the local conditions, rather than trying to fight them. Many of the outstanding gardens in Australia have been created upon sites which were once major problems. Landscaping a steep housing block usually presents one or two main problems: when the land falls sharply from the street down towards the house, and when the opposite occurs, and the house is well above the street.

These two situations present completely different problems. When the house is below the street, there can be serious lack of privacy, because passers-by can look down into windows facing the street. Often, because this is the side without a decent view, the rooms facing the bank leading up to the street are bed and bathrooms and this tends to increase the need for privacy.

An obvious solution is a fairly dense screen of plants located between the house and the street, tall enough to overcome the privacy problem. On some sites the steepness of the bank will make it difficult to plant trees and shrubs, especially if there is little topsoil.

There are several ways to deal with barren, steep places like this but they are almost impossible simply to top dress with imported loam, because it keeps sliding down.

Building a series of terraces out of rocks, bricks or other materials is one way of ensuring stability, but care must be taken to provide sufficient drainage or 'weep' holes to prevent moisture build-up. This can eventually cause even solid structures to collapse, or at least crack, as the pressure mounts, leaving an unsightly mess.

Simpler ways can be found of providing secure places for plants in such situations. Hacking out a large pocket in the bank in the place where each shrub is to be planted, then placing a semi-circle of rocks, well bedded-in, on the outer rim of the pocket, provides stability. At the rear of the pocket, against the bank, more rocks can be placed. Backfill with at least thirty centimetres (one foot) of topsoil, and you will have a lovely secure place for a plant to gain a good hold.

One way to topsoil a steep bank is to spread a thick layer of wet soil over a deliberately roughed up surface. The wetness of the soil will help to hold it in position for a while. Then, before it dries out, spread a ten-centimetre-thick mulch of woodchips or shredded bark over the surface. To secure this combination, stretch ordinary chickenwire tightly over all parts of the surface, pinning it down into the bank with pieces of bent fencing wire driven in with a hammer. To plant, simply cut a cross into the chickenwire, fold back the four points, dig away the mulch and plant directly into the exposed soil. Afterwards, make good the mulch

---

In the vegetable garden plant broad beans, radish, English spinach, turnip, broccoli, cabbage, leek, lettuce, white onion, silverbeet and cauliflower. Raspberry plants too can be safely transplanted from now onwards, or old beds broken up and reorganized. All berryfruit plants seem to thrive if a thick layer of old straw, mixed with manure, is laid around them to gradually rot down during the winter.

and gently bend back the chickenwire to close the opening without scratching the stems of the plants.

These methods can be used with any steep slope, and in the case of a house being much higher than the street, the only difference is the size of the plants you need. In other words, because privacy is rarely a problem on that side of the block, a whole range of smaller plants, even rock plants, can be used. When rock and alpine plants are chosen the type of mulch must be quite different. Organic mulching material can be harmful, because it will cause most tiny rock plants to decay, so small stones or blue-metal gravel should be spread over the topsoil instead.

Continuous mulching fabrics, such as 'Earthmat', can also be secured to slopes to prevent erosion and suppress weeds while plants establish themselves. A layer of organic material spread over the fabric looks more attractive.

Consider the use of trailers, creepers and weeping plants as groundcover for slopes.

MAY: LAST WEEK

Australian Plants Play a Special Role

The great strength of Australian plants lies in their ability to withstand a wide range of growing conditions, climates, soils and temperatures. This is fair enough, after all, this is their own environment and they ought to thrive here. However, many of our most beautiful trees and shrubs also do well in other parts of the world and in many countries they seem to grow better than in Australia. This is probably because of the lack of pests and diseases which are specific to this country.

However, wherever Australian plants are grown, their special needs, likes and dislikes are similar. Australian conditions, long periods of dry, hot weather, ancient soils and browsing animals have caused our plants to develop in a unique way.

For example, many native plants, especially eucalypts, wattles, grevilleas, banksias, hakeas, she-oaks and westringias, develop an extensive root system as small plants. This is a major reason why many wild plants, triumphantly brought home after a bush trip, seldom succeed in the home garden. A tiny seedling wattle, only a few centimetres tall, will already have grown a spreading root-system up to a metre in diameter. These roots are brittle, they do not renew themselves easily and it is difficult to transport a large, fragile rootball. This is why attempts in the home garden to transplant specimens which have established themselves over a season or more are doomed to failure. It is much better to begin again with a new plant rather than wait for a damaged, stunted plant to renew its vigour after transplanting.

Another dislike of many Australian plants is to be tied to a stake. This is the most common error in both public and private gardens. Vigorous trees and shrubs, treated in this way, will grow with enormous speed, virtually climbing the stake, then become top-heavy. Comes a windy day and they snap their stakes, finishing up flat on the ground with their roots badly torn.

When these plants are growing naturally they are unsupported and thus grow sturdier. In addition, when young they are constantly nibbled by animals so they seldom become long, lanky and vulnerable to unexpected winds. In fact this browsing makes them bushier as animals seek out the tender growing tips.

In the garden we must be prepared to give our native plants similar treatment.

The richer growing conditions and extra water causes Australian plants to make new growth to a degree rarely seen in the bush and this must be regularly pinched back to keep the plants secure. Even with newly planted trees and shrubs which have been grown in containers, this ruthless treatment must be carried out. The ability of these plants to renew their top growth is a result of their long history of surviving bushfires. In fact at the base of the stems of many Australian plants is a distinct swelling, often in the form of two wart-like lumps. These lignotubers, as they are called, contain valuable reserves of energy and dormant buds. They will quickly sprout into growth if the rest of the canopy is burnt or removed.

Native plants seem to prefer a soil which is slightly acid. Using lime around them can cause serious problems and even lead to the death of some of the more sensitive acid-lovers. A common cause of failure in home gardens, especially newly-established ones, is the planting of natives into soil which has been unbalanced as a result of mortar or cement being mixed there during construction.

Australian soils are generally deficient in phosphorus and our plants have learned to survive with only tiny amounts of this major element. While the addition of superphosphate will certainly stimulate their growth, the long-term effects of this type of fertilizer are not yet fully understood. My own preference is to avoid using superphosphate and to concentrate on slow-acting, organic fertilizers such as blood and bone during the first two or three years.

While most container-grown native plants can be planted out at any season, now is an excellent time for it. Winter rains and cooler conditions help to reduce loss and by the start of spring, good root-systems will have formed which will ensure survival during warmer periods.

Even though young plants are best left unstaked, they should have wooden markers driven into the ground next to them. This helps warn people of their presence and avoid trampling or mower damage.

Australian plants mix easily with exotics, although there is still a strong trend to grow them separately. Apart from their superbly beautiful flowers, foliage and form, they attract an amazing number of birds into the garden. A weeping bottlebrush in full bloom and covered with hundreds of tiny honeyeaters is an unforgettable sight.

Selecting the Best Deciduous Plants

Some time ago, I shamelessly intervened and succeeded in dissuading an elderly lady from buying a dead standard rose in a supermarket. None of my business I know, but neither she nor the assistant knew any better. The leaves had been prematurely stripped off the tree and its dried-out roots were concealed inside a brightly-coloured plastic bag. There were plenty of rose trees remaining, but one in five of these were also dead. They had died because they had been lifted too early in order to grab quick sales.

This destructive competition to try and get deciduous trees and roses into retail outlets before the dormant season, seems to be becoming worse every year.

When deciduous plants dry out and die in winter, there are no leaves to indicate what is happening. That's why so many people mistakenly buy them dead. The bark tells the story. It shrinks around the stems. Long, vertical wrinkles form along the dead or dying branches and the bark sets hard. It is obvious when you know what to look for and sad that so many people don't.

Too often, the dead plant is proudly taken home and carefully planted. When nothing happens in spring people tend to blame their own lack of gardening skills.

Deciduous fruit trees are often mishandled. Because of pressure from retailers, many growers are being forced to try and hasten dormancy by ripping the leaves off their trees. Peach and nectarine foliage is inclined to hang on longer than other fruit trees, so they suffer the most.

Growing young fruit trees is a highly skilled operation. Growers work hard and most of them are proud of the quality of their plants. Selected stock material is propagated, then as this develops, grafting or budding is carried out the following year. More than a year later the trees are ready for lifting, as soon as the leaves have been cast. Just before this occurs, each tree draws from its leaves all surplus carbohydrates and other essential substances, and stores them in the trunk and roots. That's why the leaves change colour before they fall. When the trees are lifted too early they are deficient in stored reserves, and if leaves are still on them, they 'sweat' their lives away, the bark shrinks and goes hard.

It must be heartbreaking for a grower to see the results of almost three years' work jeopardised like this, for no sensible reason. After all, there are about ten weeks from the middle of June during which excellent tree sales can be made.

Another problem affecting young fruit trees for sale, occurs during lifting operations. These days, machines are normally used to carry out the process. Unfortunately, the number of strong, healthy trees which have had their roots virtually sheared off seems to be growing each year. The most important roots of a young tree are the 'fibre' or fine, feeding roots. If there is only a few remaining after lifting, the chances of the tree making a good start in spring are reduced enormously. This problem becomes aggravated by the demands of some retailers for as many branches as possible to

> This week in the vegetable garden sow broad beans, spring onions and radishes. In warm areas well-sized seedlings of spring cabbage, broccoli, cauliflower and edible kales can be planted out in well-drained spots. Continue to sow cover crops of ryecorn, Algerian oats or horse beans for digging-in and enriching the soil later. Houseplants such as cyclamen should be gently fed with weak liquid fertilizers, and the leaf debris cleaned away from all other houseplants. Place gloxinias and their containers on their sides to dry out gradually, ready for restarting in spring.

be left on the tree, in order to make it look more attractive. Consequently, we have the sad sight of large vigorous-looking trees, some more than two metres tall, with hardly any roots. One justification for this reduction in roots is to save on transport costs.

Most growers try to overcome this problem by encouraging the trees to form a dense, smaller root-system. Long before the trees are to be lifted, outer roots are severed, at the same time irrigation and fertilizers are concentrated close to the main stems. Tight masses of fine, feeding roots develop producing a compact feeding system which can withstand the shock of transplanting.

But if these trees are dragged out of the ground while they are still in leaf, they will become badly desiccated and much of the care and attention they have had, will be wasted.

To obtain the best quality bare-rooted trees and roses, choose the ones which are sturdy-looking, have plenty of fibrous roots and have a healthy, greenish, soft bark. Prune hard as soon as possible, soak the roots in water for an hour, then plant. If they cannot be planted immediately, place the roots in a shallow hole and cover them with moist soil.

If you have already bought a plant which has few roots, or has the tell-tale vertical grooves in the bark, then take it back to where it was purchased and get your money back.

If we all did this, I'm certain there would be a little more self-regulation in the industry.

Protecting the Soil with Mulch

The best way to make gardening easier is to mulch the surface of the soil between and around plants. The most commonly used mulching materials are shredded bark, woodchips, old straw, spoilt hay, seaweed, leaves, sugarcane trash and even sawdust.

Lawn clippings, unless mixed with other, coarser materials, are of limited value. They either become slimy when applied too thickly, or form a dry crust if spread thinly. Hedge clippings can be useful in the ornamental garden, where they slowly rot on the surface.

A mulch should always be left to decay on the surface, never dug in. Most of the bacteria, moulds and fungi which break down organic matter exist close to the surface of the soil and they operate with great efficiency at that level. Digging in any coarse, undecayed organic matter can seriously unbalance the soil, causing nitrogen deficiency.

Mulch can be spread over weeds without having to dig them out first. Even if weeds are beginning to go to seed, the warm, moist conditions within and below a mulch can prevent seeds ripening. Weeds which do germinate are rarely able to penetrate the ten centimetre thick pad.

Even persistent perennial weeds such as couchgrass, docks, catsear, sheep's sorrel, bindweed and dandelion can be controlled by means of a mulch, preferably of straw or seaweed. Once the problem weeds begin to poke through the mulch, it is a simple task to slide a garden fork below it, then gently lift the matted mass just high enough to clear the weeds. These, being rooted in the soil, remain attached to the ground. The mulch is then lowered on top of the collapsed weeds. A large area can be quickly covered using this method and, after three or four such 'lifts' over a two month period, the weeds become too weak to try again, are smothered and become part of the mulch.

Areas which have been mulched are resistant to soil erosion, even those with unstable soil or steep slopes. Very steep sites may cause the mulch to slip downhill unless it is secured with chickenwire, as described on page 71.

Using mulch massively reduces evaporation from the soil. It seals in the moisture, while controlling any sharp fluctuations in soil temperature during day and night. Plants grow strongly, even though much less water is used. Fertilizers can be sprinkled over the mulch and raked in. They gradually filter down to feed the soil.

The cheapest type of mulching material is sawdust. (Although sugarcane trash can be free, apart from cartage costs.) It makes little difference whether the sawdust is aged or fresh green, provided it is not mixed with the soil. The addition of animal manure, blood and bone or compost will increase the speed with which sawdust breaks down. This makes it suitable for use in the vegetable garden. The instability of sawdust in windy districts can be a problem but a thin layer of coarse sand spread over the surface will stop it from being blown about.

Seaweed can be taken directly from the sea and used immediately as a mulch without washing. It contains very little salt and if there is a problem, it is the sand which clings to it. This can be too alkaline for those plants which prefer an acid soil. Seaweed, like most other materials, is better as part of a general mixture, rather than on its own.

All mulches must be kept clear of plant stems, otherwise they may cause mould upon the lower bark. Exceptions are tomatoes, sweetcorn and rose plants.

Plants which do not like being mulched with organic matter include onions and rock plants. Onions are best left to grow in uncovered soil, while alpine and similar rock plants can be mulched with a five centimetre layer of fine bluemetal screenings.

Watering is substantially reduced by mulching, but it must still be carried out regularly and deeply. Otherwise the roots of trees and shrubs will tend to congregate near the surface of the soil where the moisture lingers, causing instability.

No-dig gardening, using mulch, is the easiest, most intelligent way I know of growing things, because it constantly improves the most precious resource we have, the soil.

Ornamental gardens are treated differently from vegetable gardens because they remain unchanged for many years. Therefore, the mulching materials need to last for a long time before they begin to break down. That's why woodchips, pinebark, pebbles or metal screenings are of such great value when they are spread thickly between and around plants in the ornamental garden.

They play the dual role of suppressing weeds while sealing in soil moisture, allowing trees, shrubs and other plants to grow strongly with little competition, right from the start. This type of long-lasting mulch also prevents soil erosion, keeps the soil temperature stable and prevents the surface developing a hard, water-repellent crust.

Low-maintenance gardening has become common during the last two decades, especially in municipal parks and gardens. The days when teams of gardeners worked ceaselessly around parks and gardens, weeding and digging, have virtually gone forever. Such time-consuming and expensive garden labour has generally been replaced by mulch gardening coupled with the use of modern herbicides.

In the vegetable garden the no-dig revolution has not been as extensive. This is a pity, because there is no better way of improving the shallow and often impoverished soils found in many parts of Australia.

With a newly-made no-dig vegetable garden, the rate of decomposition is relatively slow at first, especially in hungry soils. As micro-organisms, moulds, fungi and worms multiply in the soil, the organic matter on the surface disappears at an increasing rate.

By constantly adding to the mulch as it is drawn down, especially during the warmer growing seasons, the rate of enrichment accelerates. It soon becomes possible to push the mulch to one side and comfortably drive one's fingers deeply into a transformed, sweet-smelling, friable soil which, even during the hottest days, remains pleasantly warm. If the air temperature drops sharply during the night, the soil is still warm beneath its protective, nourishing blanket.

Simple Rose Pruning

Correctly pruned roses bear better quality blooms, are less likely to be attacked by insect pests or diseases, are more vigorous and present a tidier appearance. If they are badly, brutally pruned, they still show their forgiveness by producing some good blooms. If they are left unpruned altogether, the flowers will be smaller and poorer, and the plant will suffer from diseases aggravated by congested growth.

Now is a good time, in most districts, to prune roses. In areas prone to heavy frosts, it may be better to leave this job until August to avoid stimulating new growth.

This is how to prune the most commonly-grown roses.

Hybrid-tea or floribunda types

Bush and standards are pruned the same way. After all, a standard rose is only a bush rose on a stick. Remove all dead or weak wood plus all growth which heads into the centre of the bush. Cut off flush to the branch without leaving a stub. The growth should now look a bit like a wineglass, with plenty of open space in the centre. Cut out all small, twiggy growth, then prune back the main branches to the top well-developed, outward pointing bud. The finished plant won't look pretty, but it will appear leaner and more sparse.

Suckers grow from below the bulge where the graft took place and are best cut off below the soil if necessary, even if part of the root from which they are growing is also removed. Watershoots, the vigorous new growth from above the graft, are different. They are important because they are the basis for the continued framework of the plant. Their growth is soft and rank, so they must not be pruned hard. Only the tips need be trimmed to remove seed capsules.

Climbing hybrid-tea and floribunda roses

Start from the base. Cut out all main branches more than four years old and carefully disentangle them. The remaining young canes are left unshortened if possible, but the masses of twiggy growth sprouting from them is best trimmed away, leaving a bare, whippy growth to be tied in a fan-shape to the trellis or support. This type of pruning means that climbing roses will have most of their wood replaced over a four year period.

Miniature or hybrid polyantha roses

The easiest of all to prune. Simply cut to a few centimetres above the grafting union, or, if ungrafted, just above the ground. Don't bother trying to look for suitable buds, but clean out all dead wood. Cuttings of these small roses will strike easily in moist sandy soil, often growing into better plants than grafted ones.

Shrub and other old-fashioned roses

Remove weak or dead growth at any time. Prune lightly, but occasionally cut out some of the older branches from the base to prevent congestion.

Weeping standard rose trees

Usually a floppy, rambling rose grafted on to the top of a two metre high standard. They are often mispruned dreadfully by people who think they should be converted into a stubby mini-skirt. The correct way is to thin out some of the long, arching canes, retaining the healthiest to weep to the ground. All weak, short canes should be cut out, plus any growth which wants to grow skywards. Twiggy sideshoots are best trimmed away. A correctly-pruned weeping standard rose tree is left with about a dozen or so canes trailing the ground and virtually all other growth removed.

All prunings and dead leaves should be raked up and either carted away or burned, in order to reduce sources of infection. The plants can then be sprayed with a fungicide such as Bordeaux mixture.

JUNE
GUIDE TO ACTION

Ornamental Garden

Lift dahlia tubers as tops die back or are frosted. Store under cover. Lift and divide perennials. Make or lay lawns. Re-organize garden. Plant new roses. Select and plant deciduous trees. Liliums, bulbs and perennials can go in. Clear exhausted flower beds and cultivate roughly, apply lime if needed. Prune late-flowering shrubs such as buddleia, hypericum, tibouchina, margueurite daisies and *Spiraea* 'Anthony Waterer'. Other flowering plants to go in now include: alyssum, aquilegia, arctotis, calendula, candytuft, Canterbury bells, carnation, delphinium crowns, dianthus, foxglove, geum, gypsophila, lupin, myosotis, ornamental kale, pansy, penstemon, polyanthus, Iceland poppy, oriental poppy, shasta daisy, stock, sweet William, sweetpea, paeony and, in warm districts, lobelia, begonia, mignonette and statice.

Vegetable Garden

Plant asparagus and rhubarb crowns. Sow broad beans, peas (frost-free areas), spinach and white onions. Garlic cloves can be planted into well-drained, limed soil. Install drainage pipes. Use liquid fertilizers in cool areas. Dig all potatoes and bag. Potato onions go in on the shortest day for harvesting on the longest. Prepare onion beds for next month's sowing of long-keepers. Pick sprouts from the bottom, snapping off lower leaves as you go. Check for late cabbage caterpillars and spray with Dipel for safe control. Make compost. Mulch weed growth to smother it. Plant Jerusalem artichokes. Sow seed, under cover, of brassicas, lettuce and onions in cool districts, for spring and summer crops. Keep sowing green manure and dig mature crops into the topsoil before they become too stalky. Early tomato seed can be sown in warm conditions under glass.

Fruit Garden

Prune deciduous fruit trees, berryfruit bushes and vines. Avoid cherry, apricot and, until after flowering, male Chinese gooseberry. Plant new fruit trees and berry fruit bushes. Strawberry runners can be planted into well-drained ridges, but make sure they have been certified. Plants more than three years old should be replaced. Clean up around trees and bushes, burning all debris. Ensure all mummified fruit is destroyed.

Houseplants

Don't overwater. Allow soil to become slightly dry. Check for leaf-burn near heaters. Mist plants in warm, dry rooms. In frosty districts, keep tender plants away from window contact.

JUNE: FIRST WEEK

Pruning Fruit Trees and Bushes

This is a busy time in the garden. Pruning deciduous fruit trees is a simple task for home gardeners. Some, such as sweet cherries, European or Japanese plums and apricots, can be left virtually untouched, apart from the removal of dead wood. They will still continue to bear good yields, although apricot trees respond to summer pruning, after the fruit has been picked.

Peach and nectarine trees must be pruned regularly, so new growth is stimulated. They bear their fruit on the previous season's growth and if unpruned will gradually become straggly and unproductive, with small fruit.

Pruning consists of removing about fifty per cent of the previous year's growth, cutting out internal-growing branches and thinning or eliminating weak side-shoots.

Apple and pear trees are pruned in a similar way to each other. Usually, internal, inward-growing branches are taken out to form an open-centred shape, without leaving stubs. The days when these trees were given an annual crew-cut have gone forever. Now, all that is needed is to shorten the side-shoots to leave three or four buds, while the long, whippy leaders are either left untouched or lightly tipped. A trend these days is to tie down vigorous growth so that it is as horizontal as possible. This acts as a brake, while forcing it to become fruiting wood. Pear trees often become overcrowded with old fruit-spurs. These can be thinned to leave fifteen centimetres between them.

Old, neglected fruit trees can be brought into bearing again by cutting a third of the main branches back hard every year for three years, thus effectively reducing the height of the trees without too much of a shock. New growth will develop near the point where each cut was made, often in the form of a broomhead. The best shoots are retained, while the rest are rubbed off during the spring.

Pruning berryfruit bushes is a simple task. See page 53 for some details.

Chinese gooseberry vines will bleed if pruned in late winter. Male plants are best pruned hard after flowering in October, while the females, which bear the fruit, are tip-pruned during summer, with fruiting wood cut back to a few buds in winter.

Grapevines also need hard pruning. The fruit is produced on the previous season's growth, but if this is left untouched fruit quality will be very poor and diseases rampant. Cut out most of the previous year's growth to leave short, three-bud spurs at twenty centimetre intervals along the main arms of older wood. The effect appears devastating with enormous quantities of vine taken out, but it is necessary. With sultanas, don't cut back so hard, but leave rods containing a dozen buds sticking out from the main arms.

After pruning operations, rake up all the pieces and burn them. If left lying around, many will be a significant source of infection, especially in spring when their buds swell.

Spraying with winter oil is normally carried out after pruning deciduous trees. This is an effective means of eliminating many pests lying dormant at this time. However, the later this is applied before bud-burst the better, because it will catch many insects when they are at their most vulnerable, just as they are emerging. The entire tree should be sprayed, with the trunk given special treatment, especially crevices in the bark.

Reorganizing the Winter Garden

If there is one job in the garden which is perfectly suited to this time of the year, it is reorganizing or redesigning an old, established garden. This is because almost any plant can be transferred to a new position at this time, whether it be an evergreen or a deciduous one.

All gardens need to be regularly thinned out by removing old, diseased or unsatisfactory trees or shrubs. Sometimes, as the weeks or years sneak by, we tend to take our gardens for granted and fail to see badly overgrown or untidy, straggly trees and shrubs. Some of these plants, which seem to have lost much of their early vitality, can be rejuvenated by careful pruning or re-siting.

There are many reasons why plants gradually lose their vigour and ability to produce good displays of bloom. Excessive competition from more aggressive, dominant shrubs or trees is one of the most common reasons why flowering diminishes in some plants.

A few years ago I was asked to have a look through a very old, beautiful, but overgrown garden. Seedlings of cotoneaster, common ash, black wattle and crabapple had grown relentlessly over years of relative neglect, so that little sunlight reached the smaller plants.

I was told that there were large numbers of non-flowering daffodils, paeonies, nerines, belladonnas, zantedeschias, achilleas, agapanthuses and bearded irises somewhere in this lovely old, wild garden.

However, in spite of the great charm of the place, it needed some rather drastic treatment. Most of the cotoneasters, all the wattles and all but one of the seedling crabapples were the first to go. Then, in an amazingly newly-lit garden, many of the remaining older shrubs, which had become drawn-up and were only half-alive, were pruned ruthlessly. Some were too far gone to do anything with, the only choice was to grub them out.

Those perennials which were still overhung were transplanted to new locations, as were some miserable-looking azaleas, camellias and rhododendrons. The final result, after the bonfire had consumed most of the woody debris, green or dry, was an open, sunny but slightly devastated garden. Afterwards, when the ash had been spread around the perennials or the vegetable garden, the entire area was given a good dressing of blood and bone with ten per cent added potash.

The first year produced astonishing but bushy growth. Some blooms appeared, but not many. There was no doubt about the return of great vigour and health, while the initially severe appearance had been well covered with a mantle of green.

The following year the garden never seemed to stop blooming. The bulbs and perennials took on a new life and many plants which had been concealed or ignored during the earlier clean-up, unexpectedly produced long-forgotten displays of colour and fragrance.

Within two years, a leafy, shady, but pleasantly dull garden had been returned to its youthful vitality.

So if you've been wandering around your own garden, slightly dissatisfied, wondering what happened to this and that plant over the years and yearning for the garden that was, you really couldn't pick a better time than now to get cracking.

However, it can be very difficult to make decisions about what to move, which tree or shrub to discard, or even how to get started on the reorganization.

Many people stare at their unsatisfactory garden, and, while aching to get to work on something, never seem to get started because they don't know where to begin. The unhappy garden is untouched and the frustration and dissatisfaction remain.

So, here are the simple rules-of-thumb to get started on redesigning that garden of yours.

1. Walk through the garden, and mark every plant which you dislike, or has been unsatisfactory. Then get rid of them all by grubbing them out and carting them away.

2. Examine all the plants that are left, and where two or more of them are madly competing for space and light, make ruthless choices about which ones are to be removed altogether and which transplanted to another spot. Naturally try and retain the most attractive and expensive. For example, if the choice is between a well-sized rhododendron and a much more vigorous cotoneaster, you would be mad to chuck out the rhodo. The chances are that a place for the cotoneaster can be found somewhere else in your garden.

3. With the clearing out done the sun will be shining into areas which have not seen bright sunlight for years, and this will give plenty of scope for some totally different types of plants. Try belladonnas, nerines, Cuban lilies, jonquils

> A special hint for pruning time: when cutting back diseased limbs, do so in stages until clean wood is reached. Wipe the blade of the saw with methylated spirits between cuts to prevent infection being introduced lower down.

and daffodils. You could also consider paeonies, dianthus, and the superbly beautiful gypsophila. Two years ago I dug up a gypsophila which had remained stunted and concealed under a heavy, dense shrub, and replanted it in an open spot into well-limed soil. The growth which occurred was extraordinary, developing into a bush over a metre in height and width.

4. Having made a shrub clearance, turn your attention to the lawn. It is here that all sorts of dramatic changes can be made to totally transform the character of an old garden. Most lawns, particularly in some of the older gardens, are squarish, boring, and occasionally dotted with miserable-looking shrubs which always seem to be partly dwarfed by the constant competition of the surrounding grass. Many of these plants, because of their stunted state, are very easily transplanted into the shrub garden. Lawns are best left as open as possible, because this helps to make even the tiniest garden look larger. The shaping of an old lawn, even by cutting off any sharp corners and by developing gentle, flowing curves, will have the double advantage of making the garden appear more spacious and interesting, while eliminating corners which are difficult to get at with a mower. Extra planting spaces will also be created.

5. Some plants can be transplanted even if they have been growing in one place for many years: rhododendrons, azaleas, camellias, dwarf and medium sized conifers, ericas, most deciduous trees and shrubs during winter, and a host of other plants. The main characteristic of many of these plants which can be moved from one place to another without major setback, is the tight, compact rootball in the case of the evergreens, and the easily arranged bare roots of the deciduous plants in winter.

The plants which resist transplanting, unless they have only recently been planted, are many Australian native plants, all brooms, cistus, ceanothus, laburnum, established roses, podalyria, nerium and very old climbers such as wisteria.

Transforming an old garden into a new one is one of the most exciting and satisfying of all landscaping operations. At the end of each day's work the changes which have taken place can be quite dramatic, so much so that once the mood gets a grip, you can hardly wait to get back to work again the next day.

Wind Damage

When wind damages a plant, it does so in several ways, most obviously when a branch is broken or torn off. Some trees are more brittle than others. Apricots have a tendency to split down their trunks, leaving half a tree. The wound should be trimmed immediately and smeared with Bordeaux paste, made from the fungicide powder mixed with a small amount of water. Don't ever bother trying to nail or tie the two split halves together. They rarely knit to heal but can become a source of infection and a haven for insect pests.

Broken branches should be neatly and carefully cut back to the nearest junction or almost flush with the main stem and, if the final cut is vertical, there should be little need to paint the wound. Sometimes, a little heavy grease is enough to make the wound waterproof until healing takes places.

The constant movement of a plant in wind can have a disruptive effect on the root system. Every time new roots try to extend into a new area, they become torn again. With roses, which are generally top-heavy, this constant root damage is the major cause of suckering and the same is true about many other plants which are grafted on to vigorous stock. Unfortunately, once suckering starts, all that can be done is to keep cutting the offending shoots off, well below the ground, or they will eventually take over.

With many other plants, wind damage is not so noticeable, apart from a drastic slowing down of growth. This is common among some native plants, especially eucalypts, which have been planted out in a so-called 'advanced' state. These extra-large plants are rarely as stable as small plants. Invariably, the little ones overtake the big, expensive ones, sometimes within a couple of years. The larger plants are also vulnerable to wind-rock damage. This can be seen as a circular 'well' surrounding the trunk, in the soil. It means that the outer roots have been progressively torn and the tree has lost its stability.

The 'well' is where the constant movement of the trunk occurs, pushing the soil back a few centimetres. Some eucalypts develop a swelling just above the ground, known as a lignotuber, which becomes much larger than normal when wind-rock problems exist. In these circumstances, it is better to reduce the top-growth to encourage the development of a sturdier plant, than to secure the tree to a stake. Firming the soil around the stems is a help, but in windy districts, it is better to place large stones directly over the roots, flush against the stem, in order to hold things in place.

Other plants which have brittle stems, such as delphiniums and tomatoes, can be secured to a stake or, if the plants are large and multi-stemmed, several stakes. The main thing is that these supporting stakes should be of wood. Metal ones, such as steel pickets or old water-pipes, transmit excessive heat and cold to the roots, often with a definite stunting effect.

A simple, cheap windbreak can be made with three or four stakes driven into the ground close together, so that they are almost touching. If they are slightly staggered, they will stop even a gale dead in its tracks. Actually, this arrangement shatters the wind rather than deflecting it. This is one of the reasons why tea-tree fences, even with gaps wide enough to put your hand through, give such perfect garden shelter.

Gardens which are subjected to constant prevailing winds will never thrive, unless the planting is confined to a special kind of tough plants, or a windbreak is established. However, it is the unexpected winds in average gardens which can do the real damage. Some of the measures described here will help.

JUNE: SECOND WEEK

Fallen Leaves

The effects of short days and cold soils are starting to become apparent. Lawns have virtually stopped growing and have taken on a slightly yellowish appearance. Most deciduous trees have shed their leaves and when they cover large parts of the lawn for more than a week, the grass underneath begins to die from lack of light.

Leaves should never be burned. They contain enormous quantities of valuable organic matter which can be fully used by the soil. The easiest way of disposing of autumn leaves is to rake them up into piles, then spread them thickly around trees and shrubs to gradually rot down. Even emerging bulbs are not suppressed by a moist, heavy layer of them. Oddly enough, the dead foliage of most exotic broad-leaved trees such as oak, ash, liquidamber, elm or sycamore, is not really suitable for digging directly into the vegetable or ornamental garden. They take too long to break down and, like other coarse materials, can actually rob the surrounding soil of nitrogen. Most of this rough material seems to break down much more rapidly, and harmlessly, on the surface where there are more active soil bacteria and other micro-organisms. If a few handfuls of blood and bone or animal manure are also sprinkled over the leaves, the breakdown is accelerated and the topsoil enriched.

In many cases, provided there is sufficient quantity, autumn leaves can be an effective weed suppressor if they are laid directly over them. Even twitch-grass will eventually be weakened, becoming more vulnerable as it sends its rope-like runners under the moist layer on the surface.

The slow-rotting character of autumn leaves is of considerable value when they are used as a mulch around newly planted ornamental or fruit trees. Young plants are often severely checked during the summer following their planting, mainly because their roots have not been able to develop enough to tap deeper sources of moisture.

Ornamental Trees

This is the main time for planting deciduous trees, and the way this operation is carried out now, while the soil is moist, will make plenty of difference later on. The great advantages of planting during the dormant period are the easily examined, bare roots. They can be pruned to remove damaged or infected areas and you can spread them effectively at planting time.

The range of beautiful flowering trees available at this time seems to become larger every year. The flowering plums are all tough and disease resistant. *Prunus blireana* is one of the delights of early spring, with a profusion of rose-pink, semi-double flowers completely covering the canopy of this small tree. *P. elvins* is only half the size, but makes up for its lack of height by an extraordinary display of brilliant white blooms, right to the tips of every branch.

Japanese flowering cherries thrive in cooler districts providing a breathtaking sight in any garden. *P.* 'Shirofugen' bears thousands of soft-pink buds which open to fully double pure white flowers. A medium-sized, spreading tree, it is perfect for growing in a lawn with an underplanting of spring bulbs. The popular *P. serrulata* 'Kanzan' is a vigorous, upright tree bearing masses of rich-pink double blooms. Perhaps the most gently spectacular of all the Japanese cherry blossom trees is *P.* 'Shirotae' (Mount Fuji) with its hanging clusters of snow-white, semi-double flowers. In our climate it is a medium-small tree, seldom exceeding three metres but spreading widely.

Unusually beautiful is *P. serrulata* 'Ukon' known as the green cherry. The blooms begin with a superb lime-green colour, gradually changing when fully open to a buff-green.

All the Japanese cherries grow strongly in well-drained soils and can even stand a fair amount of clay provided there is plenty of good topsoil. However, constant prevailing winds will stunt their growth, and sea winds virtually destroy them.

> In the vegetable garden this week, the last sowing of broad beans can take place until the end of July in cool areas. Most berryfruit bushes can be planted into enriched soil, rhubarb crowns divided if necessary and asparagus crowns planted.

The flowering crab-apples are among the hardiest of all flowering fruit trees, and there are few places where they do not thrive. They will also grow strongly in a wide range of soils, including heavy clay. *Malus floribunda* is an old favourite, with enormous quantities of pink flowers, opening to white. A weeping form, usually grafted on to a two metre high standard, makes an unforgettable sight in any garden as its blossom-laden branches droop to the ground.

Lilacs always do better when they are planted into soil which has been well limed. However, they need plenty of summer watering during the first two years if they are to succeed. Their colours range from deep purple red to snowy-white, and they seem quite happy in protected positions with some shade.

Laburnums, known as golden chains because of their hanging racemes of brilliant yellow flowers, are an excellent tree for the small garden. While they will grow easily from seed, the variety *L.* 'Vossii' is far superior with its 'chains' three times as long.

JUNE: THIRD WEEK

Selecting Fruit Trees

It probably has a great deal to do with the remarkable growing climate we have in Australia, but the ease with which many seeds of various fruit germinate and grow, is astonishing.

Yet in some ways this can be a disadvantage. There is hardly a garden which does not have a seedling peach, nectarine, plum or even apricot growing from some stone, cast or spat out a few years ago. These trees take up room which could be occupied by a good quality, named variety of fruit tree.

Some people will still point with pride at the seed-grown tree, which produces 'quite nice' fruit every season. How many people realize, though, that even if the seed of the most delicious peach is sown, the resultant plant will generally be a fairly wild thing, bearing reasonable, but generally mediocre peaches?

Some fruit will reproduce from seed better than others. While nectarines, peaches and even plums aren't too bad, apricots can be almost non-productive for years, and then start to bear very poor quality, relatively tasteless fruit.

Plants are easy to grow from a lemon pip, but the resultant tree is often so massively armed with thousands of long, sharp and aggressive thorns, that even the coarse, rough, tasteless 'lemons' are almost impossible to pick. This dramatic reversion is also common to other types of citrus.

Pear trees which are grown from seed are almost totally useless. The fruit is usually small, without flavour, and woody. In addition, the tree can be covered with hundreds of blunt, thorn-like growths. Apple trees can occasionally be grown from a pip, but the apples produced are, at their best, of low quality.

The point of all this is to explain that when you grow fruit trees from their seed, you immediately wipe out generations of careful selection and breeding. The new plant virtually goes back to square one and, because there are so many such inferior trees growing in backyards all over the country, many people never have a chance to taste the superb quality of carefully bred fruit.

On very rare occasions a good fruit tree will germinate from a stone or a pip, but it is so unusual it isn't worth waiting for, especially with a large tree occupying part of the garden.

Here are some fruits, the trees of which can be planted out now:

Peach. Starking Delicious, Anzac. Christmas to mid-January: Briggs Red May, Elberta, J.H. Hale. Mid-season bearing: Golden Queen. Late: Tatura Sunset.

Nectarines. Early Rivers, Goldmine, Masterpiece.

Plums. Early to late bearing: Santa Rosa, Narrabeen, Burbank. Early to late bearing European types: Early Orleans, Jefferson, Angelina, Greengage, Coe's Golden Drop, Prune D'Agen.

Apples. Early to late bearing: Gravenstein, Cox's, Jonathan, Bramley's Seedling, Golden Delicious, Mutsu, Sturmer Pippin and Granny Smith.

See page 201 (Appendix) for information about cross-pollination and fruit trees.

Planting in Containers

The advantage of planting trees, shrubs and other plants into containers is that they can be moved freely from place to place to obtain the maximum effect.

Tubs, half barrels, pots, or anything which can contain soil and plants, can transform some of the most boring places in the garden into areas of great character. These places include large areas of concrete or asphalt, balconies, verandahs, parking areas and the outer edges of barbecue or outdoor living areas.

There is a huge number of suitable, highly attractive plants which can look marvellous in containers. The important thing to remember is to choose a pot or tub which will blend with the landscape, and in no way compete with the plant it contains. That's why skilled gardeners deliberately choose containers which are often fairly drab, or which they paint in dark, earthy colours.

However, there are hundreds of containers to choose from at garden centres; some plain concrete, others studded with a variety of pebbles, while many are made of terracotta. Plastic ones are easy to handle, because they are so light in weight, and will last for years, particularly if they are composed of black plastic.

The best containers have plenty of well-spaced drainage holes, usually located around the outside of the base. The presence of perfectly drained potting soil is the secret of successfully growing beautiful tub plants.

Many people soon discover the futility of using ordinary garden soil in containers. Unfortunately, it behaves very badly once it has been placed in a tub or pot. Unless the soil is fairly sandy and free draining, it will collapse into a hard compact mass within a week or two. One reason for this is the absence of active soil creatures such as worms, which are constantly activating and aerating the soil in the open garden.

By mixing good quality garden soil with granulated peat and coarse sand, a free-draining mixture will be obtained. This will not pack down hard, but will allow the roots of plants to extend easily to all parts of the container. An easily mixed potting soil is: one third each of coarse sand, good soil and granulated peat. For each bucketful of the potting soil, add a desertspoonful of superphosphate, half a cup of blood and bone, and a quarter cup of potash.

One of the most important tasks when preparing a pot for planting, is to ensure that the soil is not washed out gradually through the drainage holes. This is why it is necessary to spread a thick layer of stones or broken pots, over the base of the pot.

Then fill the pot up to about one third its depth with the potting soil, and arrange the plant centrally so that the rootball starts just below the rim. Finally, fill with the rest of the soil, tucking it in to eliminate air pockets, and water gently. This watering will cause the surface level to subside a little, and the plant may also sink a fraction. Complete the operation

> Take hardwood cuttings of last season's wood from many deciduous plants. Sow seed of cabbage, cauliflower, broccoli, lettuce, onion and silverbeet, but not in the open garden in cooler districts. Sow into containers under glass, in order to develop the young seedlings under protected conditions, for planting out at the end of July or August. Side-dress broad beans in the garden with woodash.

by adding enough extra potting soil to allow for a rim exposure of about three centimetres. This will enable further watering and feeding to be carried out without spillage.

All feeding from now onwards should be in the form of liquid fertilizer, preferably in a well-diluted, complete form, with a little seaweed concentrate added.

Many tub plants fail to grow, or become diseased and die, mainly through lack of water during the summer. Once the potting soil has been allowed to dry out, it shrinks, and any subsequent watering only gives the impression of penetration because it starts to run out of the drainage holes within minutes of the water being applied. Periodic, deep slow trickling, especially during the warm weather, is the only sure way to keep the rootball permanently moist. With deep, moist conditions, most plants will thrive, looking attractive and healthy all the year round.

Here are some easily-obtained attractive plants which are ideal for growing in tubs or other containers outside:

Shady spots. Ferns, Japanese laurel (*Aucuba japonica*), pieris, fuchsias and *Hypericum* 'Rowallane Hybrid'.

Semi-shade. Azaleas, dwarf rhododendrons, camellias, *Viburnum carlesii*, daphne, sweet bay (*Laurus nobilis*), Persian lilac, Japanese sacred bamboo (*Nandina domestica*), deutzia, *Kalmia latifolia*, and *Photinia glabra rubens*.

Sunny positions. Miniature roses, pelargoniums, dwarf flowering peach, dwarf pomegranate, juniper, yew, ericas, hebes, lavender, cordyline and countless varieties of dwarf conifers.

Conifers are particularly suitable as tub plants because they have a compact root-system which takes many years to exhaust the potting soil, and a slower growing habit.

Planting Deciduous Trees and Shrubs

The best time to plant fruit trees, roses and other deciduous plants is right now. Once they have been planted, many of them will be there for a very long time. So it pays to pick the right spot, and to be extremely fussy about how they are to be planted.

A carefully planted fruit tree will have less problems with diseases, insect pests and mineral deficiencies. How the planting hole is prepared and what goes into it, apart from the tree, will determine the continued quality of fruit, blooms or foliage right from the beginning.

Dig the hole wider than the roots. It doesn't need to be anywhere near as deep as many people think. About 400 millimetres (sixteen inches) is plenty, because the soil below this depth is usually of a poor quality. If you have to remove some of this pale-coloured subsoil from the base of the hole, replace it with good quality topsoil from another part of the garden. If clay is a big problem, and it is close to the surface, replace most of it with friable soil – but this can cause an additional problem. Digging into clay can create a kind of 'well', into which water will flow and be retained over long periods. This will rot the roots of young plants.

It is worthwhile to either plant higher, even into a low mound, or make a simple drainage channel on one side of the hole to take away any surplus water before it can become a problem.

All deciduous trees and most shrubs need to be supported for the first few years, so drive a wooden stake into the base of the hole before planting. This is safer than risking root damage by staking after planting.

Don't use steel droppers or waterpipes. They will cause all sorts of problems for the plants through heat and cold transmission, and they can be almost impossible to remove later when they are no longer needed. So stick to wood, it is warmer and even if it rots after the first season, it is easy to replace it in the same socket.

It is good if a developing tree can be slowly nourished from a 'larder' of slowly released elements. I always spread the base of a planting hole with a layer of feathers, hair, or wool-waste. Dolomite limestone thickly sprinkled over this will hold it down, and there is a guaranteed supply of calcium, magnesium, nitrogen and trace elements which will be slowly available for many years.

Place a layer of good soil, including the turves or weeds taken from the surface, over the 'larder' and you are ready to plant.

Try the tree for size, and if there are any roots which are too long, either cut them off, or enlarge the hole. Don't bend them to fit, otherwise serious problems of spiral root will develop, and an insecure, stunted plant can result. It is a good idea to make a heap of good soil adjacent to the base of the stake, and then spread the roots evenly over it.

The actual depth of the planting is important. Too deep, and the bark will go mouldy, and it is difficult to plant too shallowly because most root systems start at ground level. Shovel some good soil over the roots, then shake the stem vigorously up and down to settle the soil between the roots.

In new ground it is a good idea to sprinkle a circle of bone meal, blood and bone, or superphosphate around the inside perimeter of the hole, close to the tips of the roots. Don't overdo it, a handful is plenty, and don't let it touch the roots. Then water to further settle the soil into the roots. Finally, backfill to the top of the hole, carefully and gently tramping the soil to firm it into good contact with the roots.

Always tie the main stem to the stake with material which will rot away, otherwise strangulation problems can quickly develop as the trunk swells. Flexible, plastic ties are available, and are easily adjusted as the tree grows. Finally, attach a permanent label to the stake, or to a plastic peg driven into the topsoil near the main stem. Then prune the tree by removing at least two-thirds of the topgrowth, preferably to buds which point away from the centre of the canopy.

JUNE: LAST WEEK

The Beautiful Way to Suppress Weeds – Groundcovers

Weeds can be controlled by various means. We can use herbicides, of course, but many people are becoming reluctant to use a chemical which has the effect of killing any living thing.

The popular way of keeping weeds at bay is by heavy mulching with organic materials, which are dense enough to exclude the light from the surface of the soil, thus preventing many weeds from successfully germinating. When those weeds eventually poke through such a mulch (usually of woodchips or pulverised bark), they can be pulled from the ground with relative ease. This is because the main feeding roots of many weeds tend to concentrate near the surface, where the moisture lies. The great advantages of a mulch include a virtual end to digging. Apart from saving energy, this lack of cultivation means a rapid reduction in the number of weeds germinating. Every time soil is dug, weed seeds are brought to the surface or exposed to the light. It seems almost impossible to exhaust the number of dormant weed seeds lying in the soil. In other words, the more you dig, the more the weeds will keep on germinating. Mulching puts an end to all this and, after the first flush of weeds, the number rapidly reduces until the shrubs and trees around which the mulch has been spread, are big enough to look after themselves.

However, the most attractive way to overcome persistent weed problems is to use ground-covering plants. There are plenty of small trees, shrubs and completely prostrate plants suitable for this purpose. Many people mistakenly believe that these plants must grow completely flat on the ground, in order to do the job. In fact, any plant which has a dense enough canopy, irrespective of its size, can prove to be an effective weed suppressor.

If the branches and leaves are furnished right to the ground to form a fairly compact dome, weeds will have great difficulty in surviving. When a combination of thick-foliaged shrubs are grown with prostrate plants between them, the effects can be very beautiful, the soil takes longer to dry out, erosion is reduced and the life below the surface of the ground becomes more balanced.

Before planting a groundcover, it pays to remove as many of the surface weeds as possible, in order to give the new plants a good chance to fully establish themselves. It is not enough to simply plant groundcovers among weeds, in the hope that they will eventually overcome them. Few plants, when they are young and newly planted, can compete successfully with weeds, which have the advantages of enormous vigour, drought resistance, few diseases and, in many cases, the ability to produce anti-growth substances to fetter the development of other plants.

Once the weeds have been dealt with, the ground should be cultivated to a depth of about twenty centimetres and fertilizers in the form of blood and bone, with ten per cent potash, sprinkled over the area, at the rate of fifty grams per square metre. Finally, two or three days prior to planting, give the area a good, deep watering.

An alternative to digging out weeds is to wipe them with a herbicide such as Roundup. This will penetrate most grass, twitch and other weeds, to destroy them from within. I have used this particular herbicide experimentally and was amazed to discover dozens of worms, busily feeding off dead grass some time later. Once Roundup has been applied, many plants can go in the next day, without having to wait until the weeds become yellow and die. If the ground is given a good watering early the following day, the plants can be planted out that afternoon. This means the ground covering plants will be growing strongly, while the weeds are dying off. Roundup becomes inactive as soon as it contacts the soil.

Here are some useful, hardy shrubs which can be used as weed-suppressing groundcovers:

Grevilleas. G. 'Crosby Morrison' (tight-foliaged, sprawling shrub, with grey-green leaves and red flowers). *G. rosmarinifolia* (Rosemary grevillea, tough, dense, slightly prickly, drought resistant and bearing red spider-flowers most of the year). G. 'Clearview David' (similar to the Rosemary grevillea above, but can stand some shade. Compact growth). *G. gaudi chaudii* (outstanding prostrate plant with large, bright-red flowers and handsome leaves. Pre-weeding needed).

Acacias. *A. vestita* (a superb, semi-weeping wattle with masses of bright yellow flowers. Very hardy and drought resistant. Grows to about two metres with a much wider spread). *A. pravissima* (Ovens wattle, well known small, ground-covering tree, with brilliant display late winter. Withstands cold, wet winters and dry summers).

Banksias. *B. spinulosa* (Hairpin banksia, named because of the hundreds of glistening black, hairpin-like styles. Three metres tall, tough and withstands heavy frosts. Best used in association with any of the above-named ground-covering plants). *B. ericifolia* (Heath banksia, furnished to the ground. Bright, honey-coloured or red spikes of bloom. Outstanding, hardy ornamental plant).

Other ground covers include hardenbergia, long-leaved wax plant, *Hebe hulkeana, Ceanothus impressus, Hypericum calycinum* (a good shade plant), prostrate junipers, *Correa decumbens*, hydrangeas and prostrate rosemary.

Protection from Possums, Dogs and Cats

There are certain garden pests which cause a great deal of damage, but we rarely read about how to control them, or protect our plants.

They are possums, dogs, cats, birds, farm animals and a few others which sneak in from the bush. It all depends where you live of course. City dwellers are more affected by domestic animals.

Possums seem to be doing more damage to trees, shrubs and other plants than ever before, especially during the warmer months. In cool weather they seek warm, dry conditions and if they can break into a roof and make themselves at home, all hell breaks loose every night.

How then, can we control this beautiful animal which can be such a destructive pest? How can we prevent it from eating every leaf from our favourite trees and shrubs, pinching the fruit we have carefully grown and breaking branches too?

Trapping them is easy enough.

National Parks and Wildlife Service in some states will lend traps for a couple of weeks and these can be baited with a piece of apple and placed near the possums' activity. Usually, they have to be carted out to the bush before they are released, far away from other dwellings. Unfortunately, in an area where there are lots of possums, others just flow into the the newly vacated areas. Special licences can be obtained, under special circumstances, for the possums to be shot by skilled marksmen. The carcasses must be safely disposed of, with neither the skins nor the meat salvaged.

The most effective way is to enclose the garden with a fence, topped by an electric fence. Even a standard-sized fence, reinforced with well-secured chicken-wire, will prevent newcomers from entering. The ones inside can then be trapped or destroyed, overhanging trees cut back and that's virtually the end of the problem.

Spraying with the extraordinarily bitter quassia-chips liquid, made by boiling 100 grams in five litres of water for half an hour, straining off the liquid and spraying the foliage under attack, certainly works. The only trouble is the need to re-spray every time it rains.

Dogs can be a serious problem unless they are confined to a certain area. Other people's dogs are the biggest headache. They will defecate on lawns, vegetable gardens or anywhere else which is well away from their normal living area. Some highly active dogs, such as setters or young German shepherds, will pull out newly-planted trees or shrubs and dig up freshly bedded-out seedlings. Usually, the main reason for this is not wilful destructiveness, but the tantalizing smell of blood and bone.

Anyone with a large active dog and who wants it to run free in the garden, must be prepared to put up with the mess and damage. However, most dogs are far too intelligent to want to dash around all the time. They don't need a large area,

> In the flower garden, trim lawn edges after the grass has been given its last cut for a few weeks; check drainage conditions and install subsoil drainage pipes if necessary. Divide perennials such as cannas, perennial asters, astilbe, achillea, lupin, shasta daisy, chrysanthemums and polyanthus. Lift dahlia clumps and store out of frost and cut back all dead stalks to the ground. Apply an old straw or spoilt hay mulch to herbaceous perennial borders.

just a few square metres and daily exercise. However, don't allow your dog to mess up someone else's garden, or let it run free in the local park or children's play area.

The best controls are first to restrict the movements of your own dog, then, if the problem is caused by someone else's, a bold knock on their door to politely explain the situation. There are various devices which are supposed to repel dogs, but I have yet to see them work consistently. If one particular dog is the problem, an unexpected fright works wonders. It sounds a bit silly, I know, and probably looks even sillier, but if a dog is given a shock just as it enters the garden, by someone suddenly leaping from a concealed place and making a loud noise, it is never forgotten. Dogs have long memories and will avoid places with unpleasant associations.

Cats love freshly-dug soil and seem to have a special preference for newly-sown seedbeds. They'll come from great distances for the sheer pleasure of using your precious garden as their lavatory. The simple answer to this problem is to keep the freshly cultivated area fairly wet until the soil has settled and seeds germinated. If a small square of dry, loose soil is available nearby, they will prefer this to getting their paws mucky and wet. With a serious invasion of cats, new seedbeds can easily be protected with a length of chickenwire laid flat upon the ground, over the seeds. This is lifted when germination has occurred and the settled soil is no longer attractive.

Birds of all kinds are more pest-eaters than pests. That's why many of them scratch around, especially in areas which have been mulched. But this is little consolation, when one constantly comes across enormous quantities of straw or hay thrown all over paths and drives. Blackbirds in particular are major culprits and they get cracking long before anyone is up and about. Other birds destroy, rather than eat, fruit and berries, and it is a heartbreaking sight to see perfectly good fruit, with one little peck on each, lying thickly beneath a tree.

The answer is to make them too nervous to hang around. Netting can be awkward and expensive, while lengths of fishing line stretched between the outer branches of a tree or vine work effectively for a short time. If this type of deterrent is erected just before fruit becomes attractive to the birds, its effectiveness will usually carry over until we get our share. Simple bird-scarers made from aluminium drink containers rammed together, with one can feathered to form a simple windmill, are excellent when they are mounted on a piece of wire to revolve erratically.

There is little point in trying to grow fruit, vegetables, or an attractive garden unless you are prepared to go to the trouble of defending them from these innocent vandals.

JULY
GUIDE TO ACTION

Ornamental Garden

The days are now getting longer which means plants will respond as soil warms up. Choose new camellias while they are in flower at nurseries. Plant early gladioli. Don't prune flowering ornamental trees. Sprinkle blood and bone around spring flowering plants. Clear, weed and cultivate old flower beds. Lightly prune ericas as flowers wither. Watch out for the fragile tips of emerging spring bulbs. Plant all container and bare-rooted plants. Don't prune off frost-damaged foliage of tender shrubs, leave it to provide protection. Prune native plants as they complete flowering. In the flower garden plant seedlings of alyssum, aquilegia, arctotis, calendula, candytuft, Canterbury bells, delphinium, dianthus, foxglove, geum, gypsophila, lupin, myosotis, ornamental kale, pansy, penstemon, Iceland poppy, oriental poppy, shaster daisy, stock, sweet William and divisions of perennials such as paeony rose.

Vegetable Garden

Plant sets of potato onion, shallots and garlic. Sow long keeping onions' seed or in cold, wet districts bring on seedlings under cover for planting out later. Early peas can be planted in frost-free areas. Cold, wet conditions retard growth during this month but green manure can be dug in and badly-drained parts of the garden dealt with. Cover developing cauliflower curds with broken outer leaves to prevent frost browning. Pull out the roots of all brassicas after cutting to avoid diseases such as clubroot. Sow seed under glass, or on a windowsill, for spring seedlings, especially of brassicas. Rough dig vacant beds and lime if needed. Clear all plant debris and compost it. Plant lettuce seedlings on ridges and in cool districts cover them with plastic-bag 'cloches'.

Fruit Garden

Prune deciduous fruit trees but delay winter oil spray until just prior to budbreak, to catch emerging pests. Keep planting out new fruit and berry plants. Don't try and cultivate wet soil. Check and replace plant ties where necessary. Use old hay or straw to mulch thickly around all fruit-bearing plants. Keep mulch just clear of the stems of trees. Continue to plant strawberry runners and remove and destroy all old leaves from established plants. Mulch strawberry beds with clean straw.

Houseplants

Keep grooming away old leaves. Water sparsely. Bring bulbs in bowls inside, if they are budding up. Feed flowering plants with weak liquid fertilizers. Move any plants which are in harmful draughts.

JULY: FIRST WEEK

Winter Jobs

Although the days are perceptibly longer, the next two or three weeks are usually the coldest of the year. But don't let that put you off, because this is a very busy, productive time indeed. Winter weeds are taking full advantage of the cool soil and spreading rapidly. Yet to try to dig them out can be a frustrating experience because the soil sticks to them and no matter where they are thrown, they will probably continue to keep growing. I'm a great believer in smothering them out of existence.

If bales of spoilt hay or pea straw are left, uncovered, in the open, they soon become completely saturated. While this makes them too heavy for easy lifting, the wet straw can be pulled off in compact flakes for laying directly on top of weeds. This type of mulching is perfect for weed-control around roses and can be tucked in around the stems without problems.

In the vegetable garden at the moment, the plants vulnerable to competition from weeds are broad beans and these too can be given a tight mulching. The results of this kind of organic layer over the soil is a bigger worm population. That means healthier plants.

If drainage is a problem in parts of the garden, the effects will be showing up now. Generally, if water tends to be still lying around a day or so after it has stopped raining, there is a problem of poor drainage. See page 68 for some advice on laying subsoil drainage. As this is a muddy operation at this time of year, you could make a note of poorly-drained areas now, for treatment in drier weather.

While you are thinking about pruning deciduous fruit trees at this time, remember that some native plants will also benefit. Many wattles have almost completed their flowering, so this is a good time to lop or prune them. Usually, it is nothing more than the removal of the tips of the branches, including the spent blooms. If this treatment is carried out when the blossoms of most wattles have started to fade, the trees will be more compact, sturdy and will live much longer. Grevilleas too can be clipped or pruned back now if they are getting out of hand. Many of them will keep producing flowers for months, so a pruning will hardly spoil this display, but will help secure and tidy-up straggly plants.

Vegetable gardening at the moment is restricted to planting cool-weather plants such as onions, broad beans, Jerusalem artichokes, asparagus and in warmer soils, brassica seedlings.

English spinach is one vegetable which grows well during winter, provided the right soil conditions are prepared. Many people have given up trying to grow this useful vegetable, because the plants have either failed to grow or bolted to seed. This is usually caused by insufficient lime in the soil. Acid soils need much more lime than most people realize and a good, heavy application, even now, will make all the difference. Soil which has been well fertilized for a previous crop such as peas, beans or root vegetables, and which remains well-drained at this time, is excellent for spinach because lime will not react. Seedling spinach is useless to transplant because it bolts. Direct sowing is the only method and the seed will germinate at temperatures as low as 2°C. A short row of about two metres in length will produce over thirty plants. Side-dressings of poultry manure as the plants develop, will ensure lots of leaves.

It is still a little early in cool areas for sowing peas. They detest excessively-wet soils, and flowering must take place after the last frosts or there will be little, if any, yield. However, the soil can be prepared now, by adding lime if necessary and raising the beds so that they drain easily. Later, a couple of bags of sheep manure, partly raked into the surface, will provide plenty of nourishment for the growing peas.

Plants for Winter Colour

If you want to avoid having a colourless garden during winter, a little planning can make all the difference. The great range of trees, shrubs and other plants, which not only flower during the coldest months, but actually thrive during this period, is truly astonishing. The added advantage of many of these plants is that they can fill the garden with their fragrance, because so many are sweetly scented. Now is the time to look around nurseries and gardens to make a selection for winters to come.

Here are just a few of these valuable delights.

Chimonanthus praecox. This is the magnificently scented wintersweet, sometimes called calycanthus. It will grow to a straggly three metres, and in the middle of winter will produce, on bare branches, masses of almost transparent, yellow flowers. Be generous to yourself when cutting the blossoms for inside, because this is also the best pruning time. The plant likes a situation protected from strong winds, and can stand some summer shade.

Daphne odora. This common and popular garden plant, known for its fragrance, grows to perfection under favourable conditions. Best results are obtained if plenty of afternoon shade and lots of morning sun are given. This daphne dislikes lime, but loves plenty of old manure gently worked into the surface under the dripline.

The small, winter flowering iris, *I. unguicularis* (stylosa) will produce a non-stop supply of lilac-blue flowers, each with a golden centre. Here is an excellent plant for a dryish bank. They are one of the toughest of all plants and, once established, need very little care. Just the same, it is a good idea, just before winter, to cut back all the leaves hard. This will allow the flowers to display themselves more conspicuously, while removing hiding places for slugs and snails.

Among the many other winter flowering perennials, is the shade loving *Bergenia cordifolia*. It displays 200 millimetre high spikes of rosy-red blooms, surrounded by shining, heart-shaped leaves.

Another excellent winter bloomer is *Chaenomeles*. Also known as the Japanese flowering quince, it can be obtained in a range of colours from brick-red through pink to snowy white. It will grow virtually anywhere and thrives in extremely cold districts.

Buddleia salvifolia is an evergreen, strong-growing, four-metre tall shrub. It has large, dark green, sage-like leaves and during June, July and August will produce great panicles of sweet-scented, pale-lilac flowers. Like most buddleias, it responds strongly to a heavy pruning during and after flowering.

Winter is the time when a big range of ericas show their flowers. From completely prostrate plants to metre high, bushy shrubs, ericas will produce so many blooms that the foliage is completely concealed by them. In addition, there is their sweet, honey-like scent, which, on a sunny winter's day, can fill a small garden. My favourite is *Erica canaliculata*. It will grow to at least a metre, and the urn-shaped, rosy bells have a conspicuous black centre.

All ericas are acid lovers and prefer a peaty, moist, well-drained soil. If they are allowed to dry out during summer, they just die, so keep them well watered.

One of the most unusual and popular winter-flowering shrubs is the tassel bush (*Garrya elliptica*). The male form produces a huge hanging mass of yellow-grey catkins, which cover the shrub from top to bottom. Even a newly planted tassel bush will start to produce these attractive flowers, and the plant is hardy enough to withstand the most savage frosts. This is one plant which makes an ideal lawn shrub and creates an astonishing and beautiful effect during midwinter.

So far I haven't mentioned the great source of winter colour, Australian native plants. Wattles start to bloom from late autumn, and continue beyond Christmas. They are a rich, golden feature of our landscape and are easy, quick growers. The Sydney golden wattle will develop rapidly to form a round-topped, five metre high tree. This, *Acacia longifolia*, is available at almost every nursery, and may be planted out at any time during the year. But try to obtain small plants, because they will live longer and establish themselves into a more attractive shape than so-called advanced specimens.

The banksias too are great ones for winter blooms. They also attract the birds, and this means less insect pests in the garden. One of the most attractive is *Banksia ericifolia*, the Heath banksia, with its huge, honey or red spikes and narrow leaves. This will grow to several metres if allowed, but a ruthless pruning will control it and allow for the formation of a more compact shrub.

There are many more winter-flowering plants of course. There are the camellias, crotalaria, eriostemon, grevilleas, hakeas, hebes, *Luculia gratissima, Magnolia stellata*, most of the proteas, flowering almond, Indian hawthorn, thryptomene, and at least two viburnums.

Through careful selection of plants, even the most bare and drab garden can be transformed into a place which will make winter something to look forward to.

How to Raise Seedlings

The most fascinating and, in some ways, seductive job of all in the garden is growing plants from seed. The extraordinary sight of a successful germination, relentlessly erupting through the soil, never fails to send a tingle down the spine.

Propagation from seed is the cheapest and easiest way of increasing the number of plants in all parts of the garden. There is a much wider choice available, allowing for all sorts of experiments. Direct seeding into open ground produces healthier, drought-resistant plants which can grow unchecked from the start. In fact many common vegetables such as carrot, parsnip, spinach or beetroot, must be directly sown, otherwise they would bolt to seed after being transplanted.

However, greater control is achieved

> It is the easiest thing in the world to convert from chemicals and poisons to relatively natural or non-toxic ways of growing things. Sometimes, if the soil has been ill-treated over a number of years, it becomes hooked on chemicals and when these are no longer used, it appears to go through a kind of withdrawal period.
>
> Get rid of all the poisons. Most municipal garbage disposal sites have a special place for toxic wastes, so use these rather than pouring the stuff down the drain.

with most plants, when their seeds are germinated into containers and the seedlings transplanted, either to open ground, or into larger containers. By this method, light and moisture needs can be met and the seeds or seedlings protected against pests and diseases.

The type of soil and the way light and warmth are made available, are the keys to success with container-grown seedlings. Garden soil is not suitable for any but the most viable or vigorous of seeds and seedlings. It contains too many harmful organisms, many of which multiply rapidly when placed into containers. In addition, garden soil quickly loses structure, collapsing into a hard pad often within hours of being placed into a pot. The relative lack of organic matter in most garden soils causes it to continually dry out in a container, making seedling production very difficult and frustrating.

However, good-quality garden soil can be kept friable, by adding equal parts of coarse sand and granulated peat. This allows for a good moisture-holding capacity, while providing sharp drainage. The soil can be treated to destroy most weed seeds, eelworms, insect pests and harmful fungi or bacteria, by pasteurizing it.

This involves holding the soil in a moist condition, at a temperature of about 90°C for half an hour. Don't be tempted to use a higher temperature, because it will not only destroy many protective, beneficial organisms, but will also cause serious soil toxicity.

The alternative to using garden soil is to use a soil-free compost of equal parts of sand and peat, with a handful of blood and bone, a fistful of sulphate of potash and, for most vegetable seeds, a good handful of dolomite per bucketful of mix. If you have access to virgin bush soil, this is better than garden soil, because it is less likely to be contaminated. Just the same, the soil-based mix should also include added fertilizers and minerals.

Peat is hard to get wet when it has dried, so add plenty of water to the mix, then leave it in the shade for a couple of days to mature, while draining away surplus water. It is then suitable for spooning into punnets, pots or perforated margarine containers ready for the seed. After settling, the surface should be gently pressed level, so that it is about a centimetre below the rim.

Seed should be sown thinly and as evenly as possible. Very fine seed, which can be difficult to handle, can be mixed with fine sand to bulk it out. The seed should then be covered with its own depth of the seed-raising mixture and gently pressed into contact. Very fine seed is best left uncovered amongst its sand. The most critical part of the sowing medium is near the surface where the seeds are lying. It is more likely to dry out and, should this occur, the partly germinated seeds will dry out. This is the most common cause of seed loss.

By covering the containers with a sheet of glass, or placing them inside a plastic bag, the danger of drying out can be averted. However, a close moist atmosphere, while perfect for seed-germination, is also ideal for the growth of harmful moulds and fungi. This is why an initial pasteurization is so important.

Above all, the germinating seeds must be kept out of the sun at all times. Sunlight is a killer of germinating seeds and young seedlings. When germination takes place, full light must be given, but never sunlight. It must be an even light, not from one side, otherwise the seedlings will emerge sideways; while if the light source is too far overhead, they will quickly become stretched and weak.

The glass or plastic cover is best removed within a week of germination, to allow the tiny seedlings to become hardened to a less close atmosphere.

The sooner these plants are transferred to another container, where there is more room between them, the better. The first leaves which appear are the seed-leaves and if the operation can be carried out before the true leaves appear there is less chance of any transplanting shock. 'Pricking-out' simply means making small holes in the compost in the new containers, then carefully lifting the seedlings from their overcrowded situation and placing them into these holes. The lifting can be done with the tip of an ice-cream stick or the handle of a teaspoon, to keep the fragile roots intact during the process. If they have to be touched, it is better to hold on to one seed-leaf rather than risk crushing the stem. After being firmed into their new locations, the seedling can be watered with a fine mist spray and placed in the shade for a few days. Any attempt to give them direct sunlight at this stage will cause immediate wilting, but after they have settled in they can gradually be introduced to brighter light, then an hour of morning sun and finally, after a gradual hardening-off period, full sun.

Container-grown seedlings have compact rootballs. Transplanting them into their permanent positions is much less of a shock than it is for those germinated in open-ground seedbeds. All handling should take place out of the sun, on cloudy days or in the evening.

JULY: SECOND WEEK

Foliage Plants for a Year-round Display

Well planned gardens, while taking full advantage of the main flowering time during spring, also allow for a constantly changing background of foliage plants.

I always regard flowers as a special bonus which last only a few weeks on most plants. A really deep satisfaction and pleasure comes from an all-the-year-round colour and shape given by a huge range of shrubs, perennials and trees.

The colour comes from the leaves, bark, grass, earth, rocks, and even the lichen which grows upon the rocks. The variation is enormous, because apart from the many shades of brown, green and grey, plant foliage can be gold, red, purple, silver, blue-grey, bronze and scarlet.

Here are some easily obtained plants, the leaves of which can be used to create superb colour schemes in the garden.

Silver and grey shades. *Stachys lanata* (lamb's ears) prostrate, spreading, with silver-white, woolly leaves and lilac spikes of bloom. An excellent weed suppressor for a sunny bank. *Alyssum saxatile*, a vigorous ground-cover plant with bright yellow flowers. *Santolina chamaecyparissus* (cotton lavender) grows into a small, tight, silver bun. If its insignificant flowers are removed before they open, the plant will remain neat and compact. *Senecio cineraria* (dusty miller) silver-white shrub, growing about one-metre tall and about the same width.

In addition there are many varieties of artemisia, dianthus, carnation, helichrysum, and, among the larger plants, some species of protea, acacia and leucadendron, all of which display characteristic silver-grey leaves.

The special advantage of almost all these silvery-leaved plants is their marvellous ability to withstand sea winds and extremely sandy soil. In districts away from the coast success can be obtained in very well drained, open situations.

Golden-foliaged plants. The golden elm (*Ulmus procera* 'Vanhouttei') is quite outstanding. It grows to a medium-sized vase shaped tree and can be accommodated even in small gardens. The leaf-colour, from the time they emerge, is lime-yellow, gradually becoming soft gold as the season progresses. A friend once told me he could instantly pick out his own home, from the air, by the bright yellow of the leaves of his golden elm. Here is a plant which will tolerate most soils, is attacked by few diseases or insect pests in Australia, and requires little care and attention, apart from the pruning of dead or weak wood.

There is a whole range of golden conifers. Some, such as the completely prostrate golden juniper (*Juniperus communis* 'Depressa Aurea') will gradually change to bronze during winter, while others (especially *Chamaecyparis* 'Crippsii'), remain bright gold all the year. Among favourites are: *Thuja occidentalis* 'Rheingold', a lovely, low-growing, bun-shaped delight, pink-gold during warm weather, turning bronze-yellow in winter.

The Golden Ash (*Fraxinus excelsior* 'Aurea') is the ideal small tree, best planted out on its own where it can show off its yellow-green leaves until they become clear yellow in autumn. Even during the winter, when the golden ash is leafless, the branches and twigs have a distinct orange colour, and it creates a beautiful sight with velvet-black buds at the end of each twig.

Red-purple foliage. An outstanding tree, which grows particularly strongly in cooler districts, is the purple beech. There are many forms of this rich red-purple tree, all of them a beautiful sight in any garden with good drainage and some protection from destructive winds. In autumn the leaves take on colours of rust-red, gold, purple, and soft yellow.

Of course there are plenty more of these plants which are grown mainly for their outstanding leaves, and it is worth a trip to a nursery to see some of them growing.

Growing Onions and Garlic

The difference between shallots and potato onions is that while shallots can be grown both from seed and divisions, potato onions don't go to seed, they simply multiply. This is probably why potato onions are relentlessly disappearing from our gardens as people fail to replant every year. It would be a tragedy if we lost this useful, mild, disease-resistant and long-keeping onion. I believe Australia is now one of the few places in the world where it is still grown. So, if you have a few 'sets' left over from last year's crop, why not plant them now?

Shallot and potato onion sets are planted into any open, well-drained part of the garden, simply by gently screwing the bottom half of the bulbs into the cultivated soil. The necks are left sticking up out of the ground. At harvest time, usually around Christmas, the single set will have increased to at least ten and occasionally more than twenty bulbs.

This is the month for sowing long-keeping onions. Seed germinates readily at anywhere between 2°C and 27°C, and early-sown crops are heavier, with larger individual bulbs. This is because the growing plants seem to concentrate upon growing additional scales until the longest day in December, then they bulb-out dramatically. The more scales they can grow, the bigger they will be. Direct sowing is the best way of obtaining evenly-sized yields with less chance of the plants bolting to seed.

The bolting process is often triggered by planting too early or rough transplanting of seedlings. Once an onion bolts, it develops a 'bull-neck', loses its strength and flavour, and won't keep. The idea is to try to grow them so they have only a thin neck, ensuring good, long keeping.

Onions are lime-lovers, so if the soil has not been limed for a year or so, give it a good whitening now. It is better to choose a place where onions have not been grown for about five years, preferably one which has been fertilized for a previous crop of another vegetable. It is not a good idea to apply fertilizers at sowing/planting time, especially manure or blood and bone. They can cause problems with maggots – sometimes a serious pest with onions.

High-nitrogen fertilizers also make the developing bulbs big and soft, seriously reducing keeping qualities. This doesn't matter in the case of salad onions such as White Spanish, because they are usually grown for immediate use.

The ground into which onion seed is to be sown should be worked to a fine tilth, then raked and walked upon until only the surface is loose, the rest being firm. If you have room, make the drills at least half a metre apart. This may seem too wide a gap, but later on, a row of carrots can be sown between each row of onions. This type of companion-planting produces better yields with less disease problems.

Sow the onion-seed with a little sea sand to bulk it out, making it easier to handle, and dribble the mixture into the shallow drills. Then apply a fine covering of sand or soil, pressed into contact with the back of the rake. Germination will take place within two or three weeks, depending upon temperature. If your soil is too wet, or unprepared, the onion seed can be sown first into containers. A friable soil-mix with plenty of lime will do

> Over-vigorous, non-productive fruit trees, especially plums, can be forced into bearing by severing their outer roots with a sharp spade now.

the trick. Later, when the plants have developed enough, they can be planted out into the open garden. If you have any seed left over from previous seasons, throw it out. Use fresh seed every year with onions.

When the young seedlings emerge, they are at a great disadvantage competing with weeds and other plants. Their small, thin, grass-like leaves can soon be swamped by more aggressive plants, so make sure the ground is as clean as possible prior to sowing seed, and get ready to carry out the tedious task of removing competing weed seedlings while they are still tiny. This is why early planting or sowing is so advantageous. The worst of the weeds don't begin to germinate on a large scale until early spring, so if you can get your onions up and moving, their chances of survival are greater.

The best of the long keepers are Brown Spanish and Creamgold. Both varieties can be sown from this month, but late sowings produce small bulbs.

Harvesting takes place about the end of February or March when the tops begin to die back a little. Onions can occupy the most valuable part of the vegetable garden for long periods, but if they are grown correctly, the long keepers will last well into the following spring, especially if the tops are allowed to dry out naturally and are not bent over.

Garlic is another type of onion which now seems to fascinate people. I'm still mystified why we have to import such large quantities from overseas when we can grow such good-quality cloves in Australia. Like other onions, they will not grow in acid soils, so be generous with the lime. The best source of cloves for planting purposes is any vegetable shop which sells the good quality, small, aromatic garlic cloves. Pull the clusters apart, and push the individual cloves into the soil so that they are just below the surface. They tend to sprout within days and, in good, well-drained conditions will make strong growth. Unlike other types of onion they will go to seed, but this will not affect keeping qualities or yield.

Creating a Rock garden

A rock garden can be an absolute delight. They can be small enough to fit into a large container, or big enough to cover a substantial part of the garden. Correctly built and planted, they rarely get out of hand and are easy to maintain. With carefully-placed dwarf conifers, interesting rocks and every crevice filled with tiny, creeping, tufted or drooping alpine plants, a miniature landscape can be created which will be a constant source of pleasure.

Rock gardens must be in open sun and the drainage perfect. They cannot succeed in the shade. Even the dappled conditions of an overhanging tree, with plenty of good light, can be a disaster for some alpine plants. The destructive drip of moisture from above means a lingering death for these normally tough plants.

Slopes are a great advantage when building a rock garden, but the soil in flat areas can be built up into an irregular mound or two to increase the planting area and improve drainage. One of the most effective I have seen was on both sides of a garden path which became a winding valley between two superbly-planted mountains.

The secret of success lies in the soil mixture. Most rock plants originate in alpine areas and grow in a mixture of small stones, decayed plant material and a little soil. These tiny mountain plants develop a long root-run, well-protected from excess heat and cold. Good quality garden soil, relatively free from clay, with large quantities of fine road metal mixed into it is ideal. These small stones can form up to fifty per cent of the total volume. If generous amounts of granulated peat-moss are also added, the final

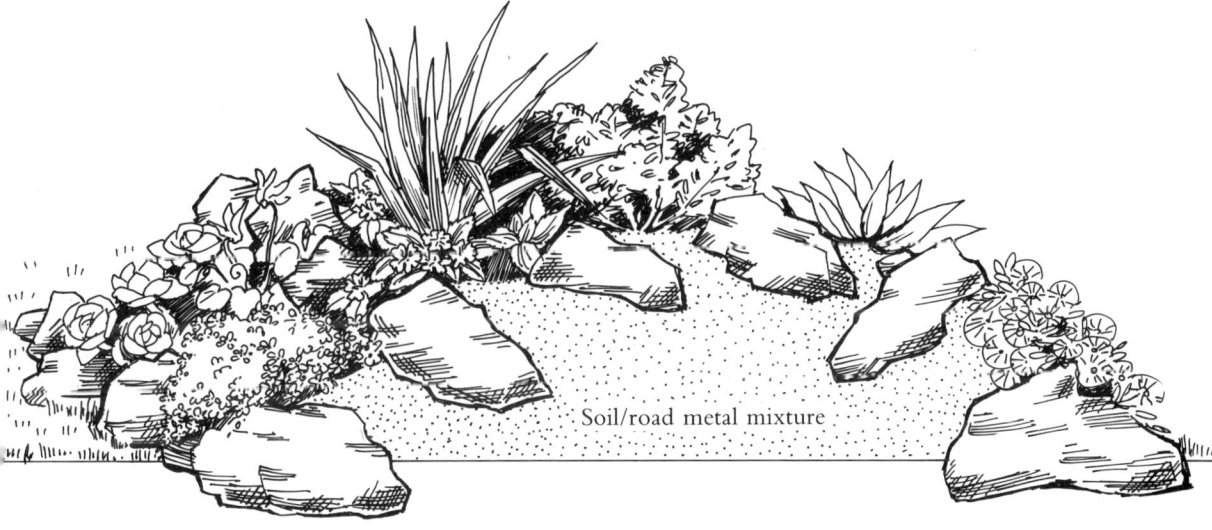

A Rock Garden Mound

mixture should resemble the enriched scree in which alpine plants naturally grow.

The advantages of this mixture are: water-holding capacity, easy handling, coolness and easy weeding. After the soil has been prepared it can be moulded into a flat-topped mound, perhaps with an off-centre saddle. Any perennial weeds or clods should have been removed during the mixing. If the soil is acidic, dolomite-limestone at the rate of a double handful to the square metre can be worked into the top thirty centimetres. Old pulverized animal manure and blood and bone can also be added.

The rocks used should be as large as it is possible to handle. Small rocks are of little value because they always appear insignificant. If the large rocks are also weather-worn and covered with lichen and moss, they will add enormously to the character of the garden. However, even freshly-spalled quarried stones can be used because the plants will soften their angular shapes. If the water in which potatoes, rice or even spaghetti have been boiled is allowed to cool, then sprayed or painted on to the surface of bare rocks, lichens will soon appear, along with other primitive forms of life.

The aim, when placing the rocks, is to try to imitate natural rock formations. Try to avoid the 'plum-pudding' look by locating the rocks in clusters, obviously relating to each other. Above all, don't stick a group of pointed rocks on the top of the heap, unless that's where your taste lies. We must cheat a little when trying to duplicate nature, by ensuring that all gaps and crevices are wide enough to insert a hand or trowel into. Placing rocks in a new rock garden is also creating spaces and bays for the plants. Above all, try to keep the 'face', that is the most attractive side of the rock, upwards, and lay flat rocks down to allow creeping plants to take them over, rather than having them balanced precariously on their edges.

Once the rocks are in position and secure, the soil between them can be smoothed and then mulched. However, unlike other parts of the garden, alpine gardens are not mulched with pine-bark or woodchips. Organic materials like this will eventually cause the death of many of the plants. The mulch to use is fine bluemetal screenings or similar, spread to a thickness of about five centimetres. This will allow air to circulate around the sensitive base of the plants, while suppressing weeds and sealing in moisture. After forming the garden, fertilize with blood and bone and, if the soil is acidic, add a good handful of dolomite-limestone to each square metre of surface, then water well.

If there is a rule about planting a rock garden it is this; avoid those plants which have large leaves. They make rocks appear small and the whole effect can be lost. Use small-leaved plants, such as dwarf conifers, low down the sides.

Fortunately, rock and alpine plants are still inexpensive and many are easily propagated. Some garden centres have a special section, devoted to these plants, although care must be taken to choose non-invasive species. Crevice lovers like the androsaces form into tiny tussocks which produce pink or white primrose-like flowers. Alpine asters, campanulas, prostrate silvery-leaved chrysanthemums, diminutive brooms, daphne and a whole range of clove-scented alpine pinks are all easily available.

In addition there are many bulbs, corms and tubers suitable for colonizing pockets in a rock garden, some growing to perfection in the sharply-drained soil.

JULY: THIRD WEEK

What are Companion Plants For?

In many ways, plants, like humans, are discriminating about the company they keep. They have their likes and dislikes, and the way they can be successfully associated, especially in the vegetable garden, is known as 'companion planting'.

There is nothing mystical about this relationship. The depths to which certain plants send their roots, the amount of foliage grown by others and the extent to which they can suppress the growth of adjoining plants, all have an important influence on the way plants tolerate each other. Some plants produce substances which limit the growth of their own seedlings, others encourage the growth and development of particular, unrelated species.

Here are some common relationships between vegetable plants which can be utilized in order to obtain better quality yields less likely to be attacked by insect pests and diseases.

French or dwarf beans. They seem to grow better in company with cucumbers, cabbages and strawberry plants.

Beetroot. Likes the company of French beans, cabbage, kohlrabi and onions.

Cabbages. Clearly dislike strawberries, but grow well alongside tomatoes, lettuces, beetroot, sage, dill and chamomile.

Carrots. The wonderful relationship between onions, leeks and shallots on the one hand, and carrots on the other is well-known among organic growers. There is no question about the better results when these good friends are planted adjacent to each other in alternate rows. The fact that onions have thin leaves which do not compete, while their roots feed at a different level, partly explains this useful friendship. Carrots also like lettuces, peas, radishes and chives. However, after lifting, carrots should not be stored next to apples.

Cauliflowers. Seem to grow particularly well next to celery. Their mutual love of soil which has been recently limed may explain this.

Chives. Have been used for years to help control greenfly on roses. They grow strongly when planted between the bushes, making an attractive semi-groundcover with rosy-pink flowers. The smell from their leaves appears to mask the smell from the growing rose shoots, so the aphids presumably pass them by.

Celery. Grows well with leeks, tomatoes, dwarf beans and cabbages.

Sweetcorn. Thrives next to peas, pumpkins, zucchini and early-planted potatoes. Climbing beans and 'burpless' cucumber can actually be trained to grow up the developing corn-stalks, where they will continue to bear long after the corn has been harvested.

Cucumbers. Like beans, cabbages, kohlrabi, radishes and lettuces.

Lettuces. Planted next to parsley and strawberry plants seem to do very well, producing crisp, tight hearts. Other good companions include carrots, radishes, beetroot and any of the cabbage tribe.

Onions. Never happy when planted next to peas or beans. They look miserable, and often develop a bull-neck, which means poor keeping quality. However, apart from their infatuation with carrots, they also like to be with beetroot, lettuce, summer savoury and chamomile.

Parsnips. Germinate slowly from seed, so many growers plant radish seed in the same drill. They are up within a week, break the crust and can be harvested and eaten while the parsnips are still following through. They also like cabbage, silverbeet and cauliflower to keep them company.

Peas. Will sulk if they are grown next to onions, garlic or shallots, so keep them apart. However, they really respond well to sweetcorn, turnips, cucumbers, carrots and radishes and will even tolerate spuds.

Pumpkins. More difficult to get on with. They detest potatoes in particular and seldom get on with other vegetables, although they have a soft spot for sweetcorn.

Radishes. Ready to pull within a month after the seed has been sown, so they rarely have much of a chance to become picky about their company. However, for some weird reason they dislike hyssop.

Silverbeet. Grows strongly next to French beans, cabbage, broccoli, lettuce, kohlrabi and to a limited extent, onions, which grow smallish, strongly-flavoured bulbs. Silverbeet however is intolerant of mustard and climbing beans.

Tomatoes. Have a large circle of good pals. These include asparagus, parsley, cabbage, cauliflower, sprouts and, the great love of their life, basil. But tomatoes will not tolerate apricot trees or even the soil where they once grew. They also dislike fennel and kohlrabi and it seems that the feeling is mutual.

A vegetable garden can be planned so that there are plenty of happy relationships in every bed. Plants have much to teach us, if we could only open our eyes.

All About the Acid-lovers

The group of ornamental plants known as the 'acid-lovers' include some of the most beautiful and sought-after trees or shrubs. It's not so much that they have a special love for acid soils, or even that they dislike lime. Most of them are not particularly good at getting iron from the soil, and the presence of lime makes the task almost impossible. The result is usually seen in the foliage. The leaves become pale yellow, sometimes almost white, especially the younger ones. The plant loses its vigour and looks unsightly.

Sometimes rhododendrons and azaleas, when planted adjacent to an old brick wall containing lots of loose mortar, will show clear symptoms of this 'lime-induced chlorosis' as it is called. Other areas where these plants are vulnerable include sites where concrete or mortar was mixed during building operations.

The cure for the problem is to supply the iron to the plant in a way which will not be affected by the alkaline soil. In Britain and some parts of Europe, chalky soil prevented the successful growing of these lovely plants. However, when chelated iron was used, both on the leaves as well as around the plants, the alkaline soils ceased to be a problem.

Rhododendrons, depending on their size, are usually a little more expensive than other plants. Perhaps this is why there is still a sad tendency for many proud owners to publicly flaunt their prized rhododendrons in the centre of their front lawns. Too often this means full sun, and worse still, grass growing thickly over the roots, which continually robs the rhododendron of essential moisture and plant nutrients. Many of these unfortunate plants seem to remain in a permanently stunted condition, the problem being aggravated by clumsy mower operators who regularly knock chunks of bark from the lower stems.

Many of these suffering plants break into vigorous new growth as soon as they have been liberated by transplanting. A position with plenty of afternoon shade and lots of well-drained, clay-free, moist, acid soil, suits them much better.

The root-systems of azaleas and rhododendrons are in the form of a tight ball with numerous fine hair-like feeding roots. This is why even large specimens can be successfully transplanted without a serious check to growth. However, shallow rootballs make this type of plant sensitive to dry soil conditions. Once the core of the rootball becomes dry, it can be difficult to wet it again because it tends to repel water at first. Fertilizers can, if incorrectly applied, burn the tender roots. When planting rhododendrons or azaleas, fertilizers should not be mixed into the planting hole. The exception is compost which is ideal for these plants.

The range of rhododendrons grown in gardens is enormous. They vary in size from twelve metre high trees to tiny alpine species. Although most of them come from western China and Nepal, many others originate in Europe, North America, New Guinea and Australia. Some are deciduous, many are sweetly fragrant and a few are grown for the attractive leaves. Most species seem to thrive in Australia, with cool districts being particularly suitable.

Many people grow them in large containers and, given the right conditions, they will grow and flower for many years with few problems. The secret of success under these circumstances is daily watering during summer and fortnightly feeding with liquid fertilizers. Every few years these container plants can be carefully lifted and the outer soil scraped away before being replanted with fresh soil.

Although the large-leaved rhododendrons like afternoon shade, many of the small-leaf varieties are happy in full sun, provided they are given plenty of overhead water in warm weather.

The most common pests are mites, often called red-spiders. They live on the underside of the leaves, are so tiny they are difficult to see with the naked eye, and suck the sap where they congregate. They are controlled by Rogor, which is very toxic, or by the relatively safe Clensel or pyrethrum. These safer sprays require several applications.

The other common problem with rhododendrons, especially the ones grown in areas of clay soil or poor drainage, is 'marginal leaf scorch'. The outer edges of the leaves develop a black burnt-looking appearance and the plant fails to thrive. The cause is dying-back of the feeding roots due to too much moisture. The cure is improved drainage, even if it means transplanting to another area.

Azaleas, which are in fact rhododendrons, can be grown in most positions in the garden, although the large-flowering indica types prefer some afternoon shade. The deciduous mollis and Ghent cultivars also grow well, flowering better in full sun.

Anyone planning a garden should think seriously about a planting of rhododendrons and azaleas if there is a place which receives some shade during the afternoon. Mixed with other acid-lovers such as camellias, pierises and daphnes, with an underplanting of liliums, Solomon's seal, lily of the valley and daffodils, they will be a great source of pleasure.

Planting for Privacy

The most attractive way to provide a screen for privacy is by using plants. There are trees, shrubs and climbing plants for almost every position, and provided that the emphasis is upon evergreens, a dense mass of foliage can be grown with surprising speed.

Usually the most common area where lack of privacy is a problem, is between adjacent houses or gardens. The key zone seems to be at the rear, although privacy planting is often necessary when the house is situated fairly close to the street, especially if the street level is above that of the house.

Large bushy shrubs or small trees make a perfect screen, but the taller they grow, the more room they generally need, and important parts of the garden can be occupied.

However, if there is plenty of room, the effects of a mass planting of large flowering shrubs and trees can be breathtaking.

Here are examples of some of these plants, all of which can be used mixed together or alone in mass plantings.

Acacia fimbriata. Sometimes called the sticky wattle, this small tree produces an extraordinary display of golden bloom during spring, weighing down the branches to give a glorious weeping effect. Height four metres and spread the same. Very hardy and frost resistant.

Acacia pravissima. Another mass of gold during spring, and holding its blooms for week upon marvellous week. It branches right to the ground and can stand almost every possible soil condition, provided it is in the open. Areas with very wet winters and extra dry summers suit perfectly. Five metres.

Callistemon viminalis (weeping bottlebrush). Thrives in heavy clay soils, grows three or four metres and during early summer is covered with hundreds of pale-red brushes. Branches weep almost to the ground and make a splendid sight at all times of the year. Very attractive to birds.

Callistemon pallidus. Another one which seems to tolerate heavy wet clay conditions and the most savage frosts. Growing to three metres or more, it forms a much narrower shrub than many similar-sized bottlebrush, and planted at one metre intervals makes a superb screen, even in a small garden. In early summer it is covered with pale yellow brushes which contrast beautifully with the dark foliage. Can be clipped immediately after flowering.

Really narrow areas, especially between adjoining houses, can present a serious privacy problem. Large trees or shrubs take up too much room to be effective in these places. This is where

---

In the vegetable garden this week plant: broad beans, brown Spanish onions, asparagus crowns, English spinach, and in early districts, peas.

Continue pruning and winter spraying deciduous fruit trees and berry fruit plants in the fruit garden, and, if the soil is not too saturated, plant out some certified strawberry runners. Do not use runners from old, existing plants, as they are almost certainly infested with insect pests and diseases.

---

evergreen climbing plants come into their own, but it is not enough to simply grow them up the side of the fence. The use of a lattice, attached to the main rails of the fence, and extending up to a metre or more above the top, can help provide a quick-growing screen which will give relief to people on both sides of the fence.

Lattices, or trellises, should not be simply attached to the top of the fence. They are stronger if they overlap, almost two-thirds of the way from the top. Wooden ones are more attractive than metal, but once they have been covered by the climber, it doesn't really matter. Just the same, it is better with painted lattice to use a dark, earthy colour. The big mistake in using white or light colours, is that they soon begin to discolour and look scruffy, and once the climber has begun to take over, they can be virtually impossible to repaint.

Always use rustproof bolts, nuts, washers and nails when erecting a lattice, and ensure that it is capable of withstanding the great weight of many climbing plants.

Easily obtained climbing plants suitable for a privacy screen, include golden honeysuckle (*Lonicera japonica* 'Aureoreticulata'), a vigorous plant which will cover several square metres of lattice in two or three seasons. The green leaves are each covered with a delicate network of gold. It is very hardy. *Jasminum polyanthum* has pink buds opening to white. Its strongly fragrant flowers in early spring make this one of the most popular of scented plants. It will rapidly layer itself and in a very short time an effective light screen will have developed. *Hedera canariensis* is non-invasive, slightly variegated ivy which, although typically slow to start, will grow rapidly and eventually completely conceal both fence and lattice.

There are many other climbing plants which make quick, effective screens, including passionfruit, potato vines, semi-evergreen roses such as mermaid, and dozens of attractive deciduous plants which allow the sunlight to flow in during the winter months. These include clematis, campsis, tecoma, and at least two varieties of Virginian creeper.

JULY: LAST WEEK

Landscaping Before the House is Built

It's not always possible, but it is so much better if the basic lay-out of a garden is roughly worked out before a house has been built. The location of the house and the direction it will face are an essential part of the landscaping. Most modern homes are deliberately angled to take full advantage of the best views, but there are other considerations too.

When the main living areas of a home are warmed by the morning sun, they usually remain warm for the rest of the day, with considerable savings in fuel during winter. If a house is set well back from the street there is usually more privacy and reduced traffic noise, but less back garden area.

Some of the biggest blunders are made during initial excavations, especially if the site is a sloping one. Too often the area which has been levelled fails to allow enough room at the rear of the house. The result is a gloomy slot two or three metres wide between the back wall and an impoverished bank of clay, rock, or subsoil. Unfortunately, once the mistake has been realized, the house has been built and it is virtually impossible to get a machine in to increase the only flat area available.

Usually, an additional day with a large tracked excavator would have been enough to provide another twelve metres of level ground across the rear of a house, plus a stockpile of topsoil salvaged from the homesite. All the excavated materials can generally be dumped and track-rammed to form an apron of flat ground to the front of the house site. This too can be given a layer of topsoil, provided the machine operator has been instructed to reserve it in the first place.

The location of paths and the drive are also an important part of the landscaping. A nice curving drive might be picturesque, but it could be a nightmare to try to reverse along, especially at night in pouring rain. So, unless a turning area is also constructed, it is better to stick to the straight and true.

Paths are different. The way they are curved plays a key part in the final shape of the garden. However excessive twists and turns look silly and are always ignored by people who simply take short cuts across the bends.

There is still a tendency to leave the location of paths to the builders. Naturally, they take the easy way out and run the paths alongside the walls of the house. I've lost count of the occasions when I have seen such house-hugging paths, almost unusable when the windows are opened. Children are the ones who are mostly at risk under these circumstances, because they move fast and the hazards are often head-high to them.

If a garden path running from the front to the rear of a house is deliberately curved around the corners and is well clear of the walls, it not only looks good, but provides enormous scope for landscaping. The normal, angular shape of most building blocks, coupled with the practical squarish shape of most houses, can make even a large garden area appear small. Gently curving paths help to alter this square look, and they also provide valuable planting areas adjacent to the house walls.

The location of garden taps is often left in the hands of the plumbers. Unless instructed otherwise they will invariably bolt a stand-pipe to one or more corners of the house. Later on, when the garden is becoming established and water is required, it can be an expensive, tedious job trying to tunnel beneath concrete paths in order to extend the water supply. Yet the initial cost of placing two or three stand-pipes at strategic places in the proposed ornamental or vegetable garden is very small. It is no problem either, to have double-cock stand-pipes which will allow for a hose attachment on each, or one tap free. Even the height of the standard is important. There has been a tendency to make them short and unobtrusive, which is fine, but try filling a bucket or a watering-can from them.

The answer is to have a minimum stand-pipe height of half a metre, but locate them in unobtrusive positions, such as near fences or trees.

Many people, anxious to get their garden started, understandably want to start planting before building operations begin. They theorize that the trees and shrubs can be growing while finance is being raised, or the house built. It sounds marvellous, but it only works if the plants are well clear of all work being carried out.

Moving Plants Around

When alterations or extensions are made to existing homes, all sorts of landscaping problems can arise, especially with an established garden. I've long since learned that marking vulnerable plants with a conspicuous stake is never enough to save them from damage by machine operators or dumped building materials. This is not a criticism of building workers, it's a recognition of the great difficulty in carrying out any building operations, while trying to work around inconveniently-placed trees, shrubs and other plants.

The best way of protecting difficult-to-lift plants in vulnerable areas is to prune them back fairly hard and to drive two or three stakes into the ground around them at an angle. They can then be secured together to form a kind of roof.

It is much safer for the plants, and work usually proceeds much faster, if as many as possible are lifted and placed out of harm's way for replanting later on. At any time of the year, a surprisingly large number of plants can easily be lifted without setback, some continuing to grow while awaiting replanting.

The ones which suffer least from being taken out of the ground for a while, are those with shallow, compact rootballs. These include rhododendrons, azaleas, camellias, ericas, daphne, citrus, pierises, kalmias, and many of the smaller conifers. Even large specimens can be lifted, provided certain precautions are taken.

If damage to roots occurs while they are being dug out of the ground, the top-growth must also be reduced in order to compensate and restore the balance. If this is not done, the tops will die back anyway, with a high chance that the plant will either die, after struggling for a month or so, or will be permanently stunted. If the tops of these attractive ornamental plants have to be reduced, the job can still be carried out in a manner which will not destroy the overall shape. Thinning-out rather than lopping-back is how this type of pruning should be done, with most of the cuts occurring at the junctions of branches in order to retain shape, while avoiding die-back.

One way of ensuring that the soil will cling to the roots is to soak the root-zone first. Immediately on lifting, the plants should be placed out of the sun and either replanted, or covered with wet bags, straw and black plastic sheeting to prevent moisture loss. If they are watered daily, most compact-rooted plants can remain like this for months, awaiting replanting.

Other plants are more difficult to move, especially deciduous ones after their leaves have emerged at the end of the dormant season. Rapid transpiration of moisture from the leaf surfaces causes drying-out and inevitable death, especially during spring and early summer when growth is most active. However, during winter when deciduous trees, shrubs and young roses are fully dormant, most of them can easily be moved to a new site with few problems. Large plants which have been growing in one place for up to ten years or even more, can be moved after certain preparations have been made. The outer roots are pruned while the area closer to the trunks is watered and given regular feeds of liquid fertilizers during the previous one or two growing seasons. This will force the trees to develop a compact mass of feeding-roots adjacent to the main stems, although stability will be weakened. Once this treatment has been carried out, the shock of transplanting is reduced considerably.

Old, well-established roses can be difficult to move, because of their wide-searching roots. They have to be cut back drastically and most cultivars never properly recover from this. The best way of overcoming this problem is to start again, by taking current season's growth as cuttings in late summer and autumn.

The hardest of all plants to move (unless they have only been planted during the previous two or three months), are legumes such as brooms, wisteria, cercis, clianthus, erythrina, gleditsia, hardenbergia, laburnum, podalyria, poinciana, psoralia, sophora, viminaria and virgilia. They all have long, brittle roots which do not repair easily when broken, and many attempts at transplanting end in failure.

Established Australian native plants rarely grow well after they have been dug out and replanted elsewhere. This is because so many of them speedily develop wide-searching roots in order to anticipate long dry periods. Acacias, eucalypts, banksias, prostantheras, grevilleas, dryandras and many others usually collapse once they have been moved, no matter how carefully they are pruned and watered. This is one reason why so many failures occur when attempting to transfer plants from bush to the garden.

A Scented Garden Throughout the Year

There is nothing quite as honest and innocent as the scent of flowers. To stroll through a garden, and suddenly become aware of an ancient fragrance, is one of the few experiences which can send our minds back to times long beyond the reaches of our memory. The sweet, delicate, heavy, spicy, rich, subtle, peppery, lemony, refreshing, and deliciously fragrant vapours given off by plants, make a garden complete. The range of plants which are scented is enormous. So big, in fact, that it is possible to create a garden which will be a fragrant delight all the year round.

In spring, there is a glorious competition between some of the most beautiful of the garden plants, and those which produce a strong scent, often from flowers which remain fairly inconspicuous. Wallflowers haven't stopped producing their sweet heavy fragrance for months, and hyacinths, daffodils, jonquils, lily of the valley, add their scents to the garden alongside the almost invisible box (*Buxus*). Leaves have a special part to play in the scented garden, and even small evergreens such as lavender, thyme, sage, rosemary, *Melaleuca thymifolia*, eriostemon, and young eucalypts add their spicy aromas to the atmosphere.

Many rhododendrons have sweetly scented flowers. The most popular *R. fragrantissimum* thrives in most parts of Australia. The flowers, in the garden, are not overwhelming but once they are taken into the house, their sweet, spicy fragrance will penetrate into every corner of every room.

My own favourites are among the viburnums. Every year I look forward to the first blooms of *V. carlesii*, which develop from a warm, rich pink into a loose cluster of star-like white flowers. I remember seeing these plants for the first time during the Korean war, growing in the wild, and they presented an unforgettable sight. Many nurseries stock *V. bitchiuense*, which is almost identical, except that it comes from Japan, grows a little taller, and the flower trusses are not as compact as *V. carlesii*. You could also try *V. burkwoodii* which has the same fragrant flowers as *V. carlesii* but is semi-evergreen.

Right at the end of spring the lilacs bloom, with a scent all their own. However, when cutting the flowers, it is better to take only the truss, otherwise the blooms will not appear the following year. In old plants, gathering armloads of blossom-laden branches is an excellent excuse to prune them back hard, but be prepared for a disappointment the following year.

In summer, apart from the large range of scented annuals, the main fragrances are provided by sweet peas, and the lovely, slightly straggly mock orange (*Philadelphus coronarius*). We are lucky here, in that there are many varieties of mock orange available, some with open,

> Broad beans are potash-hungry now, so sprinkle a tight fistful of sulphate of potash alongside every metre of row and water-in.

cupped, single blooms, others with delicious double flowers, and golden leaves. The Portwine magnolia (*Michelia figo*), with its unusual purple coloured, rather dull flowers emits an unusually sweet, almost fruity smell. The evergreen magnolia is too large for a small garden, but its powerful lemonsweet fragrance can fill the air of half a suburb.

Roses are the greatest source of summer scent, and please don't believe the myth that modern roses don't smell as sweet as the old ones. Today's roses have been created for flowers, vigour, disease resistance, and definitely their fragrance (hybrid teas in particular), although many of the floribundas are not as strongly scented.

Then there are the honeysuckles, brooms, lemon verbena, lupins, pinks, and the magnificent liliums.

Autumn is often forgotten as a source of scents, but apart from the pungent smells, the earthy aromas which are so much a part of the recycling process at this time of the year, there are the heavily-sweet fragrances of belladonnas, chrysanthemums, autumn-flowering roses and the delicate sweetness of violets.

The fragrance of winter is varied, and universally sweet. Apart from the early wattles, there is the Chinese wintersweet or allspice (*Chimonanthus praecox*), with pale, almost transparent yellow flowers on bare branches, hollyleaved mahonias, yellow flowers, the witch hazel (*Hamamelis mollis*), and the ever popular daphne. See page 95 for other lovely winter-brightening plants.

The scents of the garden continue through the seasons.

Which Fertilizer is Best?

The demand from all kinds of plants for fertilizers is now rapidly increasing. Fruit trees, vegetables, berryfruit, ornamental plants and houseplants are starting to move rapidly, and the way they are fed, at this time, will determine how strongly and productively they will grow during the next six months.

The question is, what is the best fertilizer, for which plant?

The answer depends upon what the plant is being grown for, foliage, roots, seed or fruit. Fertilizers and manures contain different mixtures of essential elements. The dominant element will supply the major demands of certain plants.

For example, most animal manures contain a high amount of nitrogen and potassium with poultry manure being the richest and most rapidly available source. The role of nitrogen is to promote the growth of large amounts of foliage. This means that the plants which benefit most from manures are lettuces, cabbages, silverbeet, spinach, and other leafy vegetables. Certain fruit trees, particularly peach, nectarine, apricot and Japanese plum, also thrive, yielding better quality fruit, when plenty of animal manure is spread directly over their roots at this time of the year.

Houseplants which are grown specifically for their attractive leaves, such as philodendrons, ficus, aspidistra, monsteras, *Begonia rex*, coleus, fittonias, and many of the leafy trailing plants, also need generous amounts of a high nitrogen fertilizer. However, with houseplants it is best to avoid manures or even blood and bone, because of the problem of flies being attracted. Liquid fertilizers are always the best for houseplants, and the main thing is to ensure that only weak solutions are applied.

Deficiencies of nitrogen in most plants show up as a general lack of vigour, with the oldest leaves having a yellowish look. This is often seen in half-starved lemon trees, plants which thrive upon a high nitrogen diet.

Apart from animal manures, and the bloodmeal part of blood and bone, sulphate of ammonia is the major chemical source of nitrogen available to home gardeners. However, chemicals should be used with great care as the effects are much more rapid.

Phosphorus, usually in the form of superphosphate, is one of the most common soil additives in Australia. This is because most of our soils have a marked deficiency of this element. Most Australian native plants have learned to live with this shortage, but the exotic plants we grow in our gardens usually come from parts of the world where there is a much higher amount of phosphorous in the soil. Just the same, only relatively small amounts of phosphorus are needed when compared with nitrogen and potassium. The great mistake made by many gardeners is to spread large quantities of superphosphate around, on the basis of a 'more the merrier' philosophy. This causes all sorts of problems, including a serious disruption of the balance of other minerals in the soil.

Superphosphate is important in typical virgin or bush soils, and is one of the most important additives in a new garden. It helps plants develop a strong root system, and plays a special role in the early maturity of plants right through to flowering and fruit formation. Plants which seem to benefit most are peas, beans, sweetcorn, pumpkin, newly planted trees and shrubs, and newly sown lawns. The interesting thing about superphosphate, is that once it comes into contact with the soil, particularly acidic soil, much of it is rendered insoluble by the soil chemistry. The way to apply superphosphate to obtain the best response is to sprinkle it directly into the drill, next to the seed. This allows the newly emerging plants to take it in, before it becomes unavailable. The main organic source of phosphorus is bonemeal, or the pulverized bone which is contained in blood and bone.

Phosphorus deficiency shows up as a distinct blue-purple colour in the leaves, poor rooting and late flowering. Plants usually remain stunted and dwarfed as a result of this deficiency.

The rate of application when sowing seed is about half a matchbox full for each metre of drill.

Potassium is needed in much larger amounts than superphosphate, and fortunately it is present in the soil to a greater extent than many other elements. A shortage will show up in the form of leaf scorch, especially at the margins, and a curious squat appearance in many plants. Sandy soils in high rainfall areas show the greatest deficiency.

The best way to provide potassium is in the form of sulphate of potash, which looks like fine white sugar. Other sources are seaweed meal, concentrates, or woodash from the parts of the tree close to the bark. Burnt hedge clippings are another excellent source of potash, but the ash must always be raked up and stored in a container out of the weather. Even one good shower of rain upon a heap of woodash will leach out the potash content.

The plants which seem to have a special need for potassium are broad beans, French and climbing beans, peas, onions, and, in the early stages of their growth, tomatoes.

An excess of potash shows up dramatically as hard, stunted growth, and in young tomato plants as dark green brittle foliage, often cupped downwards. The way to apply sulphate of potash is to sprinkle it alongside the growing plants at the rate of a tight fistful for each metre of row and water in.

The best way to feed the soil is by using a balanced, complete fertilizer which contains a good proportion of the major elements, and trace elements. Mixed animal manures are perfect, especially if they have been allowed to break down under cover. The high amount of organic matter in these manures acts as a kind of buffer, and the chances of imbalance occurring are reduced.

The finest fertilizer of all, suitable for all plants, is well made compost, especially that which has been made of a wide variety of ingredients. This is best applied by placing a good handful into the planting hole just below the roots, when new plants or seedlings are being planted.

AUGUST
GUIDE TO ACTION

Ornamental Garden

Clean out lily ponds and divide water lilies. Sow or lay new lawns. Prune roses. Take cuttings of delphiniums and chrysanthemums. Divide perennials. Transplant evergreens to take advantage of the warming soil. Sprinkle blood and bone, with ten per cent added potash, to all parts of the garden. Layering of azaleas, rhododendrons, daphne and any other shrubs with branches which can be pressed into the soil, is an easy way to propagate at this time. Dead-head spring bulbs as flowers fade. In the flower garden seedlings of alyssum, aquilegia, arctotis, calendula, candytuft, Canterbury bells, delphinium, dianthus, foxglove, geum, gypsophila, lupin, myosotis, pansy, penstemon, Iceland poppy, oriental poppy, shasta daisy, plus divisions of perennials, can all go in now. Seeds of many tender annuals can be sown in containers under glass, for bedding out later.

Vegetable Garden

As the soil warms, sow seed of broad bean, cabbage, cauliflower, broccoli, kohlrabi, swede, turnip, carrot, leek, lettuce, onion, parsnip, peas, radish, spinach, silverbeet, salsify and, under glass, tomato, pumpkin, squash and sweetcorn. Off-shoots from globe artichokes and tubers of Jerusalem artichokes can also go in. Start applying manure or blood and bone to all parts of the vegetable garden except beds in which onions or carrots are to be grown. Mulched beds which are still cold can be allowed to warm up by raking aside the mulch for a month or so.

Fruit Garden

Spraying with Bordeaux or the even stronger Burgundy mixtures, to help control peach leafcurl, brown-rot and American gooseberry mildew, is essential this month. The fungicide must be applied before the leaves emerge, otherwise it is too late. Yet, the later the better. Do not apply on plants in leaf. Tip-prune gooseberry plants which had mildew last season, also apple trees which had been infected. Remove all prunings. Prepare to spray with winter oil, before budburst, all apple and pear trees. Feed lemon and other citrus with blood and bone or old animal manure. Keep grass below all trees cut short or wipe it out of existence with Roundup.

Houseplants

This is the best time for repotting or potting-on. Plants which have suffered from overwatering, indicated by marginal leafscorch, need to be carefully knocked out, dead or diseased roots cut away and the plant repotted into a smaller container. Prune weak or dead wood and remove all discoloured or unsightly leaves. Remove vulnerable plants from sunny windows. Gently supply liquid fertilizers as days lengthen. Check hanging baskets for drying out. Ferns will need to have dead or weak fronds removed. Watch out for scale pests and spray with weakened white oil mixture. Cut off all badly infested material.

AUGUST: FIRST WEEK

Leafcurl in Peach and Nectarine Trees

The next couple of weeks are crucial. This is one of the best times of the year to control one of the most frustrating of all diseases of peach and nectarine trees. Leafcurl causes the foliage to twist, thicken, pucker and discolour. Yield is sharply reduced because of the greatly weakened trees, caused by the disease preventing the leaves from properly functioning.

Sometimes people spray their trees with great care, yet the pestilence still strikes. Usually, the cause is rain which not only washes the spray off before it has had a chance to become effective, but also helps to spread the disease. If it rains during the period from the initial spraying to the first emergence of the tiny leafpoints, the fungicide must be applied again immediately.

If it were possible to have some kind of rainproof cover over peach or nectarine trees during the next three weeks, the disease would not be a problem. This was discovered in Britain, where these fruit trees are grown as fans against walls for extra warmth. They found that if only one branch was left accidentally sticking out into the rain, while the rest remained protected, that particular branch would be attacked and not the rest of the tree. Covering a tree out in the open is virtually impossible, although I have tried placing a sheet of plastic around the odd branch until the leaves emerged. If it is loose enough to allow the bees to get in to do their job, there will be good crops from this limb only, in districts with high spring rainfall.

The best, relatively non-toxic sprays for leafcurl control are the old-fashioned Bordeaux and Burgundy mixtures. See page 201 for recipes. Neither must ever be used on plants while they are in leaf. These mixtures can also be used to combat many other diseases, especially mildews, provided they are applied just before leaf-burst.

Jobs in the Orchard

While many stonefruit trees will be on the move very soon, apples and pears tend to lag behind by a week or so. However, many pests which have been skulking in fissures in the bark, or in debris around the base of the trees, are starting to emerge, ready to begin breeding and doing their dirty work. Winter oil, applied now, catches them with their pants down, so to speak. Pests which attack deciduous trees are now at their most vulnerable, so get squirting, concentrating upon any crevices or other hiding places. However, remember that winter oil must not be used upon trees which are in leaf or just starting to sprout.

As soon as the sap starts to rise, grafting can take place. However, the scion-wood should have been taken earlier, or, if taken now, should be immediately retarded by chilling in the refrigerator, wrapped in moist moss or newspaper. Generally, with fruit trees, stone fruits such as peach, nectarine, Japanese plum or apricot are bud-grafted during late summer. Apple, pear and some European plums can be grafted from now onwards, using scions or short pieces of last season's growth. Even if the trees are already coming into leaf, they can still be grafted as long as the scion is still dormant. If the scion begins to sprout before it has been grafted it becomes quite useless and will not take. This is because it loses moisture before it has had a chance to make proper contact with the tree to which it has to become attached.

Now is a good time to plant citruses, especially the hardier lemons. The toughest of the bunch is Meyer, which carries most of its juicy-sweetish fruit during winter. A low-growing, bushy tree, Meyer lemon makes an attractive ornamental plant for any sunny, sheltered spot in the garden. The other two common varieties are Eureka and Lisbon, both of which bear more evenly through the year, with reasonable pickings even during January.

Scale is the big problem right now. It looks as though it is a disease, with masses of soft-brown tiny humps clustered along the midribs of the leaves. With the inevitable black, sooty-mould, which always accompanies scale insects, a normally healthy tree can look a dreadful sight. The answer to this problem is quite simple, two or three sprays with white oil, all over the tree. This will smother the scale, killing it in a non-toxic way.

Plant Vegetables!

It's on for young and old from now onwards. Spring is definitely in the air and the soil is getting warmer. There are plenty of vegetable plants and seeds which can now go in, while many of our trees, shrubs, houseplants and perennials are beginning to demand their nutrients. Pruning is still being carried out, deciduous plants being planted, perennials divided, lawns made and the ground is being dug or prepared for later sowing or plantings.

In the vegetable garden, don't go silly and use up all the space at this stage. In cool districts it is still too early for tomatoes, capsicums, French or climbing beans, sweetcorn or pumpkins. But leave them plenty of room.

Plant a row or two of potatoes, either directly into the soil, or on top of the ground with a thick layer of straw and manure spread over them. Even if you decide to plant in the orthodox way, you can still place a layer of straw over the surface too. The potato tops will have no problem about penetrating it as they grow, and meanwhile weeds will be effectively suppressed.

In some well-cultivated soil, worked to a good tilth, sow seed of carrot, parsnip and beetroot. Get rid of old seed and buy new if you wish to ensure an even, rapid germination. Don't forget, carrot and parsnip seed can be a bit slow or erratic in cool soil, so don't weep tears of blood if the results are not spectacular during the next three weeks after sowing. However, you can help by mixing the fine seed with white sand and granulated peat. This provides a light, warm, moist seedbed to give them a good start, helps to deter some weeds and makes it easier to see exactly where you have sown for weeding purposes. Good types of carrot for deep soils are Western Red, Topweight and Zeno.

Clay, shallow soils are best sown with stump-rooted types such as Early Horn or other short chantenay types. Parsnips which do well include Hollow Crown or Melbourne Whiteskin. Fresh seed is essential.

Beetroot seed is much larger, about the size of a matchhead. It is really a tightly-packed group of seeds, which is why more than one seedling emerges at times.

Onion seed or plants, especially of the long-keepers, can go in now too. The rule about good fresh seed certainly applies here. Brown Spanish and Creamgold are the best of all, but like all onions they need the best soil in the garden and plenty of lime. Remember that soil which is rich, but has been fertilized for previous vegetables, is best, and avoid the use of manures or fresh fertilizers such as blood and bone at this stage. It causes problems with onion maggot, while producing onions too large and soft for good keeping. The most important soil additive for all onions and garlic is lime. So if your soil has not had any for several years, be generous.

Most of the brassicas can be sown or planted now. The earlier they can be developed, the tastier and crisper they will be. They can also be harvested long before the big caterpillars of the white butterfly start munching away. However, leafy vegetables, including silverbeet and lettuce, are great consumers of highly nitrogenous fertilizers, especially sheep, cow, goat or poultry manures, and once they start growing fast, as they will indeed, they will need a lot of water. When cabbages, broccoli or similar brassicas get a little dry around their roots, another terrible pest, the cabbage moth grub, will strike deep into the hearts of these plants. So watch out.

If your garden space is limited, use smaller types of brassicas. There are excellent miniature caulies, cabbages and broccoli which can successfully be closely-planted and there is very little waste at harvest time. My favourite cabbage is still the nuttily-sweet Sugarloaf. They can be comfortably grown four to the square metre and seed sown now will produce good yields long before Christmas.

More on Australian Plants

Any tree or shrub planted now will develop rapidly, but Australian native plants seem to thrive particularly well when they are planted at this time of the year. Even seed of a whole range of native trees and shrubs will germinate within the next two or three weeks and will be ready for pricking-out into containers during October.

The key to success with Australian plants is to place them out when they are small. They will establish themselves quickly, becoming compact and sturdy. The roots of young seedlings grow at high speed, spreading widely in all directions and deeply into the subsoil. This almost frantic root growth is necessary in the wild state, because of our moist springs and early summers, followed by long, dry months during summer.

The extraordinary vigour of young Australian plants is the main reason why they are able to survive droughts, just a few months after germinating from seed.

The best size at planting time for aca-

> If you haven't done it yet, dig-in any green manure which has grown over the cooler period, before it becomes too woody to be of value. Dig up any vacant beds to break up and aerate the soil, concentrate upon weed-control, including oxalis (which, if wiped now with Zero or Roundup will be devastated before it has had time to flower), give the compost heap a few good turns, and start to enjoy the warmer weather.

cias, eucalypts, casuarinas, viminarias and similar fast-growing species, is about thirty to forty centimetres. This is so small that most people unfamiliar with the growing habits of these plants tend to look for something larger 'rather than wait'. However, although there are plenty of extra-large plants available, some grown in dustbin-sized containers, they are invariably overtaken by the tiny plants, often within the first two years.

Smaller plants grow to a much better shape than the big ones, which usually take years to recover from their initial, straggly appearance. Also, the amount of maintenance needed by small plants is much less than for big ones. Oversized specimens succumb to dry conditions, because of their restricted root systems. They not only have to be watered often during the first year or so, they are also unstable.

It is this instability which is a major problem with extra-large native plants, which have spent years restricted to containers. If they are secured to a stake, they become weakened and even more straggly. If the stake should break, as it often does after a year or so, the grossly deformed, lop-sided tree, is blown over during the first strong wind.

The only sensible way of stabilizing newly-planted large natives is to ruthlessly prune them back to make them sturdy and more wind resistant. This defeats the whole purpose of buying a large, sometimes expensive plant in the first place.

Australian plants of any size should never be secured to a stake, no matter how windy the site. Small plants, including exotic, deciduous trees, when left to grow unsupported, develop a main stem which is much wider at the base than at the top, almost like a short whip. It is the constant movement in the wind which clearly encourages the formation of this remarkable flexibility. This protective taper is missing from staked trees, making them much more vulnerable to wind damage.

In areas which are subjected to persistent, powerful winds, even young seedlings, especially if they have been grown close together in their original containers, can be blown out of the ground or seriously damaged. There are ways to secure these plants without using a stake. The easiest is to place three large stones close to the main stem of each plant, in the form of a rough triangle.

The effect is to weigh down upon the roots, keeping them moist as well as secure. If the rocks are large enough, they will also help protect the foliage. The young plant can be whipped around by the worst gales but, being confined between rocks, will remain perfectly safe while developing flexibility. As the plant can now form a good root-system without being torn apart regularly, it will grow strongly, pushing apart the rocks against their stems as they do so.

The other advantage of placing rocks next to small plants is protection from accidental damage by people or animals.

The main competitor of young trees and shrubs is weeds, especially grass. These will relentlessly rob them of moisture, nutrients and light during the first crucial months. Later, when the weeds have seeded or the grass browned off, the vigour of the plants has usually been sapped to such an extent that they remain motionless for the rest of the summer, with the shortening days acting as a further break to growth.

Mulching with woodchips, pulverized bark, or even sawdust will effectively suppress this competition long enough to allow the plants to achieve dominance. Then the tables are turned and the growing plant becomes the dominant competitor against weeds, always winning the battle. However, black plastic should never be used beneath the mulch. It seems to prevent the topsoil from 'breathing' causing it to become virtually lifeless. As a result, serious stunting will occur among the plants trying to grow under these conditions. Most mulches need to be about ten centimetres deep to be effective, and if the ground has been wiped with Roundup first to kill weeds, especially twitch-grass, there should be few problems.

However, the main plant stems must always be kept clear of an organic mulch, otherwise they can rot. The gap left will soon grow a tuft of weeds if it is not dealt with, which will be difficult to remove. So, a good shovelful of coarse bluemetal at the base of every plant is required. This will allow plenty of dry air to circulate at soil level, while sealing in moisture and keeping weeds under control.

AUGUST: SECOND WEEK

The Dreaded Oxalis Weed Moves In

Some time ago I blundered once again. If you knew how I've suffered since. I've paid the price, cursing and whimpering every day for weeks. It was my own fault of course. Because of this I almost enjoyed the shame and misery I've brought upon myself.

You see, it happened while I was sowing the last of the seeds in a row of peas. As I bent to retrieve some I had dropped, there in front of my horrified eyes, was a small clump of oxalis. How this dreadful weed had sneaked into the garden in spite of all my precautions will never be known, but there it was, deceptively pretty, a tiny cluster of soft green, shamrock leaves.

That's when the awful mistake was made. I should have dropped everything and dug it out straight away, in a perfectly normal blind panic, but I didn't. Nor did I even mark the spot. I knew I'd remember to come back to deal with it later, so I kept on sowing.

You've guessed it. Please can I hang my head in shame? I forgot. A couple of weeks later I cultivated deeply between the rows. Still in a half-witted daze, I raked and fertilized before planting some sturdy cabbage seedlings I had been bringing on. Each was given a small circle of blood and bone, a little mat of old straw and a good watering.

It must have been about a fortnight later, when I was innocently gloating along between the rows, that I spotted the first smirking clump of oxalis leaves, metres away from the original site. Further along I discovered two more and I felt sick as I realized what I had done. *Oxalis latifolia* is its fancy name and it thrives in cultivated soil, because that's how it spreads. The root system is composed of a mass of tiny bulbils, clinging precariously to a swollen root. The slightest disturbance causes the bulbils to fall off and wherever they land, a new clump is born.

Trying to dig out a major infestation of oxalis is worse than useless. In fact it helps spread it more efficiently. However, if extreme care is taken, a minor outbreak can be controlled. It is possible to slide a trowel deep down alongside each clump to lift out a long wedge of soil containing all the oxalis roots, bulbils and leaves. The safe way is to cart the

Massed planting of bluebells and other woodland plants beneath giant oaks in a Tasmanian garden.

Old-fashioned roses make a charming, easily maintained hedge.

Mulching with old hay to control weeds and conserve moisture around Savoy cabbages and cottager's kale. Winter garden.

Unpruned climbing rose.

Climbing rose after pruning.

lot away, but if the soil is broken open only after being carried to the middle of the lawn, it is worth checking to see if there is an intact nest of deadly bulbils inside. Then they can be squashed and the soil distributed over the grass. This type of oxalis does not normally grow in lawns, because the constant cutting of its leaves causes the roots to die.

Some people, sick and tired of trying to get rid of this weed from cultivated parts of the garden, finally give up and convert infested beds into lawns. It takes about two years of mowing to get rid of the pest by this method.

Other methods of oxalis control include no-dig gardening, using the mulch-rake technique. A thick layer of old straw and grass-clippings spread over the oxalis will not smother the weed, but if the mulch is raked back and forth every week, the fragile leaf-stems will be constantly broken and the effect will be the same as in a lawn. Some herbicides, such as Roundup or Zero can also destroy oxalis, if wiped on to the leaves in early spring, before the flowers appear. However, once those pretty, violet trumpet flowers have matured, it is too late.

There are more than eight hundred species of oxalis, most of which are attractive, non-invasive garden plants. Only a few become a nuisance. One species invades turf: yellow wood sorrel (*O. corniculata*), creeps and spreads through grass, seriously disfiguring lawns. Its ground-hugging habit enables it to evade the mower blades, but if the infested surface is raked with a steel-tine grass rake, just prior to mowing, the leaves will be left cocked-up, ready for slicing off. This will greatly weaken the weed and allow the grass to compete effectively.

The fat tubers of one species of oxalis are edible, making a tasty dish when they are roasted or steamed. 'Maori potato' or 'Oka' is grown in gardens in all states and in other parts of the world. *O. tuberosa* can be found in some nurseries or even vegetable shops and can be planted in early spring for harvesting about April.

While many people would run for cover at the thought of deliberately planting oxalis, there are some species which are very beautiful, thriving in an alpine garden or as outstanding edging plants. *O. hirta* which comes from southern Africa, has hazelnut-sized clusters of bulbs which thrust themselves to the surface producing violet trumpets, each with a yellow throat. This plant grows in sun or part shade.

For years I have grown a tiny oxalis known as 'Barber's Pole' in the rock-garden. *O. rubra* produces narrow, funnel-shaped trumpets with red and white stripes, hence the nickname. This little delight comes from Brazil, is very hardy and, like many others, disappears each winter.

As for my battle of the bulbils, I think I've won. Much time has now gone by since the last clump of leering leaves appeared and now I can even bask among the brassicas without twitching.

How to Obtain Massive Yields of Peas

In three weeks we will be officially into spring. Even now, the sun has started to produce a satisfactory bite, and this is a marvellous excuse to start some serious planting or preparation in the vegetable garden.

One of the main vegetables to go in now are the peas. Soil preparation is most important, and the drainage must be perfect, otherwise the seed will rot. Peas like a soil which has been limed, and will fail to grow in sour, acidic soil. They also love to have plenty of well-decayed organic matter in and on the soil in which they are growing. If your garden area is small, it pays to practise the trenching method of growing peas. This will give you massive yields from a small area,

> In the flower garden: clean out lily-ponds and divide up old clumps of water lilies, carry-on planting roses and flowering fruit trees, divide up delphiniums, achilleas, chrysanthemums, catmint, astilbe, penstemons, perennial asters and cannas.

finishing up with your soil being much improved.

This is what to do. Dig a trench, about one and a half times the depth of the blade of the spade (forty centimetres) and roughly as wide. Line the base of the trench with layers of old newspaper, then top this up with plenty of old straw, seaweed, limestone or dolomite, and a few handfuls of blood and bone scattered well through the material. If you have access to any animal manure, sprinkle this thickly along the trench too, working it slightly into the surface of the straw mix. Then, after a good watering, backfill with good topsoil, and allow to settle for a day or so.

Sow the seed in a ten centimetre wide drill, about four centimetres deep into the topsoil, directly over the buried mulching materials, and stagger the seeds so that they zig-zag evenly along the length of the drill. Then, before covering the seed, sprinkle superphosphate (if you prefer the organic way, bone meal or blood and bone) alongside the seed, at the rate of a tight fistful for each metre of row. Then cover the seed, pressing the soil well into contact with it, by using the flat end of a rake. Water well, and the first shoots should appear in about two weeks.

There are many varieties which do exceptionally well in cool districts, but the old favourite Greenfeast is still one of the most reliable. Melbourne market is another cool climate pea which crops heavily. The old fashioned telephone will grow to more than two metres, and will bear masses of large, succulent pods. This is more suitable for growing up a tall lattice or fence, where it will take up very little room.

Most peas need something to climb on, helping them produce heavy crops which are easy to pick. For years I have used the same short pieces of fencing wire. They are bent double to form a kind of long 'U' about a metre in length. They are stuck in the ground fairly close together, so they overlap, four or five for each metre of row. After the peas have finished, about Christmas time, the wires can be easily and quickly gathered together and hung from two or three nails in a shed until next time they are required.

Carrots can now be planted in most areas, although cold, wet soil will delay germination so long that the seeds will either be eaten by pests or will rot in the ground. Work the surface soil to a good fine tilth, then, after mixing the seed with some light coloured sand, sow into shallow drills. Just cover the seed, or press it gently into the surface, and keep it moist. The variety All Seasons will germinate strongly at this time, and once the first true leaves have formed, development is very rapid. The major problem with carrot seed, apart from slow germination, is its inability to compete very effectively with weeds, the seeds of which will germinate long before the carrot seed.

Other vegetables which can be sown now include broad beans, leeks, lettuce, onion, parsley, radish, silverbeet, kohlrabi, broccoli, cauliflowers and turnip.

Jobs for the Warmer Weather

Better outside working conditions will let you tackle a big range of essential jobs in the garden this week. Lawns are beginning to sprout in the most threatening way, and so are the many weeds which disfigure them. Make sure that a grass catcher is attached to the mower when cutting the grass, and after mowing, apply lawn sand to all weedy areas. The simple way to mix this is two-thirds dry sand and one-third sulphate of ammonia. This will kill most flat weeds in the lawn before they have a chance to go to seed. Throw the dry mixture over the worst-affected areas at the rate of a good handful for each square metre of surface. With persistent weeds, such as docks, another application in about a week's time should finish them off.

It is a good time to level off any uneven section of the lawn. Simply dump a barrow load of good loamy topsoil over places where there is a slight depression and, with a straight piece of board used as a screed, level off the surface.

If there is less than five centimetres of new surface added to the lawn, the existing grass will easily grow through in a couple of weeks. However, fresh seed will have to be sown if the extra soil is deeper than this.

It is a perfect time to take cuttings of chrysanthemums and delphiniums. While clumps can be easily divided now into many new plants, the advantage of cuttings is that there is less chance of diseases being passed on. Other plants such as perennial asters should be divided up, so that individual new plants are occupying the same piece of ground. If the soil has been well manured, the size of the flowers can be much larger. Gladioli corms can also be planted now, and if they have been lifted in autumn, many of them will have tiny cormlets attached to the mother corm. These can be separated and planted out. They will not flower this season, but will develop rapidly, and many of them should produce good blooms next year.

AUGUST: THIRD WEEK

Towards Self-sufficency on a Typical Home Site

It is possible to become almost entirely self-sufficient in vegetables and fruit, in an average-sized garden. Production from small areas can be enormous, provided ample water is available and the soil continually enriched with organic matter, animal manures and other kinds of natural, balanced fertilizers.

The advantages are obvious. Great savings in food costs, plus a degree of freshness seldom experienced with bought products. There is also a tremendous feeling of pleasure and relaxation when growing food, especially when the soil you have been working and feeding becomes productive. Above all, there is the sure knowledge that home-grown vegetables and fruits are completely safe to eat, provided you choose to avoid toxic sprays and unnatural chemical fertilizers.

All parts of a garden can be used for growing food, although there can still be enough room for many ornamental plants too. Fences can serve a double purpose. Apart from giving some privacy, they can be used for growing climbing beans, peas, passionfruit, grapes and espaliered, or fanned, fruit trees. In good, well-drained, fertile soil, fruit production can be very high from trees grown like this, flat against a fence. Some apple and pear trees will carry up to a case of fruit per tree. Also different types of fruit can be chosen to provide a continuous supply for most of the growing season, with enough to spare for bottling or drying to use later in the year.

European plums make superb eating and are ideal for preserving too. The French prune, d'Agen, grown as a fan, will regularly bear half a barrow load of rich, sugary fruit. Prunes I dried several years ago are still in good condition with excellent flavour. Apricots will dry well if they are halved and stoned first. All fruit placed in the sun to dry should be covered when rain threatens and every night, because the water or dew will cause some of them to ferment.

Japanese plums are suitable only for eating fresh. They don't dry and when bottled, some cultivars become bitter, especially the early-bearing, very juicy varieties.

The most important of the vegetables are those which contain the most energy. Potatoes top the list, but they take up more room than any of the others, up to half the vegetable garden. If space is limited, it is better to concentrate upon an area measuring six metres by eight metres. If grown under straw, organically, this area can produce well over 100 kilograms of clean, tasty spuds.

Peas are magnificent. In well-drained, enriched soil, containing lots of organic matter, the production rate is enormous, especially with some of the taller-growing varieties. Peas can be eaten fresh, podded directly into plastic bags in the garden for immediate freezing without messy blanching, or left to dry for long storage in air-tight jars. French beans can be frozen in the same way and in compost-rich soil will bear enormous quantities of fresh pods. When you are sick of eating or freezing them, they can be left to dry on the bushes. Some years ago I grew such a prolific crop of Hawksbury Wonder that after eating and freezing as many as possible, I could still harvest ten kilograms of the dried beans. We are still eating them.

Carrots, beetroot, parsnips and swedes can be left in the ground for pulling as required throughout the year, provided successive rows are sown every few weeks. Brassicas such as cauliflower, broccoli, and cabbage can easily be grown all the year round in most parts of Australia. So can onions, although it pays to select varieties according to season and district.

Pumpkins can be kept until the next season's crop becomes available, while sweetcorn freezes to perfection when it is stripped from the cobs directly into plastic bags as soon as it is picked. Tomatoes can be eaten fresh throughout most of summer and autumn, with any surplus used in pickles, chutneys, concentrates or just popped whole into freezer-bags, the air sucked out and the lot frozen for later use.

With a good, four or five year rotation system operating, all organic waste recycled back into the soil as either compost or a mulch, regular applications of animal manures and an adequate supply of irrigation water, the amount of useful production from even a small back-yard can be staggering.

Above all, there are enormous health benefits to be reaped from this satisfying combination of gentle relaxation and productive work.

Growing Juicy Carrots

It's easy to grow carrots. Even if you only have a tiny area in which to sow seed, the yield is surprisingly high. One square metre of the deep, sandy loam they prefer, can produce up to four buckets of carrots. After all, some of them go down a long way.

These are among the most valuable of all vegetables. Children, with their uncorrupted taste-buds, instinctively prefer them raw, especially if they can pull and wash them under the garden tap themselves. Carrots can be made into an extraordinary number of dishes and drinks. In soups, stews, puddings, cakes, and wine or, best of all, quietly crunched while strolling around the garden, carrots have few equals among the common vegetables.

Even shallow, clay soils will carry good crops, provided correct varieties are selected. In most parts of Australia, seed can be sown now, although in cold districts it is better to wait a week or two.

Unlike most other vegetables, carrots grow best in soil which contains no recently added manure or large amounts of organic matter. Too much of this material causes forking of the roots, which not only spoils the appearance but makes a lot of waste.

Carrot seed will germinate in soil temperatures as low as 6°C, but it can take up to a month before the first leaves appear in cold-soil conditions. This is a major cause of failure, because pests and diseases often have a field day during this long period. Under normal, well-drained, warming soil situations, the first tiny, narrow seed-leaves are showing in a couple of weeks. Even so, the relatively long germination time means that many weeds will have already emerged and staked their claim, before the carrot seedlings appear. This usually puts survival at risk, because carrots are poor competitors at this early stage.

The best way of dealing with this problem, without squirting kerosene all over the place and risking tainting, is to work the soil first, allow the weeds to germinate, hoe them out of existence, then sow the carrot seed. The young carrots will at least have a start, especially if the seed has been bulked-out with white sand and granulated peatmoss.

The advantages of the sand-peat mix are many. The small seed is easier to handle, better spaced in the drill and easily seen for pin-prick weeding; while the peat will prevent the surface from drying out too quickly.

If possible, each seed should be about two centimetres apart. If any closer, the carrots will either be very small, or entwined around each other in a close but distorting embrace. The depth of sowing is important. The seed should be just below the surface, or covered with a little sand and pressed into contact. The main job after sowing is to prevent the soil from drying out until germination. In warm, dry areas, this means at least two gentle waterings every day. Once the first fern-like leaves start to develop, watering can be slowed down to encourage the roots to move downwards.

Normally, the distance between rows is about thirty centimetres, but if this spacing is doubled, there is room for a row of onions too. There is a special relationship between carrots and onions. They are the good companions which help each other yield better while strengthening resistance to diseases and pests.

No-dig Potato Gardening

The easiest way of growing potatoes is under straw. There is no digging, weeding or earthing-up and watering is enormously reduced. The potatoes are clean, easily harvested, tender and absolutely delicious. There is almost no work involved, apart from the initial preparation, and the yield is usually higher than with the orthodox method of growing. Anyone can do it in most parts of Australia right now, irrespective of the quality of the soil.

The site must be well-drained and in an open sunny position. Even a tiny back-yard can be used. If the ground is infested with weeds, there is no need to remove them. If you are sick of mowing the lawn, give yourself a break and use it for growing potatoes under straw. You'll lose the lawn of course, but there will be a lovely crop of spuds instead, and you might begin to enjoy the garden.

First mow down any rank growth such as long grass or weeds. Leave the wilted materials lying around on the surface. Use certified 'seed' potatoes of a variety suited to the district. I prefer Kennebecs or Russet Burbank because they taste

> Feeding the soil is vitally important right now, especially around rhododendrons, azaleas, camellias, citrus, stone and pome fruits. I mulch relentlessly for the last three or four weeks of winter and manage to smother large numbers of growing weeds, without much physical effort. Every fruit tree will receive half a barrowload of sheep manure, plus lots of half-decayed, spoilt hay. The main thing when carrying out this type of mulching, is to leave the main stems of the plants clear, so that they don't go mouldy.

good and keep well after harvesting.

The 'seed' tubers are not planted into the ground, but simply placed upon the surface of the grass, mown weeds or bare ground. Make sure they are about thirty centimetres apart, in rows sixty centimetres apart. They look a bit silly sitting there on the surface, but this is only the start.

Next, cover all the potato 'seed' and the entire bed with a very thick layer of straw. Make sure there are generous overlaps at the edges of the bed. Any kind of straw material can be used, such as pea or bean haulm, wheat, barley or oat straw, or even spoilt hay. The depth of the mulch should be at least half a metre, especially if the straw is fluffed a little during the spreading process. Then, give the entire bed a good watering to help settle the straw.

Once the straw has been well wetted, sprinkle blood and bone, with about ten per cent added potash, over the bed at the rate of a good handful for each square metre. Then start to spread any kind of animal manure, especially sheep, goat, poultry or pulverized horse or cow droppings. A couple of shovelsful for every square metre is plenty. Then water again, and this, plus the weight of the manure, will reduce the thickness of the mulch by about half. Seaweed, if available, can also be added, or even sawdust. This will help to exclude the light from the growing tubers, bulk-out the manure and add important trace elements to the mixture. Finally, water again and tidy up the edges of the bed, throwing any surplus straw on to the top.

After about three weeks, the first growing tips of the potato foliage will appear. By this time, the straw mulch will have settled down into a warm, moist and highly nutritious pad about fifteen centimetres thick. If it seems a little thin, avoid the danger of light getting through by adding more straw, but this time, leave the potato tops clear to keep growing.

This is what is happening: the grass or weeds down below are smothered by the mulch. They rot and add to the food supply. The 'seed' tubers quickly sprout in the perfect conditions and the shoots easily penetrate the straw covering, at the same time sending out roots close to the ground. These roots will soon begin to form the new potatoes. In the mulch, the animal manure breaks down quickly and, mixing with the decaying straw, creates a magnificent larder containing food and moisture for the growing plants. Once the plants begin to flower the young potatoes will grow rapidly.

Within two or three months, with just an occasional watering, it will be possible to lift up a corner of the 'carpet' and not only see the delicious harvest awaiting and continuing to grow, but the larger spuds can be removed for early eating. Meanwhile, the rest keep on growing.

That's all there is to it. However, the greatest benefit of all comes after the harvest.

The soil, which may have been hard-to-work clay, sandy or just impoverished, will have been enriched to an astonishing degree, and our greatest animal friends, the earthworms, will have multiplied in every part of the bed.

If you've never tried this form of gardening before, do it now. You'll not only enjoy the most superb potatoes you've ever eaten, but you'll never want to mow the lawn again.

Gladioli and Dahlias

Gladioli are among the most useful and beautiful of all our flowering plants. It's a pity they have become such an object of mockery by one of Australia's most talented comedians, because I feel sure that this has contributed to a fall in their popularity here. It takes somewhere between ninety and a hundred days for a newly-planted corm to develop into a superb display of flowers. In other words, corms planted this week will be starting to reward you sometime in early December.

I always soak gladioli corms in a mixture of water and Clensel, at the rate of ten of water to one of Clensel. After about an hour, the corms can be briefly rinsed and planted in an open, sunny, well-drained spot, to a depth of around ten centimetres. If the soil has been enriched with compost, or very old, fully-decayed cow manure a few weeks before planting, the size of the flowers will reflect these conditions. However, it is essential to keep any manure or blood and bone fertilizer well clear of the corm, in order to avoid damage to it.

If some corms which were lifted last season for storing under dry, airy conditions have a ring of tiny cormlets attached, these can also be planted now, preferably in a separate bed. They will come true to the parent plant, but will not flower until next, or even the following, summer.

The great problem with gladioli these days is thrips. These tiny insects can so weaken the plants that leaves become disfigured with yellow streaks and the flowers are either inferior, or fail to develop. The pre-planting soak helps to effectively control this pest, but should any signs of attack occur later on, spraying will be necessary. Gladioli should not be continuously replanted in the same place year after year, nor should they be left in the ground too long once they have flowered. Plenty of overhead watering while they are growing is a good safe way to keep thrips at bay.

Dahlias too are always much healthier when the tubers are lifted at the start of winter. Most people store them out of the frost, leaving plenty of soil adhering to the clumps. The big threat during storage is about now, when they can begin to dry out. A few shovelsful of moist sand thrown over the clumps will prevent this occurring, and if early development is required, the tubers can be started into growth soon by plunging the tubers in moist earth, sand or even sawdust. Young shoots which emerge can then be removed and struck in a sand-peat mixture for extra plants.

AUGUST: LAST WEEK

Harlequin Bugs and Scale Insects

Harlequin bugs have some amusing habits. When they are courting, they not only become very attached, but cement the relationship by sticking their backsides together. This intimate embrace lasts so long, that the weaker of the two spends the rest of the season walking backwards. If you are silly enough to squash them, or even pick them up, they take their revenge by filling the air with a particularly revolting smell. Even starving chooks blink and turn away when they are confronted by these colourful clowns. They quickstep around the yard, flaunt their orange and black zoot-suits and seem to have most birds bluffed.

Anyone whose garden has been invaded by these sap-sucking hordes will find it hard to be amused by their antics. They breed in their thousands in piles of wood, old fences and badly overgrown areas. Marshmallow weeds have a special fascination for harlequin bugs, which may explain why the more attractive forms of hibiscus are a target for their destructive attention. They will also spoil and soil tomatoes, figs, grapes, melons, oranges and other fruit. In the flower garden they will dance ceaselessly over helichrysums, snapdragons, stocks, painted daisies and dahlias, often causing the collapse of these plants.

Control of these gaudy pests starts with destroying their breeding places. Masses of dry, weedy surface-growth must be ruthlessly cleared and stacked to rot or for later burning. Gaps between fence palings should be sprayed with contact killers such as Clensel or winter oil and the same treatment given to cracks and crevices in old sheds or wood-heaps. A regular spraying programme at fortnightly intervals for about two months should wipe out most of them, leaving any survivors to jig to another tune, in someone else's garden.

Another common pest is quite different. At first, it seems as though some terrible disease has struck. A black, sooty mould covers leaves and branches. The plant is listless and ants frantically charge up and down the branches. The culprits are scale insects and they too are sap-suckers. While feeding off a wide range of plants, they protect themselves and their eggs under waxy domes, secretions or woolly substances.

Some scale insects constantly produce 'honeydew' which, after falling upon the upper surfaces of leaves and branches, goes mouldy. Hence the sooty appearance. Ants get into the act as they attend the scales in order to harvest the 'honeydew'.

Soft brown scales attack camellias, citrus, oleander, sweet bay, olive, fig, daphne, holly and ferns. They cluster along twigs and the midribs of leaves, sometimes half piggy-backing each other in their close-packed colonies. They multiply rapidly, especially on plants which are unthrifty or have had a growth-check.

White oil emulsion is relatively safe to use. When mixed with water at the rate of fifty to one and sprayed over infested plants, it will suffocate the pests while preventing many of their eggs from hatching. The same amount of pyrethrum added to this mixture will make it more potent and three sprays at weekly intervals should do the trick. Badly infested fern fronds or small twigs should be cut off. The sooty-mould gradually wears off as it breaks down and rain or watering finishes it off.

Hydrangeas are invaded by a different type of scale insect in summer. This too looks like some sort of disease at first, with leaves and branches flecked with white, woolly particles. Hydrangea scale is easily identified by this fluffy cover and the insects will often spread to adjacent plants, especially American dogwood (*Cornus florida*). Watch out for this in the summer months and spray with the white oil mixture to control the pest.

Among the most disfiguring scale insects are the hardwax types. They form unpleasant crusts on leaves, twigs and fruit, but without the tell-tale sooty-mould. Oranges, lemons and other fruit develop a mottled, scabby appearance, leaves start to drop and entire branches die back. Best control is obtained by spraying with white oil at the first signs of infestation. These are often on parts of the plant which have become overcrowded or excessively shaded. Pruning away badly affected foliage and opening up congested growth, will also help to introduce predators.

White wax scale occurs in warm districts and old, unpruned and neglected citruses will have branches and twigs covered with blobs of what look like candlewax. Sooty-mould clogging leaf-surfaces adds to the misery of the trees. It is hard to get at the insects, because of their protection, but home gardeners can brush off much of the waxy material and if this is followed by two or three white oil sprays, plus some careful pruning, the problem will be solved.

Pruning Neglected Lemon Trees

The effect pruning has on many plants is to stimulate them, mainly by activating dormant buds lower down. If frost-tender trees and shrubs are pruned during winter, the flush of new growth often appears much earlier than usual and can be severely burned. This is the main reason why citrus trees, passionfruit vines and, in very cold districts, roses, are not pruned until it is safe to do so.

Citrus trees don't need pruning very often, but when they do, the effects, especially with some lemon varieties, appear devastating. This is one of the best times of the year to prune them, because by the time new growth has appeared, the danger of frost damage will have passed.

Orange, grapefruit, cumquat and one variety of lemon, the Meyer, all have a fairly dense canopy. This is needed to some extent, particularly in hot districts, to protect the trunk and roots from sunburn. The best way to prune them is to thin out most of the non-productive twiggy growth from within the canopy. If they are still bearing heavily, the pruning can be postponed for a couple of months until the fruit has been harvested. However, it is important to remember that lemons are best clipped from the tree just before they have ripened, then stored in a box under cover, to complete the process. This can take a few weeks, but the fruit is much juicier and the skin becomes thinner.

Lemon trees, such as Eureka or Lisbon, usually carry some fruit for most of the year, although the main cropping period is late winter and spring. These are common varieties planted in Australia and now is the best time for planting them.

Over a period of five or more years, the top-growth gradually becomes congested with masses of small branches and twigs. This not only restricts healthy air movement, but provides numerous hiding places for insect pests. All kinds of diseases can also gain a foothold under these conditions, while birds and other predators are unable to penetrate the heavy growth. Most uncared for lemon trees are infested with pests, yet are difficult to spray successfully.

When pruning is necessary, Lisbon and Eureka lemon trees can withstand much more drastic treatment than other citrus. Old trees, which have long since lost their vigour, will only produce small yields of poor-quality fruit, often small, dry and covered with black, sooty mould. These trees respond dramatically to a good, careful pruning and will bear healthy, juicy fruit within twelve months.

The method is simple. Cut off all small branches and twigs, right to the ends of the main branches. Don't leave any stumps. Rake the mass of prunings clear, then remove or burn them. The ash is excellent around peas and beans, applied

> This is the time for planting all kinds of trees, shrubs and vegetables. They will be able to form a good root-system before the dry sets in and will have a better chance of survival. Rootcrops such as carrots, parsnips, beetroot and potatoes should go in immediately. Many of them will grow and produce a good yield during the next three or more months, if they get a good start while the soil is still moist.

as soon as it has cooled. The finished tree looks quite a miserable sight, with hardly a leaf and with only the bare main branches. However, within a matter of weeks, especially if the root-zone has been given a good, deep watering after pruning, the bare limbs begin to sprout healthy new growth. The watering must be maintained, with fertilizers such as blood and bone generously sprinkled over the root-zone, then watered in, every three weeks until the end of March. During this time, the transformation from an old, sick neglected tree, into a healthy one is completed. The main ingredient is plenty of moisture during summer. This type of pruning need only take place every five years or so, provided it is needed.

Prune Passionfruits Too

Passionfruit vines, especially 'Nelly Kelly' black passionfruit, can also be pruned about now, for the same reason as with the citrus. Most vines have a relatively short life, usually about six years. Although some will live much longer, their production rate drops sharply and disease becomes chronic. Pruning helps to overcome this problem to a limited extent by giving the vines a longer, healthier life.

Pruning can be carried out with a pair of hedge-shears, using secateurs to finish off the difficult-to-get-at areas. Simply cut away the main bulk of leaves and small branches to leave the main arms of the plant untouched. Once the main tangle of growth has been cut off, the ends can be further shortened to the nearest side-shoot. The effects of this pruning will be lots of new growth and a later crop of high-quality fruit. Watering, as with the citrus, is absolutely essential during spring and summer, while regular feeding ensures steady growth and a good crop.

Hard-surface Landscaping – Patios and Paths

Open spaces, even those without plants, make all the difference in the world to the character of a garden. Outside-living or barbecue areas, driveways, turning circles, patios and paths can all look attractive, because they are all an essential part of the landscaping. If these areas can be designed to fit in with lawns, perennial borders and other planted areas, a special kind of balance is achieved, especially if the hard surfaces are carefully chosen.

A few years ago, drives and paths were usually constructed with concrete. In too many cases the results were harsh, and impossible to try and blend into the rest of the garden.

Today, the situation is quite different, with all sorts of imaginative materials available with which to cover surfaces subject to hard wear. Fortunately, most of these can be easily laid by unskilled people, in their own gardens, with an enormous saving in cost.

Concrete pavers come in several natural colours and are easy to handle. There are heavy types, suitable for driveways carrying heavy loads, while the thinner, lighter and cheaper ones are perfect for footpaths. The great advantage of the slightly-roughened pre-cast 'cobbles' is their non-slip surfaces. It makes them perfectly suitable for surfacing steep drives and paths.

The actual construction of this type of paved area is so simple that all members of the family can become involved. Once the base has been prepared, the actual laying can take place at high speed, with large areas being completed in a surprisingly short time. Here is what to do to lay an attractive path, patio or drive, using concrete pavers:

1. Level, or even-out the surface, even if it has to be lightly cultivated first to assist raking. Try to compact any areas which may be a little loose or soft and remove or bury stones or rocks.

2. Once the earth foundation has been consolidated, spread coarse sand or stonedust over the ground, to a minimum depth of five centimetres. If persistent weeds are present, black plastic can be laid first, with a good overlap at joints.

The great thing about coarse sand and rock-dust is that they can still be handled easily when they are wet. Even after drying out, they don't shrink or settle. Fine sand is difficult to work, it can blow about even in a light wind, and if you wet it an even finish is hard to obtain. Soil or clay is useless for this type of thing.

3. Spreading the base materials evenly can be difficult if just using a rake, but a straight-edged piece of wood, even a fence-paling, can work wonders. Sometimes, if two temporary wooden guides, or runners, are placed in position first, the straight edge can be rested upon them while levelling the sand. Once the sand has been levelled, it should not be directly walked over again.

4. The pavers are laid, without pressure, directly upon the undisturbed sand. They do not have to butt up against each other, but a gap of about a centimetre is plenty. If the gaps are kept consistent, by using a flat piece of wood of a suitable thickness, the pavers will go down evenly and in line. Even when laying, it is important to avoid walking over the surface of the level sand. Instead, it is much easier to work from the surface which has just been laid. If someone is constantly bringing in pavers, the person doing the laying can put them down as fast as they can be handled.

5. After the laying has been completed, dry sand can then be brushed into the crevices. A little dry cement can be mixed into the sand in order to make it more firm. This is the advantage of having decent-sized gaps. The sand easily falls into them and they will absorb a great deal of it. Many paving manufacturers or distributors will also supply a compaction machine which will even-out the finished surface. A tile-cutting guillotine is usually available so that smaller gaps at the edges can be fitted.

6. Finally, after the surface of the pavers has been vibrated, a final filling of sand can be swept in. If the whole area is then gently hosed, any last air-pockets will be eliminated.

Bricks, either on the flat, or better still on their edges, also make an attractive hard surface. Second-hand bricks have always been popular, especially if they are finished off with an abrasive disc, because of the attractive, earthy colours produced.

Glazed bricks or tiles are excellent, particularly for level paths or patios. However, on a sloping site they can be a serious hazard when frosty or wet. Steps made from this type of shiny material can be quite dangerous, unless a special anti-slip strip is placed near the edge of each step.

There are many other types of paving or materials suitable for places which receive plenty of traffic – wooden discs, slate, scoria, ironstone gravel and of course concrete, which can easily be painted or rendered to conceal or darken the surface.

September
GUIDE TO ACTION

Ornamental Garden

Spring brings enormous activity. As wattles and other flowering native plants finish blooming, prune away spent flowers. Cuttings taken in autumn will have formed roots by now, so plant some out into the garden, or pot them on for further development. Lime beds which are to grow annuals. Aphids are attacking roses and other plants, so use pyrethrum, a safe spray which will exterminate them. Plant gladioli corms. The tiny, pea-sized cormlets can also be planted to provide future displays. Divide chrysanthemums and other perennials which normally die down in winter. Spread animal manure, blood and bone and organic mulching materials between all shrubs to control weeds while feeding the soil. In warm, frost-free districts, most annual plants can be sown either directly or into containers. In cooler districts, seedlings are best raised under glass or in a protected environment, such as a windowsill. Sow seed of ageratum, alyssum, anchusa, amaranthus, antirrhinum, aquilegia, aster, bellis perennis, calendula, candytuft, celosia, cornflower, chrysanthemum, clarkia, coleus, cosmos, dahlia, dianthus, gaillardia, geranium, gerbera, geum, godetia, gypsophila, helichrysum, heliotrope, hibiscus, hollyhock, impatiens, kochia, larkspur, linaria, Livingstone daisy, lobelia, lupin, lunaria, African and French marigold, mignonette, mimulus, moluccella, myosotis, nasturtium, nemesia, nemophila, nigella, pansy, petunia, platycodon, polyanthus, oriental poppy, pyrethrum, rudbeckia, salpiglossis, salvia, scabiosa, schizanthus, statice, sweetpea, verbena, vinca, viola, viscaria, wallflower and zinnia. Many of these plants will also be available as seedlings, ready to go in during the next few months as the danger of frosts pass. Spring bulb clumps which have finished flowering are now developing next year's flowers, so don't cut the leaves or tie them in knots. If they are inconveniently placed, they can be heavily watered before carefully lifting the entire clump, rootball intact, to replant them out of the way to continue growing.

Vegetable Garden

Start mulching to suppress young weeds. However, keep the ground clear, to warm up, where tomatoes are to be grown. Plant potatoes in order to take advantage of moist conditions over the next few months. Make plenty of liquid manure. Slugs and snails must be controlled urgently. Crunching them out of existence at night by torchlight will reduce the population massively over a couple of weeks and, if the job is done properly, these pests will provide few worries for the rest of the season. Toxic baits can be laid, but beware of young children or animals eating them.

Plant or sow globe artichoke, asparagus, beetroot, broad bean, broccoli, summer cabbage, Chinese cabbage, carrot, cauliflower, celery, chicory, cress, corn salad, endive, kohlrabi, leek, lettuce, mustard, okra, onion, parsley, parsnip, peas, radish, turnip, spinach, salsify, tampala and most herbs. Seed of tender plants such as capsicum, cucumber, egg plant, marrow, melon, pumpkin, winter squash, tomato and zucchini is best sown under glass, in cool districts.

Fruit Garden

Gooseberry bushes should be continuously tip-pruned to help control American gooseberry mildew. Apple trees showing signs of powdery mildew must also be tip-pruned and all prunings destroyed. Place hessian or cardboard codlin moth grub-traps around the trunks of apple, pear and quince trees. Graft chilled, retarded scions on to actively growing wood this month. Mulch around all fruit and berry plants with old hay or straw. Spray stone fruit trees for brown-rot control with Mancozeb at full bloom, petal fall and as the withered remains of blossoms are detaching from the immature fruit (shuckfall). Old, congested lemon trees can safely be pruned now by removing all old, twiggy growth. Water heavily afterwards and spray with white oil emulsion for scale control. Feed citrus with old manure, blood and bone or enriched mulching materials. Keep main stems clear. Late-prune over-vigorous plum trees to control growth. Peach aphids will keep pace with attempts to grow. Pyrethrum will provide good relief until ladybirds move in next month. Apply weak liquid manure around strawberry plants and mulch with clean straw. Woolly aphids attacking apple trees can be wiped out with cottonwool, soaked in methylated spirit.

Houseplants

Cyclamen plants will be finishing now so allow to slowly dry off. Gloxinia is starting into growth, so bring inside and gently water. Houseplants which are rootbound should be repotted or potted-on. Large containers which are hard to lift can have potting soil replenished by scraping away top layer of exhausted soil. Replace with enriched potting soil. Weak liquid fertilizers and seaweed concentrate are well received by houseplants from now onwards. Pests include scale (white oil sprays), aphids (pyrethrum), mealy bugs (dab with cottonwool, soaked in methylated spirit) and caterpillars (Dipel sprays).

SEPTEMBER: FIRST WEEK

Crop Rotation

The human race long ago discovered that the most effective way to keep soil fertile, while preventing the build-up of pests and diseases, was to rotate crops. This ensures that the same type of plant is never grown in the same piece of ground for three or more years. All plant groups have their own special circle of parasites, pests and diseases. They gradually build up during the growing season and, if the same plants are mistakenly planted in the same place the following year, these pests etc. already have a foothold as they lie waiting in the soil.

Some soil diseases, once they have been allowed to become established, can take years to be successfully eradicated. Rotation constantly shatters the growth cycle of harmful organisms and pests. The longer the period between related plants being replanted in the same place, the more effective the system will be.

Here is a simple four-year rotation system, which is suitable for both large and small gardens. It is based upon keeping together plants which are either related or which are natural companions and like the same soil conditions.

Divide the vegetable garden into four roughly equal beds, with narrow paths between.

In bed number one: (which would have grown acid-loving plants such as tomatoes, capsicums and eggplants last season) the ground should be limed, preferably as the last tomatoes are being harvested. In autumn, or after the harvest, sow lime-lovers such as broad beans and early peas. Later, sow maincrop peas and, as the soil warms up, bush and climbing beans. As the broad beans, then later the peas and other beans are being harvested, the vacant spaces are filled with brassicas such as broccoli, sprouts, summer and winter cabbage and cauliflowers. After the beans and peas are harvested, their haulm is cut off at the ground to leave the nitrogen-rich roots waiting to feed the hungry leaf crops.

Bed number two: (which grew the pea/bean tribe the previous year, followed by brassicas.) As the last of the winter/spring brassicas are being harvested, the main root-crops go in. These are carrots, parsnips, beetroot, onions, salsify and, if enough room, potatoes. Swedes and turnips can also be sown, even though they are closely related to the cabbage tribe. This bed was limed two years ago, and the soil is still sweet enough to grow lime-lovers such as onions and garlic. Most of the rootcrops, especially carrots, parsnips and swedes, can be left in the ground for winter pulling, but the bed should be clear by late spring. A good dressing of animal manure can be applied to be weathered-in as the rows are cleared.

Bed number three: is for the good companions, such as sweetcorn, cucumbers, pumpkins, winter squash and zucchinis. These are all planted or sown at the start of the warmest period and will thrive in the well-rotted manure which has been worked into the soil. If early-bearing winter squash such as Golden Nugget are included with long-keeping varieties such as Supermarket or pumpkin Crown Prince, a continuous supply for over a year is certain. Cucumbers, such as the climbing Burpless, can be planted adjacent to the sweetcorn stalks and encouraged to grow up them to increase yield and save room, long after the cobs have been harvested. After the bed has been cleared in late autumn, it can be sown with ryecorn, annual lupins or old pea and bean seeds, for a green-man-

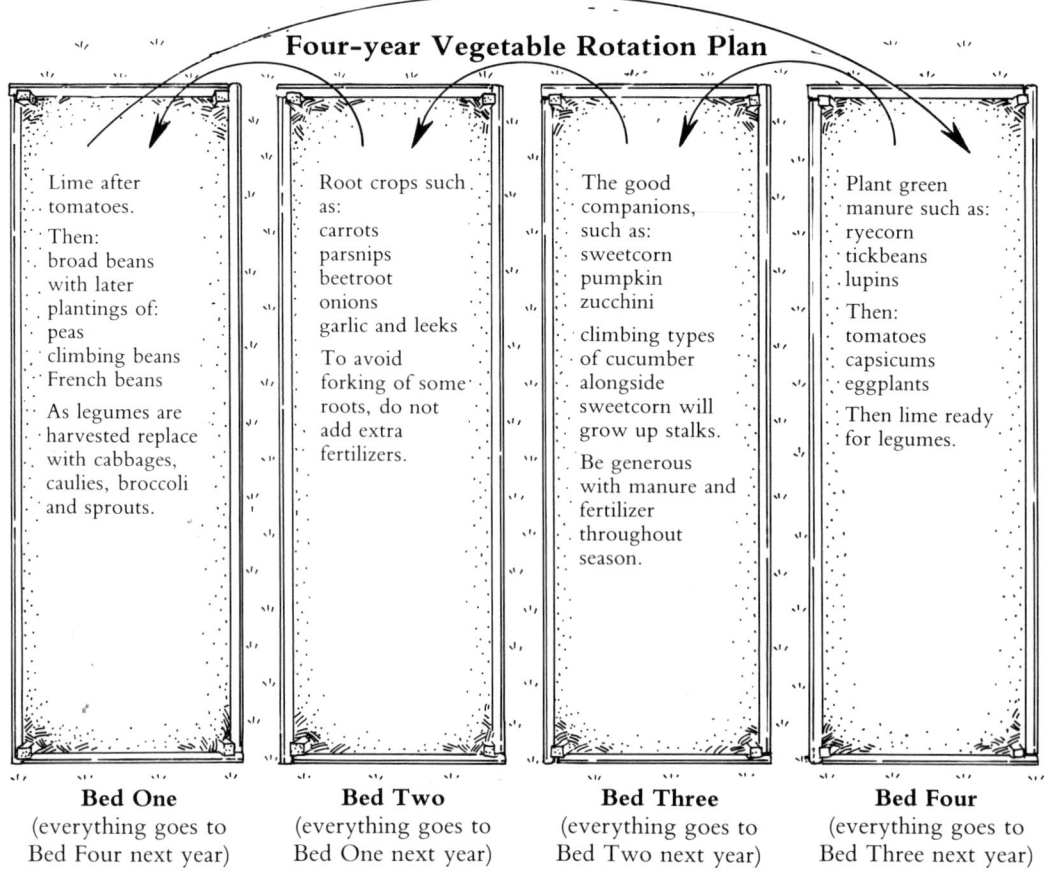

Four-year Vegetable Rotation Plan

Bed One
(everything goes to Bed Four next year)

Lime after tomatoes.
Then:
broad beans with later plantings of:
peas
climbing beans
French beans

As legumes are harvested replace with cabbages, caulies, broccoli and sprouts.

Bed Two
(everything goes to Bed One next year)

Root crops such as:
carrots
parsnips
beetroot
onions
garlic and leeks

To avoid forking of some roots, do not add extra fertilizers.

Bed Three
(everything goes to Bed Two next year)

The good companions, such as:
sweetcorn
pumpkin
zucchini

climbing types of cucumber alongside sweetcorn will grow up stalks.

Be generous with manure and fertilizer throughout season.

Bed Four
(everything goes to Bed Three next year)

Plant green manure such as:
ryecorn
tickbeans
lupins
Then:
tomatoes
capsicums
eggplants
Then lime ready for legumes.

---

ure crop for digging-in at the end of winter.

Bed number four: has not been limed for three years, so the slightly acid soil will be perfect for tomatoes, capsicum and eggplants. Last year's green-manure has just been dug-in, so the soil will be fertile, without excessive nitrogen. Too much fertilizer when tomatoes are still without flowers will mean late crops and delayed ripening. As the tomatoes and other plants no longer bear heavily, the ground between them can be covered with lime or dolomite, ready for next season's crop of peas, beans and brassicas.

Other plants such as silverbeet and lettuce can be included in any of the sweet-soil beds and rotated as room allows. Strawberries can be grown on the fringes of any of the beds, to be replaced and moved on every three years.

Turning Clay into Friable Soil

There is no garden more frustratingly difficult to keep well-maintained than one planted into heavy clay. Everything is hard to do, because of sticky, clinging soil. Weeding is virtually impossible, when roots cannot be pulled out, and if they are dug out, a whole clod comes with them. Digging can be an exhausting exercise, even for those who are at the peak of physical fitness, while trees, shrubs and other plants often remain impoverished, miserable-looking and stunted.

Well, it's not all that bad really. In fact there is a lot to be said for heavy clay soils. For one thing, in spite of the hard, tight structure, clay soils are very rich in minerals and plant foods. The big problem is that many plants are unable to get at them because the soil particles are so fine, they cling together.

There are several ways to deal with and conquer clay soils. They can be treated and eventually converted into easily-worked, loamy soils, they can be overlaid with a thick band of good quality, light sandy loam or they can be accepted as clay soils and planted accordingly.

All these methods work, but some are more expensive than others.

To convert sticky clay into good loam means breaking up the tiny particles which make up its structure. Spreading heavy dressings of gypsum over the surface, then incorporating it into the clay, makes it much easier to deal with. Gypsum is plaster of Paris or calcium sulphate, but unlike other forms of calcium, it does not make the soil alkaline. It can be freely used in the vicinity of lime-hating plants and remains effective in the soil for a long time.

If, in addition to gypsum, large quantities of sand are worked in, this will break up the tight particles even more effectively and when organic matter is also included, the transformation is complete.

When the surface of soils treated in this way are mulched with a thick layer of old hay or straw, the worm population explodes and these marvellous creatures create thousands of tunnels as they drag down decaying organic matter. I have seen a cold, heavy clay garden totally converted into an easily-worked, fertile delight within six months as a result of this type of treatment. However, the layer of organic mulch must be constantly replenished as it is absorbed into the surface.

With many new garden sites, the amount of excavated clay spread over the entire block can be very disheartening. It is virtually impossible to shift and this is probably the best time to import good topsoil. Make sure that clay which has been compacted by machinery is broken up before overlaying topsoil. The costs can be high, but these must be weighed up against a lifetime of difficult, more expensive maintenance. The added layer of topsoil need only be about twenty centimetres thick, but that means a cubic metre extra of soil for each five square metres of surface. Savings can be made in the areas designated for lawn. If the clay surface can be cultivated with a rotary hoe, preferably when fairly dry, it is a simple matter to even-out the surface. Then a successful lawn can be sown using only five centimetres of topsoil. In other words, the costs of importing topsoil can be massively reduced if it is only spread thickly over areas to be planted with trees and shrubs.

The easiest and cheapest way of dealing with clay soil conditions is to accept the situation and plant only trees, shrubs and other plants which thrive in clay. There are a very large number of them, including some of the most attractive garden plants. However, the vegetable garden will need either the special treatment, or a good layer of imported topsoil.

Here are some plants which will grow strongly in even the heaviest clay soils.

Common alder (*Alnus glutinosa*): suitable for a larger garden, this vigorous, vaguely birch-like tree is beautiful in both summer and winter. However, such is its love of moisture, that it is best kept well clear of sewerage or stormwater pipes.

Silver birch (*Betula pendula*) and *Liquidamber styraciflua,* the beautiful sweetgum tree, will both grow strongly in heavy clay soils, provided they are watered often during summer.

There is a good range of clay-tolerant, smaller plants which don't threaten drains or cause concrete paths to buckle and lift. These include many of the bottlebrushes, such as the crimson and lemon flowering forms, the woolly tea-tree (*Leptospermum lanigerum*), a wide variety of paperbarks, especially *Melaleuca spathulata, M. thymifolia* (the low-growing thyme honey-myrtle), correas such as the enchanting dusky bells, *Banksia spinulosa* (Hairpin banksia), boronia, many grevilleas, eriostemons, *Westringia fruiticosa* and most roses.

Spring Lawn Care

For those with large lawns, this is an increasingly desperate time in the garden. Nothing grows as relentlessly as spring grass. Our towns and suburbs are truly buzzing with activity as seemingly demented figures march back and forth behind the hedges.

What a sad madness it all is. The benefits of the exercise are cancelled out by the toxic effects of the fumes we suck into our lungs, as we trudge behind, or are dragged along by, our mowers.

The alternatives include hand or electric mowers, getting rid of the lawn and replacing it with ground-covering plants, or liberating it to become proper grass, lovely, long and shaggy. But, what will the neighbours say? Or the visitors?

The reality is, of course, that grass is one of the best ground-covers of all, because it is one of the few plants which can be regularly cut off, almost to the ground, yet still keep coming back for more. A well-maintained lawn can enhance the appearance of a garden, and if it is cut correctly there are fewer problems.

Unfortunately, this is the time when the worst mutilations occur, because of the terrible myth which insists that a closely-cut lawn means less mowing and little maintenance. Too often, at this crucial time, lawns are not so much cut, as scalped. This results in an unsightly, piebald piece of ground, dotted with patches of shaved earth where the high-points were.

The longer grass is allowed to grow, the deeper its roots will penetrate. When lawns are cut too short, especially at the start of the growing season, the roots become exposed to the harsh, drying effects of wind and sun, at a time when they are most vulnerable. Short grass means shallow roots and, unless plenty of water is applied every day, a rapid browning-off, long before normal.

Lawn mowers should never be operated with the cutting-blades set at the lowest point, or even the next two stops above that. Depending upon the mixture of grasses, a sensible cutting-height would be between three and five centimetres. Such a lawn would remain green and healthy for most of the year.

The work involved in mowing a large lawn can be reduced by dividing it into two types of grass. The areas close to the house can be cut regularly (about every week at this time) to develop a traditional, high-quality sward, while the less-used outer areas can be left fairly long. This tidy but slightly rough grass need only be cut about six times a year and, if there is a clear demarcation line between the two areas, it can look attractive.

Feeding a lawn is essential at this time. Slow-acting fertilizers are best because they come available as they sink down past shallow roots, inducing the roots to go down after them. Quick-acting, highly soluble fertilizers, especially those containing large amounts of sulphate of ammonia, while initially producing plenty of lush, green growth, discourage active root development. The grass then becomes dependent upon this type of feeding and is liable to sudden drying-off during hot weather.

Blood and bone, with about ten per cent added potash, makes an excellent lawn food. However, like all other fertilizers, it should never be applied to a dry surface, otherwise severe burning can take place. Immediately after rain, or at least a good watering, is the best time.

> Tip for the week: use a garden fork to prick deeply and slightly prise badly compacted ground beneath large trees. If coarse dry sand is scattered over the surface before watering, it will flow into the holes to provide long-lasting drainage plugs.

Sprinkle the blood and bone mix at the rate of forty grams (a tight fistful) for each square metre, then water again to wash any deposit off the leaves. If this treatment is carried out about once a month, the lawn will respond by producing a thick, springy, bright green sward with a resistance to drought conditions.

Hungry, impoverished lawns quickly become infested with weeds because the grass is unable to compete effectively. Once flatweeds become established, they soon learn how to escape the blades of the mower, by growing close to the ground. There are many selective herbicides available which sort out the weeds, leaving the grass to keep on growing, but the danger of spray-drift on to adjoining garden beds is a problem. Even worse, some of the herbicides can be breathed in to our lungs or absorbed through the skin, with consequences as yet unrevealed or unknown.

I've long since stopped using these selective herbicides, because I don't trust them. It is not enough to be reassured that such substances have not been proved to be dangerous, it is much better if they were proved to be safe. Frankly, anyone who uses them indiscriminately, especially near a pregnant woman, is stark raving mad.

Weeds in lawns can be killed by mixing one part of dry sand with one of sulphate of ammonia and scattering it over the weed-infested areas. Within days, the weeds start to bolt out of the ground, then eventually turn black and die. This is the old-fashioned lawn-sand used long before herbicides were invented. It is safe to use and doesn't drift.

SEPTEMBER: SECOND WEEK

More on Houseplants

This is the great rejuvenation time for houseplants. For those which have been sitting in their pots for two or more years, it's a good time of the year to re-pot or, if they are seriously rootbound, to transfer them to a larger pot. All plants are vigorously sending out new roots right now, so the slight shock of transplanting, or even being disturbed, will not prove a check to growth. In fact, what will happen, if the job is carried out correctly, is plenty of strong growth for the next four months at least.

Some plants prefer to be slightly rootbound. These are mainly the ones which also produce flowers. Wax plants (hoyas), African violets (*Saintpaulias*) and strelitzias will often fail to bloom until they start to become slightly cramped in their pots. Even tomato plants can easily be forced into flower by leaving young seedlings in tumbler-sized pots until they start to become rootbound.

With most foliage plants, we try to induce plenty of healthy, luxuriant growth and this is largely achieved by regularly replacing or adding to the potting soil.

The actual potting mix differs a little according to the type of plant being grown. For example, ferns seem to prefer a well-drained compost which contains a high proportion of granulated peat. A good simple mix for ferns is: five parts of peat, three parts of good garden loam and two parts of coarse sand. For each bucketful of this mixture, add a tablespoon of superphosphate, three tablespoons of blood and bone and a tablespoon of sulphate of potash. The whole lot must be thoroughly mixed.

This will give the ferns a good source of plant-foods which can also retain enough water to satisfy the needs of these shade-loving plants.

Desert plants such as cacti and succulents will never grow properly in a compost which does not allow for quick drainage. A coarse, gritty mixture containing a high proportion of sand or grit, and with less than a quarter peat, is more than satisfactory for these plants, especially if some good topsoil is included.

However, the majority of houseplants will grow quite happily in a simple mixture of one third each of river sand, peat and good quality topsoil, with the same amount of fertilizers per bucketful as the ferns.

Incidentally, never use the soil from the garden on its own. It may contain plenty of plant foods, but is not very porous, usually collapsing into a hard lump after a few weeks in a pot.

To re-pot, carefully knock the plant from the container by placing the flat of one's hand over the soil at the top, with the main stem passing between the fingers. Then reverse the pot and gently tap the edge against a solid surface, such as the edge of a bench. If the plant has been given a good soaking earlier, the rootball will come out intact. With badly rootbound plants, many of the roots will have gone black and died and these can be cut off. The rest can be teased out with a pencil or a small table fork, allowing the outer layer of potting soil to be scraped away. Extra-long roots, especially those which have been spiralling around the sides of the container, can be removed and some of the leaves and tops of the plant reduced to compensate.

Check for signs of decay, then replace in the original container, after renewing the original drainage materials. The potting soil is best poured into the sides of the pot in a dry form, until it reaches the original soil level. However, it should not be rammed into place, as this will cause compaction. Rapping the entire container on a hard surface two or three times will be enough to settle the level. After that, all that remains is to water the plant. This is done by placing the container in a large bucket containing enough water to come half-way up the sides of the pot. After a couple of hours the soil will be saturated and will have settled still further. If so, add more potting soil. Finally, allow to drain completely so that no more water seeps out from the drainage slots.

Potting-on to a larger pot is basically the same, except that only a little of the original potting soil need be removed. The common error is to pot-on into too large a pot, thus causing the unused soil to become permanently saturated and eventually toxic.

Quite often there is a real problem with older, more vigorous houseplants, especially monsteras or rubber plants. If they have been in a large, heavy container for a number of years, it is almost impossible to lift them from their comfortable conditions without seriously damaging them.

So, don't even try. Instead, carefully scrape away as much of the topsoil as is possible, without damaging the roots. It is surprising how much can be removed, even from between the main roots. Get rid of this exhausted material and replace with a standard potting mix. Then water slowly and persistently until the centre of the rootball has been penetrated.

If the existing soil has become dry and shrunken, any water applied to the top surface will almost immediately run out from the slots at the base of the pot or tub. The easiest way to deal with this is to soak the whole pot in a trough of water. Another way is to block the slots up with wads of moist paper or even clay, then water the surface. Leave to soak for half a day or more, then remove the plugs. If very little water runs out, do it again until eventually water runs out when the plugs have been removed. But never make the blunder of leaving the plugs in, otherwise you will soon have a dead plant on your hands.

Some Spring Jobs

It always comes as a bit of a shock when spring arrives. Winter is now over officially and it is too easy to be tricked into planting all sorts of things which are really not yet ready to go outside. So, please don't be fooled by warm, almost summery days. Remember, the nights are still very chilly, and there will be plenty of cold, blustery days ahead before it is safe enough to plant out tender plants. But there are many other things to do.

The first great flush of flowering plants is now beginning, and it is an excellent time to select and plant a wide range of trees and shrubs, while they are in bloom. Names, and even descriptions of flowers, on labels are obviously limited, so it is a perfect opportunity to visit nurseries and garden centres to choose plants while they are in flower. There is nothing wrong with planting a blooming plant and in fact it has the advantage of providing instant colour in a drab part of the garden. Rhododendrons, camellias, azaleas, many ericas, and a large number of native plants are good examples of the kind of plant which can be chosen now, in bloom, so you can obtain just what you want.

It is the start of the main plant feeding time now, as most trees, shrubs and other plants respond to the warmer conditions and longer days by making demands for regular supplies of plant food and minerals. It is a waste of time, money and effort to feed garden plants with solid fertilizers during the cool months, when they are in a semi-dormant state, but right now we can start laying it on generously. I have always been a great advocate of blood and bone fertilizer, because it contains, in a slow-release form, phosphorus and calcium, in the bone meal, and nitrogen in the blood content. However, blood and bone does not contain any potash, so this should be added to create a fairly balanced, all purpose fertilizer.

Sulphate of potash looks like fine sugar, and it is easy to mix with blood and bone at the rate of nine parts of blood and bone to one part of potash. This can be sprinkled to all parts of the garden, over the lawn, between shrubs, and around fruit and ornamental trees. The rate of application should be about forty grams per square metre, or a tight fistful, well spread out, then watered into the surface.

If this treatment is carried out every three weeks, from now until the end of March, the plants will respond and develop new flowering wood to an amazing degree. This light but regular feeding is much better than irregular applications in heavy doses, which can disrupt the soil and harm the plants.

The most hungry competitor of garden plants, particularly young trees, is grass. Newly planted fruit trees will remain almost motionless throughout the summer, even if well watered and fertilized, if there is a vigorous growth of grass around and over the roots. This quick and greedy growth always begins ahead of the tree, and so gains an important advantage right from the start. Grass, more than any other plant, robs a tree of moisture and food before it has a chance to get down to the roots.

The answer is simple to apply, and the effects are long-lasting. Old straw, sawdust, seaweed, old newspapers in thick layers, and even grass-clippings mixed with wilted weeds, all spread directly over the surface of the grass around the trunk of the tree, does the trick. The grass is smothered by the mulch and then rots down so that it becomes part of the mulch too. The resultant growth and development of a young tree can be staggering once it has been relieved of the dead weight of the competing grass, and the extra moisture retained in the surface soil reduces unnecessary watering later on.

Over-vigorous trees, especially varieties of stone fruit, can be controlled, simply by allowing plenty of long grass to grow around the base of the trunk. A light pruning, now that growth has commenced, coupled with the grass as a growth-retardant, can bring to heel the most aggressive tree, and even force it into fruit.

Some apple and pear trees will respond to delayed winter-pruning, at this crucial time, by developing more accessible fruiting wood, and trees whose fruit is usually out of reach can be encouraged to produce a more accessible canopy for easy picking, after a couple of years of this treatment.

Outstanding berry fruit is one of the advantages of cool winters. Gooseberry bushes are normally winter-pruned for best results, but a relatively new problem has arisen within the last few years which has caused us to alter this pruning habit a little. The disease American gooseberry mildew will cover branches, leaves and fruit with a pale grey powder, starting from now. It will devastate even old established bushes, and is one of the most heart-breaking blights to attack this particular berry fruit plant.

This disease is not new in Britain, where it has been common since the last century. It is also misnamed, because it isn't American. I believe it originated in Europe. But it can be dealt with by a combination of spraying and pruning techniques. First, it is significant that, like powdery mildew on apple trees, it overwinters inside tight bud scales, particularly in the tips of branches. Conse-

> For extra-quick germination of tomato, pumpkin, capsicum, eggplant or melon seeds, place them in moist potting soil, in a container, enclose the lot in a plastic bag and place on top of the refrigerator at the rear, where the warm air is.
>
> But, as soon as seedlings emerge, get them into better light immediately.

quently, the careful pruning out of all the growing tips helps to control this awful disease, and to prevent it spreading to currants which it will also attack in a lesser way.

Sprays such as Zineb or Benlate will also help to keep American gooseberry mildew in check if applied directly after pruning. But be prepared to keep on nipping out the growing tips and destroying them each time any sign of this disease appears. Don't get it confused with the common European gooseberry mildew, which doesn't attack the fruit seriously, but concentrates on the upper surfaces of some leaves, usually those in the shade.

Codlin moth grubs – which tunnel their way into the centre of apples, eat out the core, then tunnel out again, leaving an unpleasant mess of brown frass – can be controlled safely.

A band of hessian or even newspaper several thicknesses thick, can be tied loosely around the trunks of the trees. When the grubs have emerged from the apples, they lower themselves to the ground and seek a hiding place on or near the trunk. The band provides this, and if taken off, burned, then replaced every two months, next year's brood will be reduced markedly.

Tip-prune apple trees subject to powdery mildew and help control brown-rot of stone fruits by spraying the trees with Mancozeb while they are in full bloom. These trees must be sprayed again with the same substance as soon as the withered remains of the blooms are dropping off from around the young fruit.

It is still grafting time, so if you have saved any scions, make sure they are cool enough to prevent them from sprouting, otherwise success will be limited.

In the ornamental garden, seeds of many annuals can now be sown, although more certain results will be obtained by using special treated growing medium which is free of harmful organisms. Seeds to sow under glass are: ageratum, alyssum, tagetes, lobelia, phlox, antirrhinum, celosia, verbena, rudbeckia, salvia, helichrysum, and larkspur. Take cuttings or divisions from perennials such as chrysanthemum, delphinium, oriental poppy, perennial aster, and penstemon. Complete the pruning of roses, and prune flowering fruit trees as they complete their blooming. Lime any beds before being made ready for annual display during summer, and remove weeds. Wipe the developing foliage of oxalis weed with a Roundup or Zero weeding wand and touch-kill flat weeds in lawns with the same tool.

Gladioli corms can be planted out, and as early flowering jonquils start to fade, they can be carefully lifted without disturbing the rootball, and transplanted to a less used area of the garden to complete their cycle of growth before dying down. This is the time to generously feed camellias, azaleas, rhododendron, daphne, pieris, erica and other shallow-rooted plants, with large quantities of old animal manure, especially sheep, goat or cow. This will sustain the plants during the next few months, providing plenty of organic matter.

Divide up old chrysanthemum clumps, and where possible take cuttings rather than simple divisions. Shoots only ten centimetres long, without roots, placed in a sandy soil mix and kept watered, will form fresh roots within a month. This method ensures that diseases which have built up in the main root system of the old plant will not be transferred to the new ones. The same treatment should apply to delphiniums, which will develop and flower strongly this season from cuttings struck at this time.

Spring planting of vegetables is a busy operation. Many seeds sown now will develop rapidly in the next couple of months. Plant seeds of broad bean, beetroot, cabbage, cauliflower, carrot, kohlrabi, leek, onion, parsley, parsnip, peas, radish, salsify, silverbeet, swede and turnip. In greenhouses or under warm protected conditions, sow seed of celery, cucumber, marrow, pumpkin, winter squash, sweetcorn and tomato. Seedlings of most brassicas, lettuce, onion and leeks can be planted out now with good prospects for sturdy plants.

Magnolias

Among some of the plants in flower at this time are the magnolias. There are more than eighty species which grow in the wild, mainly in the northern hemisphere, and fortunately, we are able to grow some of the most beautiful of them to perfection in Australia.

Most magnolias prefer a well drained open position, although the deciduous varieties can also put up with a little afternoon shade. Generally, most species suffer badly in exposed, windy places, the major problem being a combination of severe stunting, and inability to retain their flowers, because of the wind.

Cold, wet soils also seriously retard growth, especially if there is a high content of heavy clay in the soil. So it pays to locate the young plants in areas which are fairly well sheltered.

It is the best time to plant magnolias right now, because the warming soil allows the roots to establish themselves better than a cold, wet, winter planting. I always make a point of mixing large amounts of granulated peat, or better still, well-matured compost, with the soil in the hole. A fistful or two of blood and bone scattered into the hole, and mixed with the soil, will give the young tree a good start. A wooden stake is essential in order to keep the new tree secure, and this should be driven in first to avoid damaging the roots.

The most popular of the deciduous magnolias is *M. soulangiana*. There are a number of superbly beautiful cultivars of this hybrid, with colours ranging from pure white to various shades of rosy purple. These are the ones often called the tree tulip, because the blooms look like giant tulips springing from the bare branches. These are rarely pruned, although I have seen some remarkable results from a regular light pruning, just after flowering.

Among the smaller magnolias, *M. liliflora*, which grows into a compact shrub, less than two-metres tall, is a must for the smaller garden. The blooms are surprisingly large, and are extremely attractive being rich purple with snow white centres. The even smaller *M. stellata* has fully opened, star shaped white flowers, which are borne in their hundreds, making the small tree appear as though it is covered with giant snow flakes. This breathtaking display continues for weeks, making it one of the longest flowering of all the magnolias.

My own favourite is the extraordinary 'Yulan' which has been grown in China for thousands of years, and is often illustrated in traditional paintings. Correctly named *M. denudata*, it will grow to a height of five metres with long, spreading branches. The fragrant, bell-shaped flowers are almost fifteen centimetres across, making this one of the most sought-after of all the magnolias.

The evergreen *M. grandiflora* is the largest of the species, eventually growing to a height of twenty-five metres under ideal conditions. This is grown almost as much for its handsome, glossy, rich green leaves as for the flowers. The blooms are strongly scented, and look like huge white cups, twenty centimetres across, nestling among the foliage. Unlike most other varieties, the flowers of *M. grandifolia* are carried throughout the summer months, and present a magnificent sight in many of the older gardens.

So, whether you have a large garden, or a small one, there is a place for a magnolia in it somewhere.

SEPTEMBER: THIRD WEEK

Choosing the Best Lemon Tree for Your Garden

Every garden should have a lemon tree. They are attractive plants and some varieties steadily produce useful fruit most of the year.

At least three varieties grow and bear well. The hardiest, suitable for colder districts, is the low-growing Meyer. This is also one of the most ornamental of the lemon trees, because of the contrast between the deep green leaves and the shining, rich yellow, smooth-skinned fruit. The main crop of the Meyer is borne during the winter months, when up to two hundred or more sweetish, very juicy fruit can be carried on a healthy tree.

The most common lemon tree grown is Lisbon. A large upright tree with pale green leaves, it produces big, well-flavoured lemons, mostly during the winter, but with reasonable pickings at other times of the year. Lisbon is easily identified by its upright shape, and by short spines on the branches. The only real problem caused by these spines is during picking time, when they can seriously scratch the rind, causing the fruit to go mouldy very quickly during storage.

Eureka is another popular lemon variety. This grows into a big, semi-weeping tree, which can produce great quantities of very large fruit, even during the summer. There are few, if any, spines, and fruit picking is fairly easy. The flavour is similar to that of the Lisbon, although the skin is sometimes a little thicker.

All citrus trees need an open, sunny and sheltered situation. Major problems are caused by heavy clay soil, which these plants dislike, and by constant cold winds. Sea winds can be particularly damaging, often causing the leaves to drop off completely and forcing the tree to remain stunted.

Once these trees have been planted, the ground near them should never be cultivated, because of the fine, hair-like and shallow roots. These shallow roots are easily damaged, and their nearness to the surface means that they are very vulnerable to drying out during summer. This is why summer watering on a regular basis is so essential to plant health and steady growth.

Lemon trees, like all other citrus, need regular but gentle feeding to get the best results. They have a special need for nitrogen, and also respond particularly well to foliar sprays of greatly diluted seaweed concentrate. The best time to fertilize is in spring, and blood and bone is among the most suitable of the fertilizers. A good fistful for each square metre of surface, sprinkled over the root system and covering the ground beyond the dripline, will work wonders. This treatment every month until the end of February will produce a strong and productive response. However, feeding must always be preceded by a deep watering, and followed by another one to wash the plant foods into the surface. Applying fertilizers to a dry soil can be a disaster, because the sensitive roots are easily burned.

Some Citrus Problems

The main insect pests which attack citrus are scale and black citrus aphids. Scale is easily spotted, because the leaves become covered with a black, sooty mould. The scale insects, whose droppings cause this mould, are out of sight, under the leaves. Spraying with white oil emulsion, especially beneath the leaves, will eliminate the scale pest.

Black citrus aphids are starting to multiply now, as the young, dark-coloured new growth begins. They can easily be seen as clusters of dark, almost black insects, in their hundreds, usually at the tips of the new growth. They are quickly killed by spraying with non-toxic pyrethrum, preferably in two sprays at four-day intervals.

Another serious disease of citrus is caused by planting too deeply, or by piling up organic mulching materials such as leaves, grass clippings, etc., around the main trunk. This causes the bark to go mouldy, and produces collar rot. It is treated by scraping away the mulch, exposing the trunk to the atmosphere, cutting away diseased bark (but being careful not to ringbark the tree), and applying a paste made with Bordeaux powder and a little water.

Most of the other diseases can be kept in check by eliminating congestion in the canopy, and allowing plenty of air to circulate.

Finally, don't pull the fruit off the tree, otherwise it will pull out the 'plug' at the base of the stalk. This means that the fruit may not keep. Lemons should be neatly cut off with sharp secateurs, and their skins never scratched. Like other citrus, if the skins are thick, and there seems to be little juice, don't worry. Once they have been carefully stored in a drawer or box for a week or so, the skins will become quite thin, and they will be full of juice.

So, if you haven't a lemon tree or other type of citrus in your garden, now is the perfect time of the year to plant one.

When Trees Become Too Big

There can be no more expensive blunder than planting a big, aggressive tree in a small garden. The damage inflicted on drainage systems can be massive, and, apart from the expense of having to hire plumbers to repair or replace disrupted sewerage or stormwater pipes, there can be the extra costs of having to replant a large part of the garden.

But the most painful expense caused by badly located, greedy trees, is from major damage to the pipes belonging to the house next door. Apart from the expense, the destruction of a friendly relationship with neighbours might take decades to replace.

Damage to pipes is extremely common where the systems are made of terracotta, or glazed earthenware. Modern rigid plastic pipes which have been correctly laid and sealed are generally resistant to penetration by most roots, and pose few problems.

Damage is usually in the form of a serious blockage, and tree roots cause this in two ways. Smaller feeding roots can find their way into the pipe through an open joint, and then, nourished by the delights within, expand rapidly, open the entry point wide, and let all their mates in to attend the feast.

In a frighteningly short time, a huge section of the pipe is filled with a compact, fibrous mass of feeding roots, while back at the house the lavatory bowl fills in a most threatening manner.

This type of pipe blockage is almost always caused by the roots of those trees which need plenty of water, and can tolerate wet situations. Willows, poplars, liquidambers, river she-oaks, alders, and some types of large-growing melaleucas, are all trees to plant with great caution if there are vulnerable pipes in the vicinity. In the case of poplars, fifty metres is still too close.

Another kind of damage to pipes is often caused by trees which do not need, or like, plenty of water. Their roots don't enter the pipes but, by their thickness, actually lift and therefore open up a drainage system. Earth and clay then fall into the opening, and the pipe eventually becomes blocked.

The safest approach is to make sure it doesn't happen to you, by not planting these risky trees. Most of them are illegal anyway, and most municipalities have lists of trees which cannot be planted in the district.

If the damage has already started, cleaning out the pipes will only assist for a short period. Usually, the only answers are either to poison the tree (never just cut it down, it can make things worse) or reroute the drainage system and construct it of resistant materials.

A simple way to propagate azaleas at this time, is to mound-layer the entire plant. Wound the base of each branch by removing a small piece of bark, then bury the bottom third of the plant in a mixture of soil and sawdust. Keep moist.

SEPTEMBER: LAST WEEK

Traditional Potato Planting

You can't beat the old spuds. They seem to thrive in most parts of the world. With rice and wheat, potatoes share top place as our most important food-crop. Yet they are relatively new as a general food, compared to the others. South Americans had grown them long before the Spanish occupied their lands. They were tried out in Spain around 1570, then grown in Italy and gradually in other parts of Europe as their value became understood.

In the home garden the yield can be much greater than in the field, while the methods of growing them can be more versatile. One of the great advantages of growing potatoes is the great ease with which a good crop can be obtained. They tolerate a wide variety of soils, from heavy clay to light sandy loam and, after harvesting, will keep in good condition for a long time. Their only important needs are good drainage and frost-free conditions.

Soil preparation is simple enough. Any soil containing plenty of organic matter will always produce excellent yields of healthy, well-flavoured tubers. Lime, unless the soil is very acidic, is best avoided, because it seems to encourage the development of potato scab. On the other hand, if too much nitrogenous fertilizer is added, there is a danger of the plants producing plenty of luxuriant leaves, but relatively few tubers.

Many growers are beginning to realize the great benefits of digging-in green materials such as ryecorn or Algerian oats immediately before planting the seed tubers. This seems to be an effective deterrent against scab, while ensuring a crop with particularly clean skins.

The planting site should be in full sun and exposure to plenty of breeze is an advantage because it assists in disease control.

The most important thing to remember, when selecting the seed, is to ensure it is certified, thus protecting the soil from diseases which can be difficult to eradicate. It is false economy to use the residues from last year's crop as seed: Once certain diseases become established, they can pass easily from crop to crop, in many cases spread by aphids.

The best seed tubers are about the size of a hen's egg. This will give the new plant enough nourishment, without waste or a large amount of unused, decaying material causing problems.

The tubers have a number of buds, or 'eyes', clustered mainly at one end. This is often referred to as the 'rose' end, and is placed uppermost when planting the tuber. Some people place the seed with the 'rose' end up, out in the sun to go green and encourage the growth of short sturdy sprouts. Sometimes when seed tubers are left in a bag to grow long, pale shoots in dark conditions, the store of plant-foods becomes depleted and subsequent growth is weak.

Planting can be done using a 'dibber', often an old spade handle with a blunt point. This will make a hole about fifteen centimetres deep, into which the tuber is dropped. Alternatively, a trench lined with a five-centimetre layer of lawn clippings or wilted weeds can be used with the tubers planted to the same depth, but on top of the organic material. The most effective distance between plants for good yields is about forty centimetres, with about sixty centimetres between the rows.

In areas threatened by late frosts, the first cluster of leaves should be covered with soil drawn from between the rows. Straw can also be used for protection. When the shoots are about fifteen centimetres high, earthing-up can start. Soil from between the rows is drawn around the stalks, leaving the tips uncovered. This helps increase yields while supporting the bulk of the foliage. It also prevents damaging light from penetrating down to the growing tubers and provides protection from moth attack.

If early weed-control is carried out between the rows, the dominant leafy haulm will eventually smother any following weed seedlings. This is basically why gardeners traditionally plant potatoes as a soil 'cleaning' exercise, prior to planting a garden.

The other successful way of planting potatoes, without much work, is the straw method. See page 123 for further details.

Let's Mulch Against a Possible Dry Summer

There is an increasing urgency to plant virtually the entire range of container-grown trees, shrubs and other plants right now. The rapidly-drying soil, always with the prospect of a dry summer, means that if we can get the plants into the soil before the moisture level has sunk away from the surface, the roots will be able to follow it down and the chances of survival are good.

However, when the ground has dried out to a depth below the roots of the newly-planted shrubs or trees, it requires copious amounts of water to keep the plants moving. Even then, after watering, the moisture must be prevented from evaporating away, by sealing it in.

If ever there has been a need to mulch the surface of the ground heavily around our plants, it is now. But the job has to be done correctly, otherwise all sorts of problems can arise.

The most easily available mulch, at the moment, is lawn-clippings. The only snag with them is the high moisture content which makes them cling tightly together to form an airless pad. Instead of breaking down and decaying in the normal way, fresh heaps of lawn-clippings turn into a foul-smelling slimy mess, which is unpleasant and difficult to handle. If this is spread over the soil it will cause serious problems. Slugs and snails seem to thrive on or in it and they multiply with enormous speed. The soil seems to be adversely affected, becoming acidic and sour, while much of the life within the soil can become unbalanced.

The only way to treat lawn clippings is to give them a good stir, at least once daily, while they are in a heap. This allows the air to get inside, helping the more useful forms of bacteria to do their job, so the heap can decay in the normal way. If lawn-clippings are mixed with other materials which are coarser, especially weeds, leaves, old straw or even soil, they can be successfully converted into an outstanding fertilizer. But not if they are just left on their own in a steaming heap.

All forms of organic matter can be used as a mulch. (But remember not to use organic mulch on alpine and rock plants.) Woodchips are excellent when spread about ten centimetres deep over the surface. However, the soil should first be raked to form an even surface.

If there are clods sticking up when a mulch is spread, they become a focus for unsightly weeds, which quickly spread through the mulch. By having a tight, even distribution, without gaps, a mulch can prevent weeds from coming up from below, while presenting an unattractive seedbed for those which drift in.

Woodchips are never dug into the ground, because they can cause problems of nitrogen deficiency. If they are left on the surface, they will slowly be broken down over many years. In the meantime, newly-planted trees and shrubs can establish themselves free from competition from weeds. This type of long-lasting mulch is quite unsuitable for the vegetable garden, although sawdust, if used with care, can have a valuable, enriching effect.

Because of sawdust's lack of nutrients, especially nitrogen, it needs to be fortified in order to do a good job. I've long found that sprinkling blood and bone over the soil first, at the rate of a handful to the square metre, then applying a sawdust mulch, will cause a rapid breakdown at this time of the year. Poultry, sheep or pulverized cow manure mixed into this type of mulch then well-watered, converts it into a feeding blanket which has amazing results with impoverished or heavy clay soils. Unlike woodchips, this mixture can eventually be dug into the surface to produce friable, easily-worked soil, teeming with worms and other valuable life forms.

This type of feeding mulch, known as 'sheet-composting', is one of the best means I know of improving soil structure while suppressing weeds and retaining moisture. Old straw or hay and wilted weeds can also be included.

There is a risk, when mulching, that certain trees and shrubs will be adversely affected by this moist layer of materials. The bark at the base of most plants is not designed for moist, airless conditions and will quickly go mouldy. This will ring-bark the plant and it either fails to thrive or dies. Usually, a few handfuls of coarse bluemetal around vulnerable stems will keep the air circulating. Fortunately, plants like roses will often send additional roots into a mulch, as will tomatoes and sweetcorn, resulting in healthier, more productive plants.

Spring Pruning

It is almost impossible to overestimate the value of pruning trees and shrubs as soon as they have finished flowering. Many of them immediately begin to form their seeds, and this is an enormous burden on many plants. Pruning not only cuts off the withered blooms, it relieves the plant of the dragging weight of these seeds and seed capsules.

Many wattle trees have now completed their late winter blooming, and a ruthless pruning away of all whippy and exhausted wood will have the effect of providing a valuable rest, while producing a more even but vigorous growth within a few weeks. But the main benefit of this after-bloom pruning is to extend the life of the tree enormously and help to overcome the main problem with wattles, their relatively short life.

Most native plants thrive with regular pruning, always after the flowers have finished. The advantage of this timing allows the plants to form new growth and flowers ready for next year's display. Bushy plants, such as grevilleas, can even be pruned by using hedge shears, and the result is a much more stable plant, of compact, wind-resistant density.

The greatest problem I have come across in native plant gardens which have been established for many years, is lanky, straggly and ugly growth which often spoils the planting design. I have now developed the habit of constantly pinching out the tips of the more aggressive shoots, especially of the younger plants, and the plants are obviously healthier, sturdier, and less likely to be attacked by insect pests. So keep the branch-cutters and secateurs handy from now on, and don't hesitate to use them.

In the flower garden sow or plant: ageratum, alyssum, African marigolds, phlox, antirrhinum, celosia, gypsophila, petunia, verbena, gaillardia, salvia, helichrysum, delphinium, cosmos, dahlia, sunflower, portulaca, coleus, nasturtium, campanula, dianthus, carnation, chrysanthemum and stock.

OCTOBER
GUIDE TO ACTION

Ornamental Garden

Warm soil, a diminishing threat of frosts and longer days make this month a time of frantic sowing, planting, spraying, watering, feeding, digging and desperate lawn mowing. Annual plants can now be bedded out as well-grown seedlings, although zinnias are best left a week or so in cool areas. Dahlia tubers, stored under cover for the winter, will be beginning to sprout. It is a good time to divide clumps. Cuttings of chrysanthemum and delphinium, taken a few weeks ago, will have already formed roots and can be planted out. Place a circle of lime around each plant to keep snails or slugs at bay. Roses need a slow-acting fertilizer such as blood and bone. Aphids will be in thick clusters around growing shoots, so give them a good squirt of pyrethrum and watch them disappear. Tub plants dry out with great speed during this demanding time, so keep watered every day. Weed control is essential right now because they are able to compete successfully with most ornamentals. In spite of the relentless growth of lawn grass, don't lower the blades to cut shorter. It won't reduce the number of times the lawn has to be cut, but it will make it more vulnerable to drying out later, and cause the establishment of weeds on shaven spots.

Most annual, biennial and perennial flowering plants can go in during this month as seedlings, cuttings or divisions. While seed can be sown directly into the garden, better control can be achieved if seedlings are raised in containers. Here are some flowering plants which will contribute enormously to a colourful display, especially during summer: ageratum, alyssum, anchusa, amaranthus, antirrhinum, aquilegia, aster, bellis, calendula, candytuft, celosia, cornflower, clarkia, coleus, chrysanthemum, cosmos, dahlia, dianthus, gaillardia, geranium, gerbera, geum, godetia, gypsophila, helichrysum, heliotrope, hibiscus, hollyhock, impatiens, kochia, larkspur, linaria, Livingstone daisy, lobelia, lupin, lunaria, African and French marigolds, mignonette, mimulus, moluccella, myosotis, nasturtium, nemesia, nemophila, nigella, pansy, petunia, platycodon, polyanthus, oriental poppy, pyrethrum, rudbeckia, salpiglossis, salvia, scabiosa, schizanthus, statice, sweetpea, verbena, vinca, viola, viscaria, wallflower and zinnia.

Vegetable Garden

This is probably the most important month for sowing or planting vegetables. Ahead is at least six months' growing weather. Here are some vegetable plants or seeds, which can go in from now onwards: globe artichoke, asparagus, bush beans (warm districts), climbing beans, beetroot, broccoli, Brussels sprouts, cabbage, Chinese cabbage, Chinese greens, capsicum (warm districts), carrot, cauliflower, celery, chicory, corn salad, cress, cucumber (warm districts), eggplant, endive, kohlrabi, leek, lettuce, marrow, okra (warm districts), onion seedlings of long-keepers, white onion, parsley, parsnip, peas, pumpkins and winter squash (end of month in cool districts), radish, rhubarb (seed), salsify, spinach (round-seeded), swede, sweetcorn, tampala, tomato, turnip, zucchini and potato.

Apply mulching materials such as old hay, straw or pea haulm with added blood and bone, as soon as seedlings are big enough to cope. Weeding seedling onions and carrots is a nit-picking affair, but is essential if the vegetable plants are to survive. Poultry litter sprinkled around leafy vegetables such as brassicas, lettuce and silverbeet, then watered in, will give them a valuable lift right now. Pinch out growing tips of broad bean plants. Watch out for black aphids and spray with pyrethrum if necessary.

Fruit Garden

Spray with pyrethrum against green peach aphids, unless the ladybirds are starting to become obviously visible. Usually they will develop on almond trees, before moving on to peach and nectarine trees. The safe way of preventing codlin moth grubs hatching is by spraying towards the end of this month with a mixture of one part white oil to fifty of water. Carbaryl is a deadly poison with a waiting period of around seven days. If you decide to risk using this against codlin moth grub, remember to carefully follow instructions on the container and take every safety precaution. Early applications will cause the immature fruit to drop. I prefer to use safe methods and have few problems with the grub. Apart from white oil, which is best applied at weekly intervals for about a month, don't forget a hessian band for trapping next season's grubs.

Mulch around all bushes and trees and lightly fork the ground over the roots. At least one bag of sheep or other animal manure around each tree, mixed into the mulch, will repay you with bigger, better and tastier crops. Prune old lemon trees and spray with white oil against scale. Black citrus aphids will now be appearing, clustered thickly over all new growth. Pyrethrum is a safe, effective way of contact-killing these pests. Weed and grasses growing vigorously around fruit trees will effectively rob them of moisture and nutrients. While mulching will suppress this growth, Roundup will kill most weeds and liberate the trees. Wipe it on, but don't spray this herbicide. The danger of drift is too great, besides being wasteful.

This is a good time to install drip irrigation for fruit trees. The trees will be making demands as the fruit develops and the slow-release of water is ideally suited. Lemon or other citrus can be planted now. In cool districts choose a warm, sunny, protected and well-drained spot. Passionfruit vines too can go in, preferably on a warm wall. Chinese gooseberry plants can be given a second pruning if necessary, especially the male, after flowering. The female is usually pruned earlier and not as heavily. Some slight bleeding may occur but will soon dry up. Strawberries will be developing fast now, so apply plenty of well-diluted liquid fertilizer or compost 'tea' (made by mixing good compost with water, then straining off the pale brown liquid). Look beneath each plant for signs of grey mould and diseased leaves, removing all infected material. Add more clean straw as berries mature, but check for concealed slugs and snails.

Houseplants

Many houseplants can be propagated from cuttings at this time. Coarse sand and granulated peat make an excellent medium. Repotting or potting-on of badly rootbound houseplants is now taking place. Remember, many flowering houseplants such as *Saintpaulia* and hoya, will flower better once their roots have fully occupied the pots. Hanging baskets will be starting to dry out already. They are difficult to wet again should this occur and are best dunked into a brimming bucket of water, allowed to drain fully, then re-hung. Foliar feeding is an effective way of supplying nutrients to many houseplants, but care must be taken to use only very heavily diluted mixtures.

OCTOBER: FIRST WEEK

All About Pumpkins and Winter Squashes

What's the difference between a pumpkin and a winter squash? The answer is: very little. In fact many 'pumpkins' familiar to most of us are actually winter squash. The well-known butternut or even golden nugget are both winter squashes. I remember, a few years ago while in the United States, I asked the experts to tell me the difference. They scratched their heads and looked baffled for a moment. Then one of them held up his thumb and laughingly explained that the standard test was to try to stick one's thumbnail into the skin. It seems that if the nail can go in, it's a pumpkin, if not, it's a winter squash, but as far as growing them is concerned, there is no difference.

They love warmth, full sun and a rich, well-manured soil. Any kind of waterlogging or poor drainage is fatal. The best way to grow them is to work lots of animal manure or poultry litter into a wide area where they are to be grown. They have long, searching roots and many of the runners will also take root, thus increasing yield.

Sow the seed directly into the ground, where it will germinate rapidly at this time. It needs a soil temperature of at least 15°C, or the seed will remain dormant. This is why attempts to grow them early from seed germinated in containers often fail. In a cool potting-shed the temperature of the seed-sowing medium is usually much cooler than sun-warmed soil outside. I bring them on by using containers small enough to be placed on a sunny windowsill. If the seeds are sown into an open, free-draining mix which has been moistened, and warmed in the sun, then the lot placed completely inside a plastic bag in the sun, germination will take place rapidly. As soon as the seeds emerge, however, the plastic must be removed or the seedlings will become mouldy and die. So keep an eye on them, and plant some reserves in the open ground too.

The main needs of the growing plants are shelter and water, but don't overdo the latter in the early stages of growth, otherwise their roots will rot. As the season gets hotter, increase the amount of water to the soil around the plants. Liquid manure, well-diluted of course, is magnificent for all cucurbits, and should be applied every week. Mulching with old straw, well-mixed with animal manure and blood and bone, keeps the moisture in, smothers the weeds and feeds the soil simultaneously.

The first flowers to emerge are almost always male ones. The female blooms which bear the fruit are easily identifiable by a swelling just behind the petals. They appear on side-shoots as the main runners are extending. These important side-shoots can be encouraged by pinching out the growing tips of the runners when they are about two metres long.

Bees carry out the important job of pollination, but in cool or rainy weather, hand pollination may be necessary. Break off the male flower, pull back or remove the petals and rub the anthers on to the stigma of the female.

Once the pumpkins begin to swell, increase the rate of feeding and watering a little. Harvesting can take place as soon as the outer skin starts to toughen, depending upon the variety.

Here are some easily-grown pumpkins or winter squashes.

Golden Nugget. Small, grapefruit-sized fruit which start to bear about the end of January. Good flavour. If left to mature on the vine, it will keep for months.

Large Butter. Ready to eat by the end of February. Not a good keeper (three months) but of fair flavour.

Windsor Black. Dark green skin with a fair flavour. Poor keeper.

Supermarket. Winter squash of outstanding flavour, with bright orange, rather dry flesh. Dark green, almost black skin. Needs a pollinator. One of the best ever developed. Keeps over a year if harvested correctly.

Crown Prince. Another outstanding keeper with a good flavour.

Queensland Blue. One of the great, traditional long-keepers of excellent quality.

Butternut. Small, pear-shaped fruit with the seed cavity neatly out of the way at one end. Tasty, firm flesh. Fair keeper.

Buttercup. Another winter squash, but with very dry, sweet flesh. Popular for roasting or pumpkin pie. Reasonable keeper.

Royal Acorn. (Table Queen). Small, turnip-sized, well-flavoured fruit which mature early.

Green Warted Hubbard. Another outstanding winter-squash, dark, striped-green, with a hard, lumpy skin.

Harvesting pumpkins to ensure long keeping requires great care. Try to keep them on the vines as long as possible, but beware of frosts damaging the skins. I take the trouble to cover each pumpkin with dry straw as the first light frosts begin to strike. Finally, I harvest them by cutting the runner to which they are attached, so that there is at least a metre trailing from the fruit. Then they are grouped together in the open sun to harden off fully. Every night they are covered with bags for further frost protection. These are removed as early as is safe, every morning for at least two weeks, then the pumpkins are placed under cover, in an airy shed, making sure they are not touching. With long keepers, this will carry them through the next twelve months, provided their skins are not accidentally scratched, or their main stems snapped off.

How to Make Tomato Plants Yield Earlier and Better

I'm being terribly cruel to my tomatoes again. They are being deliberately starved and receive just enough water to keep them alive. They are only very small plants, some out in the garden protected by plastic bags, others have been potted-on into tumbler-sized containers and placed on a sunny windowsill inside the house. It's the best way I know to get them to produce early crops.

Sometimes in south-eastern Australia, there is more green-tomato chutney made than usual because an unusually cool summer delays ripening. Another reason for late fruiting is the molly-coddling of young plants before they have formed their first flower-truss.

If tomato plants are planted into a soil too rich in nitrogen, from the addition of blood and bone or animal manures, they quickly go to fat. They produce masses of leaves at the expense of flowers and fruit. When the tomatoes eventually appear, it is late in the season and they can remain green for many weeks.

Being tough on the young seedlings frightens them into flowering much earlier. They 'think' they are going to die, so they desperately try to reproduce themselves before they do so. It's the same with those growing in small containers. With just enough water to keep them upright and nothing but a tiny pinch of sulphate of potash, they should be allowed to become rootbound and, once this occurs, they start to flower. That's why so many flowering houseplants are more prolific when their roots completely fill the pots.

Once they start to flower, tomato plants will never go to fat, no matter how much they are fed and watered. All their energy goes into forming fruit, so the starvation regime must be ended. Weak, liquid fertilizer is best. It's easy to make while you are waiting. A drum of water into which a few bucketfuls of compost has been mixed, produces 'compost tea'. This is a pale-brown liquid which can be watered around tomato or other quick-growing plants, to supply most of their needs. If animal manure is also mixed into the drum, the resultant brew is much darker and stronger. This is broken down with water so that it looks like weak tea, before being fed to the soil around the plants.

Eggplants and capsicums can be treated the same way, although they prefer warmer conditions than tomatoes and are easier to bring into fruit. However, they all like warm soil and, unlike most other plants, are best left unmulched until the really warm weather arrives. If the soil has already been mulched, ready to receive these plants, it will remain too cool in many districts, causing the young plants to be seriously checked. It is better to rake aside the mulch, allow the soil to be warmed for a few days by the sun, then plant out the seedlings.

Later, when it is warm enough, the materials can be laid directly up to the stems of the plants. While most trees and shrubs develop mouldy bark with this treatment, tomatoes and other plants such as sweetcorn, cucumber or pumpkins obviously love it. They send additional feeding roots into the mulch, from higher up their stems. This ensures better yields from healthier plants.

The more vigorous tomato plants should be secured to stakes otherwise the weight of the trusses can drag them to the ground or even pull them apart. A loose loop of string just below the truss, but tightly secured to the stake, will take the weight. The smaller bush-type tomato plants can be left to flop around as they grow, especially if there is a thick mulch of old straw to keep the tomatoes clean.

Excessive pruning of tomato plants reduces yield. Strong-growing varieties such as Grosse Lisse, College Challenger, or Daydream can be restricted to four main stems by rubbing off side-shoots after the flower trusses form. Smaller bush-types, such as Rouge de Marmande (early-bearing, outstanding flavour), Burnley Gem, or the plum-sized bottler Roma, can all be left unpruned.

One reason why tomatoes are subjected to leaf removal is the mistaken belief that the fruit must be exposed to the sun to hasten ripening. This is not so. It is temperature which does the job, which is why fruit picked just as the first pink flush occurs at the base will ripen perfectly inside the house away from the windows. Strong sun and heat will certainly ripen the fruit, but the flavour will be destroyed.

Once tomato plants have started to grow and bear fruit, they must be watered consistently. If the soil is occasionally allowed to dry out around their roots, the tomatoes will develop a condition known as Blossom-end Rot. A roughly circular brown scab appears at the base of each fruit as the plant tries to compensate for lack of water, by reducing the demand from its fruit. This is why mulching is so valuable, sealing in the moisture while feeding the roots.

There is a surprising difference in flavour and keeping quality between the numerous varieties of tomato. Some look ugly but taste good, others have a superb smooth appearance and will keep for long periods after harvesting, but have little real flavour. Many of the smaller varieties are ideal for freezing whole, being picked directly into plastic bags to go into the freezer immediately. It is possible, even in a relatively small garden, to grow a number of different varieties of tomato in order to provide a wide range of uses.

Here are some of the most easily obtained types of tomato, all of which can be planted straight away.

Rouge de Marmande. The traditional, early-bearing field tomato, grown widely in Europe. Flat, heavily ridged fruit which grow on a low, sprawling bush. Don't be put off by the appearance, it's the flavour which counts and this lovely, well-tested tomato has the lot.

Red Cloud. Fortunately, public demand has made sure this outstanding tomato is still available. Mid to late season, the plant establishes quickly to form a low dense bush. The fruit are large, some weighing up to five hundred grams or more, with a deep red skin. The flesh is tasty and sweet, especially when ripened out of the sun. An outstanding, high-yieding plant with particularly heavy, fleshy fruit.

Grosse Lisse. The most popular tomato grown. Vigorous plant which requires several stakes to support the crop. Late bearer, which explains why people in cooler districts often miss out due to a failure to ripen fully before the frosts strike.

Jubilee. Yellow-skinned variety containing very few seeds. Usually preferred by those who suffer from heartburn, much of which is triggered off by the tough skin and indigestible seeds of tomatoes. The yellow varieties are considered to have more tender skins and this, with the reduced number of seeds, seems to make all the difference.

Yellow Pear. Developed over the last few years, this plant produces large clusters of tasty, bite-sized, soft-yellow fruit. It makes an attractive plant in its own right. The fruit freezes to perfection but, like all other tomatoes frozen whole, will break down rapidly when thawed.

Roma. This tomato is produced on a huge scale these days. It can be eaten raw, cooked or heat-treated to produce the familiar tomato paste, an essential part of Italian cooking. Fruit is the size of a small egg, well-coloured and prolific.

Tiny Tim. This low-growing plant bears large quantities of extra-sweet tomatoes which are about the size of a small plum. They are especially good whole in salads. The plant is popular grown in tubs on balconies or patios.

There are many other tomato varieties of course, but these are the ones for which the seedlings or seed are usually available.

For the average family of about four, a dozen mixed plants, grown organically to produce good healthy yields, will produce enough fruit to eat, give away or freeze. All they need is some early protection and a place in the sun.

A Vegetable Planting Guide for Nutritious Summer Eating

This is the greatest time of the year for planting vegetables.

What we plant within the next few weeks will supply us with all we require for the next seven or eight months, if we plan accordingly. Here are some of the most easily grown, common vegetables, with the best way to obtain the tastiest yields.

Carrots. They need an open, sunny, well-drained position, and soil which has been fertilized for a previous crop of another vegetable. It is a mistake to apply manure or fertilizer to the soil with carrot seed, because it causes the roots to fork. Mix the seed with some white sand and a little granulated peat. This will bulk it out so that it is distributed fairly sparsely, the sand will also clearly define where the seedlings will emerge so that weeding can take place more accurately. Varieties of carrot to sow are: Early Horn (clay soils), Topweight, Royal Chantenay, and Manchester Table.

Beetroot. Plant the seed about five centimetres apart in rows forty centimetres apart. Germination can be erratic but the thick sowing will overcome any problems. Be prepared to thin out to ten centimetres as soon as the seedlings are up. Varieties to grow are Derwent Globe, Detroit Dark Red and Cylindrica.

Broccoli. Sow the seed either directly into the garden or in containers for transplanting later. Go easy on the nitrogenous fertilizers and in good garden soil be content with a heavy mulch of old hay or straw. Excess fertilizer causes a massive amount of foliage growth and the development of the broccoli heads is very late.

Cabbage. Sow or plant in the same way as broccoli but a more generous amount of manure or fertilizer can be given. Soil which has been well limed the previous season will prove excellent. Varieties to try are: Succession, Stonehead and Supermarket.

Cauliflower. Sow seed as with cabbage, but water the newly planted seed with a weak solution of water and sodium molybdate, in order to overcome the problem of 'whiptail', which grossly distorts the leaves and reduces the size of the curd. Caulies can be fed heavily, using plenty of animal manure. Varieties are Phenomenal Early and Paleface. The richly purple Purplehead is particularly delicious, looking a little like broccoli.

Celery. This is one of the most useful of all vegetables, mainly because it is one of the few which is eaten raw. Many people fail with celery because they do not lime the soil enough. Heavy liming, with more water than any other plant, will work wonders with this vegetable. Remember, it is impossible to overwater celery. Sow seeds into containers for best results and good control, and transplant into the garden as soon as they are big enough to handle. Water at least twice daily during warm weather. Varieties to try are: Utah Tall, South Australian Giant, and the early-maturing Golden Self-blanching.

Never use steel pipes or star-pickets to support a young tree or rose bush. The metal transmits excessive heat directly to the roots on hot days, while lowering the soil temperature sharply during cold periods. This can stunt some plants. Always use a wooden stake, even if it has to be replaced every year.

Lettuce. Sow seed directly into the garden, and thin out after germination of seed, so that there is about fifteen centimetres between plants. Storing the seed in a refrigerator for a day or so prior to sowing will give better results, especially during hot weather. Varieties are: Mignonette (green or red), Greenmor (red), Pennlake, and Great Lakes. The lettuce Narromar seems to grow particularly well under cooler conditions, with tight, crisp heads.

Zucchini or Marrow. Plant into a rich well-manured soil in a sunny position. Blackjack and Greyzini are two very good types, and among the summer squashes, the delicious Green Buttons is worth growing.

Onions. Long-keeping types are best planted out as seedlings now if size is a consideration. Spring onions can be planted at almost any time during the year. Put lots of lime in the soil first, and, with the long keepers, very little high nitrogen fertilizer, or they will develop 'bullneck'.

Parsnips. These are grown like carrots. However, fresh seed must always be used, as old seed will often fail to germinate. The best variety for good keeping is Melbourne Whiteskin, which has large, solid roots.

Peas. Plant the seed five centimetres deep into soil which has been previously limed. A well-drained bed is essential, and plenty of organic matter in the soil will ensure heavy yields. If new ground is being opened up, apply superphosphate directly into the drill, next to the seed. Varieties are Melbourne Market, Greenfeast, and the trellis supported Telephone which grows over two metres tall.

Pumpkin and Winter Squash. These are basically the same and they are planted out and grown in the same way as zucchinis. Varieties are: pumpkins – Crown Prince, Henderson Late Grey and Jarrahdale; squash – Table Queen, Golden Nugget, and Butternut.

Sweetcorn. Plant seed in open sunny bed, five centimetres deep and thirty centimetres between them. Don't plant in long rows – it is better for pollination purposes if the plants are grown in blocks. They need large amounts of water during summer, especially after the cobs have started to form. Varieties are: Golden Cross, Miracle, Candy Sweet, Terrific and Supergold.

Tomatoes. Plant seeds or seedlings now, in good quality soil, without fertilizers or lime. Varieties: Burnley Gem, Roma, Rouge de Marmande, Grosse Lisse and the yellow-skinned Jubilee and Yellow Pear.

Silverbeet. Sow seeds into well-manured soil, two centimetres deep and twenty centimetres apart. Apply plenty of liquid fertilizer at regular intervals. Leave room for January plantings for winter and spring eating. Varieties include: Fordhook Giant and Rainbow Chard.

OCTOBER: SECOND WEEK

Dividing Dahlia Clumps

If you haven't planted out your dahlias yet, do so this week. There are few flowering plants which are more rewarding, or more forgiving when a period of neglect comes to an end. Tubers, planted now, will be thrusting their new leaves well above the ground within a month and will be starting to produce the first flowers around Christmas. From then onwards it is a non-stop display, well into May, with a range of colours and blooms which can only be described as breathtaking.

Dahlias thrive in southern Australia which is why, year after year, our specialist growers produce award-winning blooms, which leave the rest of the world for dead.

There are few plants easier to grow than dahlias. All they need is a sunny, well-drained position, plenty of water during the growing period and regular feeding with blood and bone or animal manures. There are many varieties now available from garden centres and nurseries, including lots of unnamed varieties. They all produce excellent displays of bloom and make outstanding cut flowers. However, it is better to choose a named variety as they are more reliable.

I prefer to grow dahlias in their own bed, if possible. They will grow well among trees and shrubs, provided they get plenty of sun, but sometimes the brilliance of their flowers can make adjoining plants appear slightly drab. That's why dahlias should never be grown among roses. They don't suit each other and appear uncomfortable in each other's company. A well laid out bed of dahlias, consisting of a balanced mixture of flower types, in full, glorious bloom, is an unforgettable sight.

There are many types of dahlia, some with enormous, brightly-coloured flower heads. They include the popular cactus types, with beautifully quilled petals; the large and medium decoratives, with overlapping, flat petals; the water-lily or nymphae types, some with delicately split petals and the pompones, with superb, golf-ball sized blooms.

Usually, when the leaves become blackened by the first frosts of winter, the entire clump is lifted and stored under cover.

Division can take place any time from mid-winter until planting time. Many of the tubers which have been under storage will have already started into leaf, especially if they have been buried in moist sand. If the tubers are left in the ground during the winter, many of the best ones will rot and be lost.

When dividing up the tight clumps of tubers, care must be taken to ensure that each separate tuber has at least one 'eye' or bud at the neck end. Many people unthinkingly snap off the tubers and plant them, hoping for good results. Such 'blinds' are quite useless, because they are unable to produce any growth. The actual division is carried out using a sharp knife or even strong kitchen shears. The dormant buds are situated in the hard, woody base of last year's main stems. This can be difficult to cut through, especially if it has been allowed to become excessively dry. Sharp secateurs also make an excellent tool for cutting away the divisions.

Once they have been separated, the tubers can be dusted with fine charcoal to help dry the moist cut surfaces. They are then ready for planting.

The soil should be slightly moist and have plenty of very old animal manure worked into the top twenty centimetres. Dig the planting hole about fifteen centimetres deep, loosen up the base a little, then place the tuber on its side at the bottom of the hole. Back-fill with good soil and drive a marker stake next to the hole. Make sure the stake is well clear of the tuber. Delay any watering until the first leaves appear above the ground. The distance apart can be anywhere between sixty centimetres and a metre, depending upon the expected size of the plant.

After the tops have appeared, the ground around the plants should be heavily mulched to prevent weed growth and drying out. Make sure that the name label is secured to the stake and not to the plant. From then onwards, it's a case of regular watering and generous surface applications of cow, sheep or horse manure.

It is difficult to go wrong with dahlias.

Delphiniums, Canterbury Bells and Chrysanthemums

One of the cheapest ways of establishing a good display of summer and autumn flowers is to purchase the small punnets of perennial or biennial plants now available at nurseries. The cost of ten seedlings is between one and two dollars, which is incredible value when you consider how rapidly these plants develop once they are planted out. Delphinium seedlings planted now will be in bloom by the end of January, with an amazing range of colours. They love lots of lime in the soil by the way, otherwise they will lack vigour.

Equally cheap but valuable are the seedlings of the biennial campanula we call Canterbury Bells or cup-and-saucer-plant. This year they will form a large, green rosette of leaves only, but next, will bloom themselves to death, after many weeks of total delight. They too love lime in the soil.

Carnations are now available as well-grown seedlings. Liking the same sweet soil as the delphiniums and campanulas, they rapidly take off, once they are liberated from their punnets. I believe in constantly stopping the leading shoots, preventing them from forming their first flowers. They keep producing more and more side-shoots in response to this treatment, eventually forming a tight, silvery bun, usually about half-way through February. They are allowed to flower and what a staggering display they produce. This 'stopping' treatment completely controls the plants, preventing them from flopping uselessly around and having to be propped up with sticks.

Chrysanthemums can be cut back or stopped several times during the growing season also so that they form compact clumps. Then they produce a mass of smallish flowers which are perfect for either a traffic-stopping garden display, or for cutting.

Dealing Ruthlessly with Pests

Some insects get blamed for destroying seedlings or other plants just because they happen to be around in considerable numbers. Slaters seem to multiply rapidly during spring, being found in great swarms under almost every rock or similar object lying on the surface of the ground. They can be found in half-decayed wood, in tree-stumps and hollows. Their main food is decayed organic matter such as half-rotten wood, straw or leaves. They will also eat young green tips of seedlings at certain times of the year, usually in early spring and will crowd into holes in fruit or tubers made by other pests, in order to feed off the decay, as it sets in. Birds and poultry will scratch to uncover them, gobbling them up as fast as they appear. Other forms of control include removing their hiding and breeding places near vulnerable plants. Flakes of naphthalene (mothballs) sprinkled around the places where they have been seen in large numbers will keep their numbers down.

One of the most destructive of all pests is codlin moth grub, which attacks apples, quinces and pears. The moths are now becoming active, laying their eggs upon or near the fruit. In a badly infested tree it is possible to see the quick movements of the moths, in the evening, as they dart around the branches.

The safest way of controlling grub attack is to spray the trees about now with white oil emulsion, diluted with fifty

> This is the best time to control the energy of excessively vigorous deciduous fruit and ornamental trees, by pruning. However, leave the maples, birches and walnut trees alone until March. They will bleed like stuck pigs if pruned now.

parts of water. This overlays the eggs, preventing them from hatching out. If this programme is carried out every three weeks, making sure that the mixture is no stronger than specified, excellent control can be achieved, especially with trees which have not received many previous poison sprays. In my own tiny orchard, I have about seventeen apple and pear trees, mixed among other fruits. Because they have never had poisons sprayed on them, they have built up a good population of predators against moths, and grubs are virtually non-existent. There are a few 'stings' or blemishes in the fruit, where entrance has been attempted, but they are the least of my worries.

The tendency these days is to spray at the time when the grubs are hatching, or about to do so. This is anytime during the early bulbing-out stage of the fruit, but can be measured by setting traps to find out when the moths are active.

These consist of jars or cans, suspended from the trees, in which a mixture of water, sugar or honey has been added – enough to cover the bottom. This will not reduce numbers, but will indicate when they are most numerous, through daily inspections. Spray with diluted white oil, then again a week later.

This is also the time to wrap a piece of sacking around the trunks of apple, pear and quince trees. It should be removed for inspection at least three times before it is finally taken off and burnt in late February or March. The worst thing you could do would be to forget and leave it on. This would cause a massive increase in codlin moth grubs, because they would have a nice, safe place to hide. Used carefully, the sacking-band method can sharply reduce the codlin moth population around a tree, but only in the years following the treatment.

Members of the cabbage tribe are now under the worst attack from caterpillars. The simple, safe and effective spray to deal with them is Dipel, a bacteria which only centres upon caterpillars and grubs.

The white cabbage butterfly caterpillar is well-known. Even one or two small ones are able to devastate a young plant, concentrating mainly on the outer leaves. The cabbage moth grub is not so widely recognized. It burrows deep into the heart of the plants, totally ruining them with droppings and frass. As they seem to attack plants which are growing in dry situations, a regular, deep watering can be a good, safe preventative.

Earwigs can do great damage, particularly to flowers and fruit if they are allowed to multiply. They feed at night, then seek a hiding place during the day. By providing somewhere easy for them to conceal themselves, such as a flower pot, upside down on a short stick, and lightly stuffed with crumpled newspaper, their numbers can be reduced effectively. Each morning, lift off the pots and tap them sharply against the rim of a bucket containing some kerosene and water. They will drop out into the mixture where a quick death will be awaiting.

The almost transparent, moth-like passionvine hopper has become very common over the last few years. It has a distinct wedge shape, clusters on the dark side of citrus and passionvines, and hops rapidly when disturbed. It will suck sap, weaken plants, and sometimes cause a sooty mould to develop. Treatment is by spraying with Clensel, a contact killer.

Greenhouse whiteflies have now become a troublesome pest in many parts of Australia. They cluster in their tens of thousands on the undersides of the foliage of beans, marrows, tomatoes, pumpkins, and fly up quickly in choking clouds when they are disturbed. Control is achieved by contact killers such as pyrethrum or Clensel. However, both these safe sprays will need to be applied several times at four day intervals as soon as these pests are first observed.

OCTOBER: THIRD WEEK

Germinating Difficult Seed

Some seeds are easily germinated, while others need a certain amount of knowledge and understanding, plus a few little tricks, before they can be induced to sprout.

The easiest of all are the seeds of radish, peas, beans, brassicas and flowering plants such as calendulas, nasturtiums, alyssum, sunflowers and amaranthus. These can be confidently broadcast or sown in rows, with the sure knowledge that they will all be up and growing in a matter of a week or so.

But what about the more difficult ones? There is a vast range of ornamental plants in particular, the seeds of which require special conditions before they will germinate. The seeds of a number of vegetables also appear to get the sulks for no apparent reason.

The best way to find out how to germinate difficult seeds is to find out where the species originated. In other words, understanding those conditions in which the plants exist naturally, gives a fair guide to the best conditions for germination.

For example, silver birch trees come from the colder parts of the northern hemisphere. They are subjected to intense cold during winter, even though the seeds are virtually ripe during autumn. If the seed germinates at the start of winter, the tiny seedlings would be wiped out within a matter of weeks by the freezing conditions. So each silver birch seed contains a locking system which prevents it from germinating, unless it has been through a winter. The act of freezing actually unlocks it, so that by spring, when the thaw sets in, it can safely germinate.

Our winters are mild enough for a young seedling birch to withstand the cold. However, if we collect the seed from the trees at the start of winter, then apply freezing cold, it will germinate within two or three weeks of sowing. The method is no more than mixing the fresh seed with moist sand and peat, then placing it into the refrigerator for a couple of months. Then sow the seed and up come the seedlings like grass.

Lettuce seed can also be difficult at some times of the year, when it has been stored in a warm place or during warm weather. The reason is that the original wild lettuce came from the Mediterranean area, experiencing moist springs and hot, dry summers. Seed germinated just before the dry period would not survive, so the seed contains an automatic locking device which operates when the temperature rises. That's why, from now onwards, it is a good idea to place a packet of lettuce seed in the refrigerator for a couple of days prior to sowing, to ensure good, even germination by countering the effects of high temperatures.

Some types of seed have a hard, waxy coat, making them impervious to moisture. Many legumes such as lupins, brooms, wattles or sophoras are in this category. They eventually germinate, but erratically, with some remaining dormant for years. Many farmers will have experienced an unexpected sprouting of wattle seedlings from a newly-cultivated paddock which has been under pasture for decades. Sweetpea seed too can develop a hard coat, making germination erratic.

Wattle seed can be treated to soften the outer coat by pouring very hot water over it, then leaving it soaking in the water overnight. Defective seed will float to the surface and can be removed easily. The remainder will swell slightly and should be sown immediately. They will germinate rapidly and evenly.

Lupin, broom or sophora can be dealt with by rubbing with sand-paper, to take the shine off the surface, or at least cause tiny grooves to be formed in the outer layer. This will enable soil organisms to break it down quickly, allowing water to penetrate and germination to start.

One of the most complex and difficult of all seeds is that of the tree paeony (*Paeonia suffruticosa*). This is a major cause of these plants being so scarce and expensive. The seeds are like tiny beans, but when sown, send down a root first. The shoot will remain dormant unless the rooted seed is kept under very cool conditions for two or three months. In practice, this involves transplanting the rooted seed into containers, which are placed into a cool room with a temperature of about 6°C, then placing them into warm conditions for the completion of germination.

Many years ago, I planted some tree paeony seed. Finally, when nothing appeared to have happened during the next year, I threw them out. I then noticed that each seed had formed a single, powerful root. Had I known then what to do, I would have been able to produce a number of plants.

Irrespective of how the seed is treated to ensure good germination, it is of little value unless the medium in which it is sown is suitable. Garden soil isn't good enough, because it tends to collapse and set hard, and it also contains many harmful organisms and weed seeds. Good, balanced seed-raising mixes can be obtained from garden centres, either of a soil free compost, or one which has been pasteurized to kill certain organisms. When mixing my own, I use a third each of coarse sand, granulated peat and good-quality bush soil, the latter being much cleaner than garden soil. All seed should be sown either on the surface and gently pressed in or placed at twice their own depth, in the case of larger ones. Then the containers should be covered with a sheet of glass or plastic and placed out of the sun to germinate. Once this has occurred, the cover must be lifted and brighter light gradually given.

The Joys of Sweetcorn

One of the great delights of having a good vegetable garden, is to be able to wander out and pull off a few succulent cobs of sweetcorn for immediate cooking and eating.

Seed planted this week will germinate rapidly into plants which will be carrying their ripe cobs about March. Good reliable varieties include Supergold, Iochief and Golden Cross Bantam. There are also a number of supersweet types with names like Honey Sweet and Candy Sweet. The only problem with these is poor germination due to lack of starch in the seeds and extra close planting is needed to allow for this.

The secret of success with sweetcorn is well fertilized, moist soil right from the start. Fowl manure is particularly valuable, but any kind of animal manure or blood and bone will produce vigorous growth and well-filled cobs. Once the ground around the growing plants has been deeply watered and fertilized, thick wads of newspaper, overlaid with old straw, seaweed, sawdust or wilted weeds, mixed with grass clippings, can be laid thickly up to the stalks. Sweetcorn plants develop masses of thick aerial roots just above the surface of the soil, and they soon feed off the mulch, usually when the cobs are forming.

> Use weak solutions of seaweed concentrate when germinating seed. It adds trace elements at a crucial time in their growth. However, with large seed, such as that of sweetcorn, pumpkin and beans, avoid using the concentrate, because it may retard germination.

Heavy watering is essential at this stage, and as soon as the silk has started to wither and go brown, the husk can be gently parted, and the plump kernels pricked. A sweet, milky fluid indicates a ripe cob, and that's where the rewards begin. If you have the pan of water already boiling, you can't possibly go wrong.

Putting New Life into Sandy Soils

Difficult soils are those which are very sandy, or heavy, sticky clay. Sandy soils have the advantages of being easy to work and warming up more rapidly at the end of winter. But the disadvantages can be enormous. They dry out rapidly and, because the large soil particles allow moisture to pass through rapidly, they quickly become leached of most soluble minerals.

Most sandy soils will, if not corrected, become deficient in such essential minerals as nitrogen, iron, potassium and magnesium. In many parts of Australia, calcium too is an important deficiency.

The special problems associated with sandy soils also include a sharp fluctuation in temperature during hot days and cool nights. Plants trying to grow in these conditions often fail to thrive and are easily subjected to attacks from pests and diseases. In addition, when sandy soil becomes wet, it tends to form a collapsed, lifeless pad near the surface.

Sandy soils, in spite of the ease with which they can be worked, are much more difficult to manage than sticky, clay soils but they can be made extremely fertile, especially in the home garden.

The big problem is lack of clay, and the effect of adding this can be remarkable. The only sensible way to add clay to sand is in liquid form. A bucketful of heavy clay will go a long way in a sandy vegetable garden. Place it into a large container and add enough water to break the clods down to a kind of sloppy gruel. Then water this mixture around the plants. This will not only strengthen the sandy soil but give it a valuable water-holding capacity. If this is done regularly, the quality of the soil will be completely transformed and its productivity increased markedly.

Apart from an initial cultivation to remove weeds and break up the surface, sandy soil should not be dug or turned over. Instead, it is better to apply large quantities of mulching materials to the surface and allow the soil organisms and earthworms to break it down and incorporate into the top twenty centimetres. Digging is of little value to such soils, because they are already fairly loose and open. See pages 75 and 196 for more advice on mulching.

When digging is eliminated altogether and the main means of feeding the soil is by enriched mulching or 'sheet-composting' as it is called, many people become puzzled about sowing and planting methods. After all, when the surface of the soil is covered with a thick, spongy layer of half-decayed straw, where can the plants and the seeds go?

It is quite a simple matter to push aside the mulch to expose the bare soil at the planting zones, in order to place seedlings directly into it. With seed, it is slightly different. If they were mistakenly sown into the mulch most would die. The answer is to rake aside the mulch to leave a long, narrow valley of exposed earth, into which the seed is sown in the normal way. Later, as germination takes place and the seedlings begin to grow, they are protected and fed from the adjoining mulch, which tends to drift in over the weeks and months. If the straw is clean or is pea or bean haulm, there are few problems with weed seeds. However, old, spoilt hay will contain numerous grass seeds and these must be pulled as soon as they have germinated.

When straw or haulm is unavailable, other organic materials will do just as well. Pulverized sugarcane waste, sawdust, finely-shredded bark, bracken-fern or even buzzer-chips are all excellent, provided they can be mixed with other materials. This helps to avoid the formation of a wet, airless pad over the surface.

Above all, resist the temptation to dig the mulch into the ground. Sandy soils will not improve by this treatment, unlike heavy clay, which does.

OCTOBER: LAST WEEK

Beware of these Toxic Plants

Fortunately, those ornamental plants or weeds which are poisonous have a taste which is so revolting or bitter that the chances of anyone accidentally eating parts of them are fairly remote.

However, some plants can cause problems by means of toxic sap which, if smeared on the skin or, worse still, contacting the eyes, can cause all sorts of troubles. Children, especially little ones, are most vulnerable to some of these very common but toxic plants, because they are inclined to either taste leaves or berries, or rub sap upon themselves.

Here are some plants which should be treated with caution.

Nile lily (*Agapanthus oriental*). A popular herbaceous plant with long, fleshy leaves and roots and blue or white flowers on long, lush stems. Anyone innocent or naïve enough to bite the leaves, stems or roots will quickly develop a badly ulcerated mouth. The well-known belladonna lily (*Amaryllis belladonna*) has large bulbs which contain highly alkaline substances, which, if taken in quantity, will seriously affect the heart, sometimes fatally. Daffodils and jonquils may look glorious during early spring, but don't nibble the bulbs, no matter how hungry you feel. If you do, you can quickly suffer convulsions, diarrhoea and vomiting.

Among the most beautiful of all houseplants are the dieffenbachias. They don't call them Dumb Plants for nothing. If you make the blunder of chewing any part you will be unable to speak for about a week. Your tongue will swell, your lips will be bloated and, to add to your misery and humiliation, you will be continuously dribbling down your chin. So watch it!

Lily of the valley is one of the most prized flowering plants, with fragrant sprays of white, drooping bells in spring. But, all parts are toxic, causing vomiting, violent headaches and even heart failure.

Arum lilies are often associated with funerals. Lovely white flowers with soft yellow, central spikes. Beautiful but deadly to eat. They can cause death from shock and exhaustion through purging.

Euphorbias are popular house or garden plants. The well-known poinsettia (*E. pulcherrima*), is sold in tens of thousands at the start of winter, all over the world. But the white, milky sap can cause skin problems and, if rubbed into the eyes, can cause blindness and terrible pain. If any parts are consumed, delerium, vomiting, diarrhoea and even death can result.

The much-planted herb tansy can also be a bit of a weed, if it is allowed to run rampant. Some people make a type of drink from the leaves, which is fine, provided it isn't overdone. Too much will give you belly-ache, convulsions, nausea and dilated pupils. So don't slurp too much.

At one time there was a minor trend among some silly people to get stuck into the old Angel's Trumpets (*Datura* spp.). It was smoked, sucked or munched. The result, at certain times of the year, was massive thirst, irritability, incoherence and dilation of pupils, followed by hallucinations, exhaustion or even death. Stop it, or you'll go barmy.

The name of the castor oil plant speaks for itself. The seeds have an appalling effect. You'll never stop running, except to vomit as well. Also, when you do stop, your muscles will be rigid with agonizing cramps before you start to develop a blue tint to your skin. Even the lovely golden chain tree (*Laburnum anagyroides*) has its sinister side. Every part – seed, roots, leaves and bark are so toxic, that you don't even have to start chewing. Just placing a bit in the mouth is enough to cause convulsions, vomiting, muscular weakness and sometimes death from asphyxia. So admire, but don't eat or even taste.

Rhubarb (that's right) can be a problem, but only the leaves. Go easy on the stems too, but it takes a lot. The leaves can actually be boiled, strained and the liquid used as an effective killer of aphids and other insects.

Everyone loves oleanders with their brilliant pink or white flowers. Well, every part is very toxic indeed. In fact, you can't even use the wood in the barbecue, because even the smoke is poisonous. The sap will cause all sorts of skin problems, so if you decide to get rid of yours, handle with care and don't get the sawdust in your eyes.

The beautiful clusters of black, glistening berries of the common privet, once so popular as a hedge plant, are very poisonous. I once saw two horses die in agony, after feeding over a fence from a long-neglected hedge. So you can imagine the effects upon humans. The berries and other parts of English ivy are also very nasty indeed. The sap causes dermatitis, while if any parts are eaten, the result is diarrhoea, nervous excitement, paralysis, difficulty in breathing, with convulsions thrown in for good measure.

The pods and seeds of wisteria look vaguely like beans, but don't ever be tempted to try them out. You'll be bellyaching for days, while you are vomiting and running frantically back and forth from the loo. You'll never try them again and, if you eat a lot of them, you'll never be able to.

So, have a nice day in the garden. Relax and enjoy yourself. But, if you feel a bit peckish, concentrate on the vegetable patch, you'll be much safer.

Bush and Climbing Beans

The reason why bush and climbing beans are not usually sown until about now, is that they are both lovers of well-warmed soil. While they will germinate rapidly if planted as early as August or September, they will have a miserable yield, compared with seed sown into warm soil. Too often, large areas of vegetable garden space are taken up by these early-sown, non-productive plants.

Seed sown this week, with additional plantings every three weeks until January, will carry enormous crops, with enough to eat, give away or freeze for excellent eating throughout the rest of the year. Once they begin to produce succulent pods, the only strict rule is to keep on picking as fast as they come.

Beans dislike acid soil, so an area which has previously been limed is an advantage. Otherwise dolomite or limestone can be added now, at the rate of a handful for each square metre. Blood and bone is an outstanding fertilizer for beans, because its slow-release qualities suit the way these plants grow and carry their

> If making a new lawn, never make the mistake of including clover with the grass seed. Once it starts to flower, even in a closely-mown lawn, the bees arrive in their thousands and barefoot children are the main victims of stings.

pods. A heaped handful for every square metre will not go amiss and can be raked in immediately.

The best climbing beans for flavour and freezing are the well-known Scarlet Runners. There are many varieties of these, some with extremely long, straight pods. All have thick, seemingly coarse pods, but don't be fooled by this. They are tender and crisp (as long as they are picked young), thrive in cool climates and make an attractive garden plant with their bright red flowers. They need a lattice or similar means of support and, when winter comes and they start to die back, they can be cut to the ground, from where they will re-shoot next spring. A good means of support, if there is no suitable fence, is a cone-shaped cluster of strong garden stakes, each about two metres long. Some people restrict the number of stakes to four, tie them at the top, and form a traditional pyramid. Other good varieties of climbing bean include Blue Lake with tasty pods of small white beans and Purple King which are a brilliant purple until they are cooked, when they change to a normal green colour.

Bush beans take up more space than the climbers, but their yields can be enormous under the right conditions. When closely planted in rows only one third of a metre apart, they eventually merge together to form an excellent weed suppressor, while giving mutual support against the wind. The seed is sown about three centimetres deep, ten centimetres apart and watered immediately.

One of the best producers is still the good old Brown Beauty with its heavy crops of succulent, straight pods. Other well-tested varieties include Pioneer and Hawkesbury Wonder. All these haricot-type beans will be suitable for drying later on, for use during winter in soups, stews or other dishes. A popular variety for drying is the well-flavoured Barlotti, which bears exceptionally well. This too can be eaten as young pods. All the

Bean Supports

green-podded bush beans will freeze quite well, but the yellow-podded varieties are not so good for this purpose, often becoming limp and tasteless. Eaten fresh however, they are hard to beat, with Golden Wax or Majestic having outstanding flavour.

Once the pods begin to appear, constant picking is essential, even if they cannot be eaten immediately. It is better to pick and discard, than to allow the beans to mature and become coarse. Once this occurs, the bushes will stop producing.

Their main needs during growth are regular watering, side dressing with blood and bone and, as they begin to carry heavy loads of pods, support, by hilling the soil around their stems.

Delphiniums, foxgloves and other perennials thrive in cool climates.

Wintersweet *(Chimonanthus praecox)*

Wall-planting of fleabane *(Erigeron speciosus)*. Flowers for most of spring and summer.

Carnation pruned to a bun.

Companion planting. From left to right: potato onions, carrots, brown onions.

Green manure crop of ryecorn and tickbeans ready to be dug into soil in order to enrich it.

Calcium deficiency in European plum leaves. Heavy dressing of dolomite limestone needed.

Rose leaves affected by Black Spot disease. Overhead watering is a major cause of spreading the disease.

Tomatoes with Blossom-end Rot. The main cause is inconsistent watering, which allows plants to experience water-shortage.

Pear and cherry slug, grazing on leaf surface. Early sprays with pyrethrum give control.

Close-up of soft brown scale on a lemon leaf. White oil gives control.

Woolly aphids cover themselves with a protective white, fluffy material. Winter oil assists control, especially if applied in late winter.

November

GUIDE TO ACTION

Ornamental Garden

Many ornamental plants will have finished blooming by this time. Acacias, banksias, mint-bushes, thryptomenes, boronias and hakeas are some Australian plants which can be pruned now to give a bushier, more wind-resistant shape. Many exotic plants can also be either lightly pruned or have spent flowers removed. The entire ornamental garden should be given a good sprinkling of blood and bone with ten per cent added potash, but always water first, then again after the fertilizer has been distributed. Lawns can still be sown, but in districts with dry summers it means non-stop watering every day for months. Flatweeds can be controlled by using lawn sand, but if there are only a relatively small number of weeds, a pinch of sulphate of ammonia on each weed will soon destroy them. If the dahlia clumps have not yet been divided and replanted, it is urgent that this job be carried out now. Azaleas, rhododendrons, camellias, pierises and ericas have shallow, compact root systems. They dry out easily. However, if they are deeply watered and the ground around them mulched heavily with sawdust, decayed straw or spoilt hay, moisture loss through evaporation will be stemmed. Annuals and other bedding plants to go in now include: achillea, ageratum, alyssum, ammobium, anchusa, amaranthus, antirrhinum, aquilegia, arabis, arctotis, aster, aubrieta, balsam, bedding begonia, bellis, calceolaria, campanula, carnation, celosia,

cornflower, centaurea, chrysanthemum, clarkia, cleome, cosmos, dahlia, delphinium, dianthus, eschscholtzia, gazania, gaillardia, geranium, gerbera, geum, godetia, gypsophila, helichrysum, heliotrope, helipterum, hollyhock, impatiens, kochia, larkspur, Livingstone daisy, lobelia, lupin, lunaria, African marigold, mignonette, mimulus, moluccella, myosotis, nasturtium, nemophila, nigella, pansy, penstemon, petunia, phlox, platycodon, oriental poppy, portulaca, pyrethrum, rudbeckia, salpiglossis, salvia, sanvitalia, scabiosa, schizanthus, statice, stock, thunbergia, sunflower, torenia, tritoma, verbena, vinca, viscaria and zinnia.

Vegetable Garden

Even in cool districts, French beans can now be safely sown. Eggplants and capsicums can be planted as seedlings but in cool districts they are better in containers for a week or so. Under glass they will grow quickly but like tomatoes they will come into flower more quickly if they are allowed to become slightly rootbound.

Here are some of the vegetables which can be sown or planted now: asparagus, asparagus pea, French beans, beetroot, broccoli, Brussel sprouts (seed), cabbage, Chinese cabbage, Chinese greens, capsicum, carrot, cauliflower, celery, chicory, corn salad, cress, cucumber, eggplant, endive, kohlrabi, leek, lettuce, marrow, okra (warm districts), onions (seedlings, apart from spring onions), parsley, parsnip, peas (cool districts only), pumpkin, radish, rhubarb (seed only), salsify, scorzonera, spinach (cool districts only), New Zealand spinach, swede, sweetcorn, winter squash, tampala, tomato, turnip and zucchini. In addition, most herbs, either as seed or plants can also go in this month. Existing crops need some maintenance and feeding. Broad bean plants will be top-heavy with pods and will need supporting. Peas will double their yield if the plants are allowed to climb supports. Potatoes need to have soil drawn up around the foliage to reduce grub strike and increase yields. Lettuce will be crisp and sweet if it is grown quickly, using plenty of liquid manure. Cauliflowers, cabbage and broccoli need plenty of water and love being mulched. Celery cannot be over-watered. Climbing beans require deep watering and must be constantly secured to trellis. Carrots sown before winter will be bolting now but can still be kept edible for an extra two weeks by slicing off all their leaves while they are still in the ground. Young carrots, sown during August or September, will be ready to thin and eat. Weed control between the rows is essential, so regular hoeing is needed to expose their roots to sun and wind. Easier still, try mulching directly over weeds. All vegetables benefit from a weak spraying of seaweed concentrate but larger seeds such as sweetcorn or beans can be retarded if they are allowed to absorb this substance when they are sown.

Fruit Garden

Berryfruit plants are demanding plenty of water now. Raspberry plants may be showing signs of raspberry leaf rust – bright orange spots all over the foliage. Although yield is only slightly reduced by this disease, it can be controlled by Zineb and hygiene. Winter removal of all old canes and debris is a safe, effective means of control. Bordeaux mixture at budburst is a good preventative treatment with susceptible varieties such as Lloyd George or Neika. Apple and pear trees are under attack from codlin moth grub, so keep up with the well-diluted white oil sprays to prevent eggs hatching. Over-vigorous trees can be pruned now for effective control and all trees can have unnecessary, inward-growing wood removed.

Houseplants

It should be warm enough this month to give these plants a tonic, by placing them outside, out of the wind and sun, whenever it rains. The rain has a marvellously cleansing effect. However, remember how fragile many of these plants are. Extra-heavy rain or unexpected gusts of wind will flatten them, so keep an eye on the weather. Never leave them in full sun if they have been accustomed to reflected light only.

Start to increase the rate of watering and feeding. Do it gently and if surplus water starts to collect in the saucer at the base of a pot, keep pouring it off until it stops seeping from the drainage holes. Keep a few cotton buds handy, to be soaked in methylated spirit for dabbing on mealy bugs. Groom away all discoloured and withered leaves and try to keep the surface of the potting soil clear of debris. Ferns and palms need to be sprayed with room-temperature water several times daily in hot, dry districts, or they will suffer.

Cacti, succulents, kalanchoe, hippeastrum and pelargonium houseplants can withstand plenty of direct sunlight, but most of the others need to be kept clear of hot windowsills. *Saintpaulias* and other flowering plants like plenty of good light and will bloom prolifically in a south-facing window, provided they are also allowed to become a little rootbound.

NOVEMBER: FIRST WEEK

Why Remove Spent Flower Heads?

Roses and rhododendrons seem to be affected by early heat much more than other plants. Within a few days of blooming, many flowers completely blow or wither, before we have a chance to really enjoy them. The most important task right now in the flower garden is to prevent the main energy of the plants from being wasted in seed formation.

Dead-heading is essential, because if it isn't carried out, the plants will have much less strength to form the next lot of flowers. With rhododendrons this will not occur for twelve months, but if the withered trusses are not snapped off, before the formation of seed-capsules, there will be many less blooms next year.

Roses, particularly hybrid tea and floribunda types, will produce another flush of bloom during January, with a final flush during April. If the 'heps' or seed-pods are allowed to form, there will be either no more flowers or they will be inferior ones in the coming months. The act of snapping off the dead blooms is enough but if the stems are also pruned back to the next healthy leaf-junction, the next lot of blooms will be quite good. However, the January flush of roses rarely lasts as long as the first one, because of the heat. That's why many rose growers actually prune away all the blooms which are developing at that time, in order to obtain a much better show of longer-lasting flowers during April, when it is cool enough to prevent early blowing.

Apart from dead-heading, the most significant task right now is feeding and watering. Very dry soil will repel water, so the aim is to make sure this condition does not occur. The biggest mistake is watering too lightly. This means that any moisture penetrates only a few centimetres below the surface and the roots of the plants tend to come up for it, making them particularly vulnerable to the coming dry.

Watering Techniques

There's a gentle art to correctly watering a garden. More water is wasted as a result of careless use in the garden than anywhere else. If the water is applied at the wrong time of the day, it can be lost in a matter of a few hours, simply by evaporation. If the wrong amount is given, the plants can be seriously weakened and made vulnerable to drought conditions.

All parts of the garden begin to need water rather desperately from now on. Once the soil has been allowed to dry out, it has a tendency to resist being brought back into a moist state again, because it becomes water repellent. Whether you live on a flat site or a slope will make all the difference in the world to how water is best applied, and for how long at a time.

In times of water shortage, some parts of the garden can be sacrificed by virtually ignoring them, knowing that recovery is inevitable. Lawns for example: how many people were staring at their brown, withered grass last February or March, with a sense of great hopelessness, only to be cursing its relentless growth during the last couple of months?

Lawns can be helped to conserve the water sprinkled upon them by leaving more length when mowing. This shades the roots from the sun's heat as well as from the drying effects of winds. When water is applied to a thickly-grassed area, it goes straight down between the blades of grass and soaks into the soil. Even if the land is sloping, the grass will prevent wasteful run-off. Should you make the mistake of shaving the surface of the ground with your mower, it will not only dry out quickly, but a hard, water-repellent crust will form. This makes watering, especially on a slope, almost impossible.

Any kind of sprinkler can be used for watering a lawn area, although one which can cover a large area, without being constantly moved, is the best.

The most effective way of applying water to a lawn which is on a slope or has shown signs of becoming dry, is in short bursts of about five minutes at a time. This eliminates run-off, which not only causes unnecessary waste, but actually harms the surface of the lawn. When water starts to run over such a surface it fails to penetrate. Instead, the water washes away the topsoil around the grass plants, leaving an uneven and unsightly surface.

The most important parts of the garden, when it comes to priority for water, are the vegetable garden and those parts of the ornamental garden containing plants with fairly shallow roots. Young trees, especially those which were planted a few months ago, also need deep watering from now on.

The vegetable garden must be watered daily, unless it rains fairly heavily. Light rain does nothing more than settle the dust and even a solid downpour for a couple of hours will not penetrate very far into the surface. One of the most effective means of watering a vegetable garden is by using a perforated soaker-hose. They give enormous coverage and in large vegetable gardens can be joined together to extend them more than thirty metres. With reasonable water pressure, soaker-hoses will have a wetting width of over four metres. However, they cannot easily be bent around corners without a loss of direction. Cutting them in two, to connect a short length of standard hose between the two halves, will allow them to be bent double for watering short rows.

In the ornamental garden, the use of drip irrigation can be of great value, with considerable savings in water and time. Young trees and plants such as roses, rhododendrons, camellias, citrus, daphne and others which may be vulnerable to dry soil conditions, benefit enormously from a drip system. Although they have extensive roots, roses seem to thrive with this method of watering, because the chances of the disease black spot are greatly reduced.

Recently, the extended use of drip irrigation in areas growing native plants seems to have become fashionable. Unfortunately, the continued use after the first couple of seasons seems to cause problems with those plants which often prefer to avoid wet soils during summer. As a result, many attempts at landscaping using mainly Australian plants have partly failed, especially when large quantities of saturated wood-chips remain around these plants.

Many drip systems include tiny sprinklers on miniature standards. These are excellent for watering perennial herbaceous borders but are of little value with larger plants. The button-type outlet is excellent.

The only problem with drip-irrigation is on very sandy soils. Apparently, the drainage is so sharp, the moisture goes straight down in a kind of column without spreading and adjacent trees or shrubs don't get much. One answer is a plastic sheet, perforated with holes, underneath the drip outlet. If it is fairly level, the water is dispersed over a much wider area.

Watering the garden by means of hand-holding a sprinkler is good for young seedlings or other plants but for an established shrub and tree garden it is worse than useless, unless you are willing to stand in one spot for long periods. Shallow watering usually occurs, causing the roots of many plants to come upwards to where the moist soil is. This makes them particularly vulnerable to drought conditions and is a major cause of death to many plants, which would have otherwise survived a dry spell.

Generally, if there is a basic rule of watering, it is this: it is much better to water occasionally but deeply, rather than often and lightly.

Landscaping with Stone Walls

There is no shortage of rocks in Australia. They lie around all over the place. The difficult part of obtaining them is having to cart them home. Most of our rock is dolerite. It is heavy and hard. We call it bluestone and it forms more supporting walls, house foundations and, in the case of bluemetal screenings, more road surfaces than any other stone. Sandstone is much lighter and warmer.

Retaining-walls made from irregularly-shaped pieces of rock can be very attractive. They can cost a fortune to have constructed, because the process of building them is so slow. They can either be in the form of a dry-wall, in which the rocks are carefully matched to fit next to each other without the use of concrete or mortar, or bonded together with these materials. Oddly enough, the dry-wall lasts much longer than a mortar and stone one, and the evidence for this can be seen in some of the ancient walls of Europe, South America or China. There are some excellent dry-stone walls in Australia, many of them created by convict labour using rocks and stones salvaged from adjacent farmland.

The secret of dry-wall construction is in the angle of the face. With uneven, oddly-shaped rocks it is virtually impossible to retain a vertical structure. This is only achievable when mortar is used. Dry-walls are inclined inwards towards the top, and in cases when they are used to shore up a bank or create terraces, this gives them great strength.

The first job when making a retaining dry-wall, is to dig a shallow trench for the base, throwing the soil or clay uphill.

> It is better to overcrowd large containers or hanging baskets with several plants or ferns, rather than have a small plant trying to occupy a large amount of soil.

An angle of about 50° is best

Stone Wall Construction

Next, a row of large rocks, placed next to each other in the trench so that the flattest sides are in line, angled back a little. This is accomplished by ramming soil or clay underneath and around them to make them sit correctly. From then on, it is simply a case of adding to that first layer using more rocks, then backfilling and ramming as the new wall gains height.

It is a mistake to try to select rocks to fit each gap. This makes the building process tedious, while leaving a pile of rejected, almost unusable rocks at the end. Every rock should be picked up as it comes and turned around until it fits. As long as the flattest sides are to the front and a slight tilt into the slope is maintained, the wall will remain firm and secure.

It is possible to build such a wall at high speed if the rocks are handy and if there is a good stockpile of loose soil up the slope. Small rocks can be used for 'chinking', or filling-in the vertical gaps between the larger stones. However, it is not a good idea to use these smaller pieces to wedge underneath larger ones because it makes them unstable. It is always best to use soil, firmly tamped, preferably free of invasive, perennial weeds.

Because a dry-wall is inclined backwards, all rain which falls upon it will run into the crevices, which, because they contain soil, can be furnished with a wide range of plants. In fact it is better to plant some of these as construction is taking place, especially those with a substantial root-system. The advantages of having a planted wall-face are many. For a start, if nothing was planted, the weeds would move in quickly. The presence of a variety of dense, creeping plants, inserted into as many chinks and crevices as possible, deters weed infestation. Other advantages include a softening of angular rocks, a more secure wall and, above all, an extremely attractive piece of landscaping.

The plants used in such walls as this have to be fairly drought-resistant, although once they have established a root-system which has penetrated deep into the soil mixture behind the wall, most creeping plants can survive with minimal watering. Here are some of the most attractive and useful plants for these places:

Daisy of the Veldt. *Dimorphoceca*. With hundreds of white or purple daisies, they will rapidly cover a large area, flowering all the year round, even in the coldest areas in Australia. All they need is a place in the sun.

African Daisy. *Arctotis*. Very common, easily grown semi-creeper, with attractive violet, pink or occasionally orange flowers.

Sun Rose. *Helianthemum*. This is not a rose of course, but a valuable small plant producing dozens of tiny, rose-like flowers. They can be double or single, and the range of colours is astonishing. Easily grown, it thrives in a wall, forming a dense tuft if it is occasionally cut-back hard. Propagation is by division or cuttings.

Convolvulus maritima is related to the awful bindweed, but is not invasive and is very pretty. With masses of lilac-blue flowers, it makes a superb display when grown in a well-drained, sunny crevice.

Helychrysum retortum is a prostrate everlasting-daisy which is very much at home flopping down the face of a rock wall. When the hundreds of colourful daisies have finished blooming, the silver-grey leaves have a special beauty of their own.

When cement or mortar is used in the construction of a rock-wall, care must be taken to mix it carefully and correctly. A major problem has always been caused by badly made mortar shrinking away from the rocks. Unlike a dry-stone wall, where the weight and angle of the materials are its security, the mortar-bonded one is largely supported by the mortar itself. This is why they don't last as long.

A rock and mortar wall can also be used as a vertical garden. During the building process, cavities can be left here and there in the face, which go through to the soil behind it. If a 'sill' is created at the base of these holes, drooping plants will hang over them to cascade down the wall.

Solid walls which are used to retain banks must have a good drainage system inserted. Subsoil drainage pipes enclosed inside bluemetal screenings, running along the bottom of the inside of the wall, will prevent moisture build-up which could easily crack the face. If large amounts of clay are present, it will swell when wet, placing enormous pressure on the wall.

So, if you are quietly cursing the large number of rocks in your garden, why not put them to use?

NOVEMBER: SECOND WEEK

A Blaze of Summer Colour with Annuals

In their relatively short lives, the colourful and occasionally dazzling display produced by annual plants can be astonishing. They pass through every stage of growth, from seed to seed, in one season and most of that time are in full bloom.

There are few plants more adaptable and rewarding than annuals which, once established, require very little care and attention. Many have a sweet, garden-filling fragrance, while others make excellent, long-lasting cut flowers.

They can be used to fill gaps between existing trees and shrubs, or planted out in a bed of their own. One of the most effective ways of using annual plants is among herbaceous perennials where they easily fill any breaks during the flowering period. Annuals can provide valuable colour all the year round but they are mainly grown for summer display, usually coming into bloom when the first flush of other spring or summer blooms has finished.

Annuals also make fine container plants. Tubs crammed with half a dozen or less of these plants will provide an unforgettable display for month after month and their only requirements are water, regular dead-heading and the odd feed with weak liquid fertilizer.

Generally an open, sunny site is preferred by these plants and a soil which is not too acid. They can withstand dry conditions remarkably well, provided they are given a good moist start.

In most parts of Australia, a wonderful display can be started right now, either from seed or seedlings. The advantages of seed are cheapness and a choice from a much larger variety than is available with seedlings from nurseries.

Seed can be sown directly into the garden where it will germinate freely, but in districts where the climate or insect pests may prove a problem, it is better to sow into containers first. This gives much better control over the young seedlings, ensures a higher survival rate and prepares them for bedding-out at the most suitable time.

From a sowing this week, most annuals will be ready for bedding out before Christmas and should be sufficiently established to start flowering strongly half way through January.

Cunning, Safe Ways of Dealing with Pests

Let's face it, as soon as we sow or plant something in our gardens, there is a host of insect pests just waiting to go into action. There are also certain birds which seem to wait until that crucial moment when the first green shoots are emerging before they strike. They strike again when the fruits of our labours are about to be picked.

Cats too come into the picture, as they gratefully take advantage of the freshly sown seedbed as a cure for their constipation and happily scratch away the results of your weekend's work.

Meanwhile, under cover of darkness, the slugs and snails chew relentlessly at our most precious plants, leaving the bleeding stumps glistening sadly with the evidence of a cure for night starvation.

Even if they survive all these assaults, our plants are still subjected to unexpected cold, or, much worse, hot winds, leaving many of them wilted, broken and desiccated. Later on, the soil will dry out and the survivors will once again come under this new stress.

Well, if this brief list of some of the negative aspects of growing things makes you feel somewhat apprehensive, that's a good thing because you may want to do something about it.

Most common garden problems are easily solved with a little bit of ingenuity, and a few simple devices.

To begin with, all newly planted areas should be clear of weeds, as these can be a major source of pests. One of the worst is the sow thistle, which looks innocent enough, and is not considered to be all that bad, but is an important breeding ground for aphids. If you look carefully at this weed, you will often see thousands of plant lice sheltering, especially during cool weather. So get rid of the weeds, or mulch them out of existence and a good start has been made.

Birds can be a bit of a curse at times but their good, insect-eating side is the one to concentrate on. Even the simple method of stretching cotton or fishing line along the rows of young plants is extremely effective. It seems that the taut lines make them too nervous to do much damage, because they spoil the birds' ability to make quick judgements of distance when preparing to make a quick getaway. A metre-long piece of chicken-wire, about half as wide, can be easily and quickly bent to form a protective

> Smother weeds which are starting to form seeds with a mulch of old straw or grass-clippings. If they are pulled and left to lie, their seeds will ripen, but under a moist mulch they will go mouldy and die.

tunnel for covering vulnerable fruit such as strawberries.

Fruit tree crops in the home garden can be protected by the use of cheap, long-lasting black plastic nets, which, even if they do not fully cover the crown of a tree, will still be an effective deterrent. I find that a couple of long garden stakes fixed to one side of the net will help enormously when placing it into position, or removing it.

Cats are certainly a problem, because they can be so determined and single-minded. Usually, a good watering of a newly-sown bed every evening can put them off, as they detest digging in wet soil. The provision of about a square metre of nice dry, sandy soil for their exclusive use, is also an excellent diversion.

Slugs and snails are slimy pests. One of the best ways I know of to keep them at bay for longer than many poisons, is using ordinary fresh, or even old, sawdust. If you have ever handled this stuff you will know that the sap in it will do terrible things to even the toughest hands. What it will do to the soft, moist and sticky bodies of slugs and snails is nobody's business. All I know is that a layer of sawdust over the soil around young plants, will put a stop to any damage, overnight.

So things are not as bad as they might seem – the solution to many common garden problems need not be expensive or dangerous.

NOVEMBER: THIRD WEEK

Ornamental Vegetables

Many of the plants grown in the vegetable garden are so attractive they can be used successfully as ornamental plants, growing quite happily among flowers, shrubs, perennials and even around small trees. Many have attractive leaves in shades of brilliant or deep green colours and for those who have run out of space in the vegetable patch, there are great possibilities among the ornamentals.

Rainbow chard is a variety of silverbeet. However, instead of the typical dark-green leaves with white stems, rainbow chard develops brightly-coloured stems in pink, yellow and ruby-red. The leaves too, although having a greenish cast, take on the colours of their stems. The result is a great splash of colour for most of the summer and usually right through winter too. The flavour of the leaves and stems is basically the same as silverbeet, although some people assert they are a little sweeter. The plants will grow in a partly shaded or sunny position and look particularly attractive among colourful annual or perennial plants.

Edging plants are always useful, because they effectively blunt the sharp corners of concrete paths, sometimes spilling over a little to soften the whole effect. There are many ornamental plants which will form low, brightly-coloured domes, but have you ever thought about using parsley as an edger? Some of the newly developed, highly compact varieties such as Afro are very beautiful indeed, with bright-green, tightly-curled leaves. Afro has the advantage of retaining its shape for almost two years, before bolting to seed. In the meantime the leaves can be picked almost as fast as they are grown, without any drastic loss of shape. Parsley, including the popular triple-curled variety, is snugly at home among such low-growing annuals as lobelia, ageratum, alyssum, and dwarf African marigolds. Incidentally, the marigolds play a vital role in protecting other plants, especially from eelworm attacks, besides suppressing couch-grass.

Lettuces take up little room and are always handy to form the basis of a salad. The tastiest are also the most nutritious and colourful. Red or brown Mignonette develop beautifully coloured leaves, usually with a lovely reddish tinge.

They are an open-hearted type, often referred to as 'butterhead'. The leaves are refreshing to eat and particularly delicious when freshly picked and chilled. Their leaves also look good on any plate. The great advantage of the Mignonette lettuces is their relatively small size and compact way of growing. There is very little waste compared with the larger lettuces, where a good proportion is often thrown out.

These little lettuces can be planted adjacent to flowers, or even in a kind of mass planting on their own. They are excellent border plants that can be grown virtually at most times in the year. Mignonette are easily available, with many nurseries having punnets of seedlings ready for planting. The rule for growing all lettuce, is lots of water and good drainage. I usually place a ring of blood and bone around each seedling, then water it in straight away. The plants can also withstand some shade, which makes them particularly useful close to trees.

The secret of obtaining a good germination from the seed of any type of lettuce is to chill it for a couple of days in the fridge. This will unlock it, should it have become dormant.

Scarlet runner climbing beans are extremely colourful when they are flowering. Their bright red flowers will compete with many ornamental plants for a bright, cheerful display. They too will thrive in the ornamental garden, provided they are given a lattice on which to climb. One of the most effective ways I have seen them used was on the wall

> There is a huge range of plants which can go in to the flower garden now. Ageratum, alyssum, amaranthus, antirrhinum, China aster, celosia, clarkia, cleome, coleus, cosmos, godetia, gypsophila, helichrysum, iberis, kochia, larkspur, linaria, linum, lobelia, lunaria, mignonette, nasturtium, nemophila, nigella, petunia, phlox, portulaca, salpiglossis, salvia, schizanthus, statice, stock, sweetpea, ursinia, verbena, viscaria and zinnia.

of a house directly behind a rose garden. The combined display was extraordinary and the constant picking of thick juicy pods forced the beans to keep on flowering. After the tops of Scarlet Runner beans have died down, they can be left in the ground for two or more years, with the thick, searching roots sprouting again in late spring.

It may seem strange to plant tomato plants among the ornamentals, but some varieties look very good indeed. The bright red, cherry-sized fruit of some types lend themselves well to a display of colour. My own favourite are the delicious, bite-sized Yellow Pear. With a little judicious pruning and a low stake they provide a bright splash of soft yellow as they ripen. They will hold this colour for a week or so. The other advantage of these small types of tomato is the ease with which they will freeze. I simply pick them, clean from the plant, put them straight into a plastic bag and freeze them immediately.

There are other plants too which blend in well with colourful flowers or foliage – the rich purple cabbages, beetroot leaves, golden French beans and even the attractive, lilac-coloured flowers of eggplants. They all add their own special kind of interest to the ornamental garden and it is lovely to go into the fragrant clumps of flowering plants and come back with the basis for a delicious meal.

Replacing Part of a Lawn with Flowers

Not long ago I decided to try an additional massed display of annuals in my own garden, so I dug up about fifteen square metres of lawn to accommodate them. After stripping off the turf and stacking it upside down to rot, out of sight, I dug up the soil, breaking it to a good tilth with a mattock and rake. Then, because it was obviously very acid, having been uncultivated for two or three decades at least, I spread a thick application of dolomite-limestone over the surface. Lime would have been unsuitable, because it tends to react unfavourably with fertilizers. A generous handful of blood and bone, supplemented with potash, for every square metre, then raked in, was preparation enough.

The bed I made was slightly curved, so I decided to use a mixture of flowering perennials too, with the larger ones in the centre. After giving the soil a good, deep watering, occasionally resting the sprinkler to avoid damaging run-off, the bed was allowed to mature for a day or so to fully drain. At planting time, conditions were moist and warm but I still waited until late afternoon before planting out the seedlings. It is fatal to plant during a hot, sunny day. Sensitive young plants are unable to cope with the heat and collapse, often within minutes of being planted. Once the heat of the day has declined, there is only the cool night ahead, allowing the plants to remain firm enough to withstand the following day's harsh sunlight much better.

Hollyhocks went in the middle. Nothing but rosettes of leaves at first but soon their great spikes sprouted almost two metres. Bonfire salvias always provide an immediate display and a dozen were planted among the hollyhocks. Foxgloves plus a few Crackerjack African marigolds help control twitch-grass while providing colour.

Around the outer perimeter of the bed I put in lower-growing plants. Red-flowering petunias, blue lobelias, ageratum, statice, a few helichrysums, all planted in clumps of five, soon produced some fantastic colours in a crazy kind of mixture, right through summer and autumn, until the first hard frosts.

Close planting allowed them to form a dense, weed-suppressing ground cover. Once the plants had achieved a reasonable size, maintenance was low for months, apart from the easy dead-heading to keep the flowers moving.

There were still plenty of gaps in the planting, so in went Russell lupins, delphiniums and, closer to the edge, seedling carnations, some of which had already started to send out their first flowering pipes. Naturally, the pipes were pinched off, in order to prevent straggly, untidy plants developing and this simple pruning continued for two months. This encouraged the formation of compact, attractive, silvery buns which, when allowed to bloom, were guaranteed to stop the traffic.

Incidentally, seedling delphiniums, which, like lupins, are perennials, start to produce their first blooms in nine weeks. I've long ago stopped buying the large, expensive crowns, since I discovered that unlike Britain or North America, our climate is capable of stimulating seedlings to bloom in the first season, without loss of energy.

I still had the odd gap here and there around the edges, so I planted violas, in groups of about five, fairly close together. These were favoured with additional treats of liquid fertilizer through the summer, so that their flowering continued through the winter months.

When all the plants were in (an operation which took less than an hour) the entire bed was given a good watering to eliminate air pockets in the soil or around the roots.

The cost was less than ten dollars and the total time involved was about six hours. But the rewards lasted for month after colourful month during that summer, and I had the basis of a permanent herbaceous garden which will last for many years.

That's how easy it all is. So, if you feel you have run out of planting spaces, have another look at that lawn of yours and calculate how much less mowing there would be if part of it was converted into a brilliant display of flowers.

NOVEMBER: LAST WEEK

More on Safe Pest and Disease Control

It is always frustrating and disappointing to find the fruit, vegetables or flowers you have been carefully tending unexpectedly attacked by insect pests or diseases. This usually occurs just when the fruits of your labours are at their best or are about to be harvested.

Control by poisons or other chemicals seems to offer an immediate solution and in some cases appears necessary. But in the home garden there is enormous scope for doing things in a more balanced way.

For example, a simple three or four year rotation system, during which plants are not planted in the same bed, is remarkably effective at preventing a mass build-up of disease organisms and pests. Their growth-cycle is constantly interrupted as one type of plant is replaced by another.

Timing of planting is another means of good disease and insect control. Late plantings of peas, cucumbers and zucchinis seem to be more seriously affected by problems of mildew, than early ones, while carrot seed which is sown too early, when the soil has not yet warmed, will often be attacked by soil-borne pests.

The relentless removal of 'suspect' plants which show signs of behaving abnormally is essential. A tomato or lettuce plant which suddenly collapses must be immediately removed and destroyed before other plants can be similarly affected. Even brassicas, after being cut, must have their roots hauled out of the ground if club-root problems are to be avoided. The sight of rows of lopped cabbage or cauliflower stalks in a vegetable garden is particularly saddening and when they are accompanied by dozens of radishes which have become too coarse and hot to be of further use, the problems of disease are compounded.

Fruit which falls to the ground early is usually diseased or contains an insect. Constant removal is most important, and the affected material should be buried deeply or destroyed. All plant debris is best composted or buried. However, the composting must be done correctly. It is not enough to pile it into a heap to slowly rot down. See page 28 for detailed advice on composting.

Weeds are a nuisance not only because they are competitors for light and nutrients. There has been a great deal of rubbish talked, within some organic organizations, about the value of weeds. As a conditioner for exhausted, impoverished soils, they are first on the scene and their vigour, hardiness and deep-rooting qualities undoubtedly play a valuable role. However, in the garden they harbour pests over winter and, because so many weeds are closely related to cultivated plants, they will infect them with many diseases. A garden in which weeds are not allowed to become dominant is healthier, with fewer pests.

The good thing about weeds is the superb compost they make, because they are crammed with the minerals they have stolen.

Most gardeners soon learn the value of observation. An oddly-twisted leaf-cluster will reveal a breeding-ground for aphids. Sometimes, with vigorous trees such as sweet cherry, it is enough to cut off the cluster and destroy it, without causing problems. On eucalypts, revolting masses of squirming caterpillars present a terrifying sight to those who have never seen sawfly larvae before. With large trees, the problem is not serious, but these pests will defoliate young eucalypts. Cutting off the cluster and burying them deeply with a good dusting of lime will fix them, but do it well away from the trees. Spotting a potential problem before it begins to develop, is the easiest way of pest and disease control.

The greatest friends we have in the garden for pest control are the birds. Some people who see the mess they can make when they are scratching around may disagree, but they are after insects, many of which are pests. Some small birds will eat thousands of insects every day. Not long ago, I watched with amazed delight as a small group of white-eyes completely cleaned up a large climbing rose which was heavily infested with green-fly.

The most effective way of bringing plenty of birds into the garden is to plant lots of native trees and shrubs. I planted about a thousand trees and shrubs, all Australian natives, around my tiny three hectare piece of land. They control the wind, keep the soil from drying-out and add great beauty all the year round. They are also a haven for thousands of birds which live off insects in the garden. Only a tiny fraction of the fruit is damaged, with the exception of some newly-planted blueberries.

Some pests have to be dealt with more directly, because we cannot always wait for their predators to get to work. Pear and cherry slug devastates the leaves of many trees. The old-fashioned method of mixing sand and lime to throw over the tree is effective, but messy. A standard mix of pyrethrum, laced with a little Clensel, will kill these pests instantly, but the treatment must be repeated several times over a five week period for best results.

Summer pruning, especially of fruit trees, by removing inward-growing branchlets, will open-up the centres to light, air and birds. With peach and nectarine trees, most of the earlier leaf-curl problems will have virtually disappeared with the warmer weather, but the disease is quietly continued by means of the odd leaf, here and there. Just picking them off during summer will help to reduce the virulence of this disease.

Brown-rot of stone fruit begins as a small brown patch, then rapidly spreads over the entire fruit, which in turn infect adjacent fruit. Search your trees now for signs of the disease and remove and destroy infected fruit immediately. Never allow mummified fruit to cling to the trees over the dormant period and cut off any branchlets which are showing signs of gumming.

All we need in our gardens is a balance, preferably our way. We can achieve this by sensible hygiene, weeding, keeping our plants moving, avoiding disruptive chemicals and occasionally applying a few squirts of relatively safe sprays.

Vertical Gardens and Retaining Walls

Few gardens are on perfectly level ground. This helps to give interest and character to the landscaping and if a slope is facing the sun, it receives much more of the warming rays.

There are many ways of designing an attractive garden on a sloping site. Some people simply accept the situation and have a sloping garden, with all the advantages and disadvantages.

The general trend however, has been to try and correct a slope, at least here and there, by constructing level areas. In most gardens this is accomplished by using a retaining wall to prevent the earth from slipping down. On steep sites, a series of such walls can often be seen, so

> If tomato plants are mulched heavily with moist straw or sawdust mixed with blood and bone or old manure, they will send out extra feeding roots from their stems to produce a much higher yield of fruit.

that the land becomes composed of a number of large, irregular steps. Some of the most attractive of all gardens have been constructed in this manner, so that, by solving the slope problem, the owners have created something beautiful.

Retaining walls can be of brick, stone or timber. The most expensive are the brick walls, partly because they require a skilled tradesperson to do the job, but also because they need to be thick to withstand the pressure of the earth packed behind them. If there is a fair amount of clay in the back-fill, it will swell up when it is wet and few walls can resist the enormous force which develops.

A common error, which aggravates this problem, is a failure to install weep-holes at the base of a wall. These should be at least one metre apart and large enough to keep flowing even if a little clay becomes lodged in them. Rock walls too, if they have been secured with mortar, need similar drainage-holes to prevent water build-up.

Dry-stone walls are much easier to construct and last much longer than those which are laid and mortared like bricks. The oldest walls in the world, some more than two thousand years old, are of dry-stone construction. See page 171 for more about dry-stone walls.

Timber walls, especially with treated pine logs, are quickly and easily constructed. However these too should always be inclined into the slope, otherwise they will gradually lean outwards from the top in an untidy, uneven sprawl. The main means of securing such walls is with strong posts, driven as deeply and firmly as possible into the ground. With high timber walls, used for retaining earth, it is necessary to anchor the top deeply into the bank by means of long steel rods, each with its base fixed into a buried concrete block. Concrete walls used for terracing can be hard to construct on steep sites, because of the work involved in trying to wheel heavy barrow-loads of wet concrete uphill. In addition, they need to have particularly deep foundations, or relentless pressure will inevitably force them to topple outwards. When they crack, the unsightly appearance is hard to conceal and the stark, bare slabs across the garden can make landscaping more difficult.

If crevices are left here and there in the face of any of the different kinds of retaining walls, an additional attraction can be incorporated into the garden. The walls can be planted with a large number of creeping, weeping and climbing plants, so that a kind of vertical garden is created – a mass of easily-maintained, colourful plants, either protruding from the retaining walls, or flopping over the tops. Many of the plants suitable for such places seem to have the ability to bloom for long periods, winter and summer.

Here are some of the easily-obtained perennials which can be used for furnishing retaining walls, either from special crevices, or growing down from the top. When used in a dry-stone wall, most of them will gradually spread out, eventually joining together to form a dense, attractive, weed-suppressing blanket.

Alyssum saxatile. Silver-grey leaves for most of the year, with brilliant splashes of close-packed bright-yellow flowers. Tough, drought-resistant and startlingly beautiful, they will grow anywhere that drainage is perfect.

Erigeron speciosus. This is a well-known plant which thrives in temperate areas. The colours of the many hybrids range through violet-blue, deep mauve, clear pink to carmine-crimson. Perfect for a wall.

Dianthus allwoodii. Better known as border pinks, they will form tight silver mounds on a wall, provided they have plenty of root space through to the back. Clove scented, they are a familiar sight in most flower gardens, but are unsurpassed as a wall-plant.

Lithospermum diffusum (Heavenly Blue). One of the most sought after of all creeping alpines. It produces masses of dazzling blue flowers and will hang down a two-metre retaining wall, almost to the ground.

Grevillea 'Crosby Morrison'. Only grows about a third of a metre high, but it will flow down an inclined retaining wall like a pale-green waterfall. With its red spider-flowers and extra-dense growth, it makes a beautful mat, covering up to two square metres.

There are many more similar plants which thrive in the sun-baked face of a wall, so if yours is a sloping garden, think about the advantages of a retaining wall here and there to provide pleasant level places to sit, while creating a garden with a totally different aspect.

End-of-the-month Jobs

Here are some important jobs to do in the garden this week.

In the flower garden, start pinching off the tips of annuals and perennials which are starting to throw up their first blooms. This will strengthen the plants, make them more bushy and compact, and will force the plant to produce more blooms later.

Chrysanthemums, if they are being grown for garden display, should have their growing tips nipped off. This 'stopping' takes place on three or four occasions during the growing season, and causes the plant to produce a dense mass of flowers.

Carnations too will benefit from this type of pruning. Normally, they are left unpruned and the result is a sprawling, untidy and straggly plant, with only the blooms being attractive. If the vigorous, flower-bearing shoots are continuously pinched back to prevent flowering, the plant will gradually assume a tight, compact, silvery dome shape. Then it is allowed to flower (this season or next) and the effect can be extremely beautiful, with a solid mass display of smallish blooms.

Watch out for the ugly presence of borers in some of the trees. Both ornamental and fruit trees are now under attack. The main targets seem to be ornamental and sweet cherry trees, and occasionally, birches. Evidence is the presence of masses of dark brown, sawdust-like debris, usually in the junction of two branches. This waste matter, which clings together to form a kind of rough cover over the borer hole, is easily wiped away to reveal the entrance. The borer itself is an extremely active caterpillar, which is naturally out of sight down the hole, boring away. Deal with these destructive pests instantly.

A short piece of wire thrust vigorously into the hole will do the trick. You know you have got the pest because the wire suddenly comes out wet. Then move on to the next hole. There are usually only a few holes to deal with per tree, but these insects can wreak great damage at this time.

In the vegetable garden keep up successive plantings of bush beans, lettuces, sweetcorn, spring onions, radishes, peas, silverbeet and carrots. Be prepared to give all parts of the garden a good, deep soaking before the soil becomes so dry that the growth of plants is brought to a halt. Watch out for caterpillars on cabbage. They are hard to spot but the holes they make, plus their copious droppings, give them away. Hand picking at this time can achieve good control without having to spray. The young cabbages and other seedlings are the ones which are most vulnerable because only one caterpillar is enough to devastate each one.

The flower garden is entering a period of rest, now that the initial flush of spring bloom is finishing. Complete the pruning of straggly-looking flowering trees and shrubs and dead-head roses as fast as their blooms wither. Bottlebrushes, if pruned ruthlessly as their flower spikes fade, will become dense and bushy, and next season will produce an even greater number of flowers. Boronias should be reduced by at least one third at this time, to keep them more compact and to prolong their lives.

In the fruit garden apply plenty of water and liquid fertilizers around berry fruit plants. Apple trees should have their codlin moth-controlling hessian bands inspected, cleaned out, and replaced immediately. Watch for plant lice in sweet cherry and peach and nectarine trees, and spray with pyrethrum before they multiply beyond control. All fruit trees should be heavily watered at this time. They are producing both fruit and foliage, and their moisture needs should be constantly satisfied, otherwise weakness will set in, diseases strike and yields lessen.

December

GUIDE TO ACTION

Ornamental Garden

It is a sad fact of life that this month, although one of the most important for vigorous, actively growing plants, is also the month in which many people desert their gardens to go on holidays. The sooner vulnerable plants are deeply watered, then heavily mulched, the better. It will save a lot of worry and time later. In most gardens the great flush of spring and early summer flowers is just about finished. It is the time for relentless dead-heading and cutting back where necessary. Many plants will flower again and again if their seedpods or capsules are prevented from forming. Roses will urgently need to have faded blooms and any seedpods removed. Black Spot, the dreaded disease of rose leaves, can be kept in check by using drip-irrigation rather than sprinklers which wet the leaves and spread the disease. Young developing annuals can be watered with extra-weak liquid fertilizers and they will respond quickly. In the shrub garden, deep watering is necessary now in most parts of Australia, apart from the wet tropics. In temperate and cool parts of Australia, this is without question the best time of the year to bed-out annuals for a long-lasting summer display. Here are many of the flowering plants which can be planted or, in many cases sown, in containers or directly into permanent positions: acrolinium, achillea, ageratum, alyssum, anchusa, amaranthus, anaphalis, antirrhinum, aquilegia, arabis, arctotis, aster, aubrieta, balsam, bedding begonia, bellis, browallia, calla, campanula, carnation, chrysanthemum, cineraria, clarkia, coleus, cosmos, dahlia, delphinium, dianthus, dimorphotheca, gazania, gaillardia, geranium, gerbera, godetia, gypsophila, helichrysum, heliotrope, helipterum, hibiscus, hollyhock, impatiens, ipomea, kochia, larkspur, linaria, Livingstone daisy, lobelia, lupin, lunaria, marigold (African and French), mignonette, mimulus, moluccella, myosotis, nasturtium, nemophila, nigella, pansy, penstemon, petunia, phlox, platycodon, oriental poppy, portulaca, pyrethrum, rudbeckia, salpiglossis, salvia, scabiosa, schizanthus, statice, stock, thunbergia, tirenia, verbena, vinca, violet, viscaria, viola and zinnia.

Vegetable Garden

Some of the most important vegetables for sowing this month include those which will not fully mature until the cooler months. Leeks and Brussels sprouts need time to develop strongly over the next few months, in order to produce maximum yields, while being large enough to withstand the cold during their main growing season.

Seed is best sown into boxes or punnets and the seedlings pricked off as soon as they are large enough to handle. If they are then grown, well-spaced, in other containers, they will be ready for planting out during January or early February. Other vegetables for sowing or planting now for summer, autumn and winter supplies include: bush beans, beetroot, kale, broccoli, cabbage, Chinese cabbage (cool districts), capsicum, carrot, cauliflower (three, four, five and six month varieties), celery, cress, cucumber, eggplant, kohlrabi, lettuce, marrow, okra (warm districts), spring onion, parsley, parsnip, pumpkin, radish, salsify, swede, sweetcorn, tampala, tomato, turnip and zucchini.

One of the most persistent pests of brassicas now is the cabbage moth grub. Unlike the much larger caterpillar, cabbage grubs burrow deeply into the hearts of plants, making them inedible because of the large amount of messy, unpleasant frass they produce. Use Dipel. Swedes need plenty of room, otherwise they will be too small, so thin out ruthlessly. In cool districts, force tomato seedlings into flower before planting out. Any seedlings looking or growing in an abnormal way should be turfed out with great speed. Water and feed the soil generously during these long, warm and sunny days. Mulching materials will be rotting down quickly now, so keep replenished with lots of old straw, hay or seaweed.

Fruit Garden

Pear and cherry slugs are easily controlled, but if they are left to damage and strip leaves, the effects are felt for the rest of summer. Pyrethrum with a dash of Clensel will decimate them this month, just as they are becoming active. A further spraying will be required during January to keep them under control. Another spray of weakened white oil to control codlin moth grub will be needed for trees which have become infested with these pests over a number of years. Stone fruits, especially peach and nectarine, will need plenty of blood and bone, manure or similar organic fertilizer with a high nitrogen content, spread over their roots. Don't forget to water first, then again heavily afterwards. Sucker growth of brambles will need to be tied together carefully and secured to one side of the trellis, usually the opposite side to the canes bearing this season's berries. Raspberry canes should be mulched and watered deeply now the fruit is forming. Blackcurrants will be harvested towards the end of the month, so pruning can be carried out as soon as this is finished. Melons and canteloupes can be planted as well-developed seedlings at the beginning of this month.

Houseplants

Large leafy plants in containers dry out with surprising speed at this time. Be prepared to top up with water twice daily if necessary and add weak liquid fertilizer at least once weekly with big, vigorous plants. If you are going away for a few days during the break, start bringing some plants away from windows, so that they become used to duller light. Cuttings or layers of many houseplants can be taken now but ensure they are placed in a close environment in the shade. Potting operations can still be carried out, but always out of the direct sunlight. Withered or dead leaves can be a source of infection or pests, so constantly clear away all plant debris. Ferns and palms find it hard to cope with warm, dry conditions. Keep a filled mister spray handy and give these plants a good going over, several times daily if needed. If a tiny amount of seaweed concentrate is added to this water – just enough to produce a weak-tea colour – an excellent foliar feed will also be provided. Houseplants, newly purchased or received as gifts this month, may show some signs of the shock of a new environment, by dropping some of their leaves. Be prepared to stand some of them on a large plant saucer, filled with small stones, topped up with water. This will reproduce the more humid conditions found in most nursery glasshouses. Wipe the leaves of plants with a glossy foliage using a soft cloth and warm water. Then spray with water to make them really clean. Cacti and succulents will appreciate a good watering this month, but make sure they are able to drain their roots fully. Pointed tweezers can be used for the odd mealy bug. Otherwise use methylated spirit, soaked in a tiny ball of cottonwool to deal with these pests.

DECEMBER: FIRST WEEK

Essential Summer Jobs

There is always a distinct change in our weather about this time of the year. Ahead of us lies a long, hot period, which usually comes to an end about Easter. Every day has already started to get a little shorter, but there are at least four good months ahead which will be frost-free, and during which the soil will remain warm.

All this means excellent growing conditions in most parts of the garden. The main vegetables for planting or sowing include dwarf beans, beetroot, silverbeet, carrot, swede, turnip, Chinese cabbage, lettuce, radish, spring onion, broccoli, Brussels sprouts, celery, celeriac and Florence fennel. Well-sized and sturdy tomato, capsicum and eggplant seedlings can also still be planted out, although it is generally too late to plant the seeds. The easiest way of preparing for winter and spring brassicas is to sow the seed into containers. Make a medium by mixing together equal parts of sand, soil and granulated peat, and to each bucketful of this, add a good handful of dolomite or limestone, and an equal amount of blood and bone and potash. Keep the seeds away from the sun during germination, and make sure they don't dry out.

In the flower garden, dahlias are growing well. However, the top-heavy, leafy growth is very brittle and it only needs an unexpected wind to destroy most of your efforts. Staking is the answer, and it doesn't have to be unsightly. Thin, black, flexible bamboo supports are cheaply available, and they are strong enough to comfortably carry the weight of most dahlia plants. Don't drive them into the ground too close to the tubers, otherwise damage can cause the introduction of all sorts of diseases. All parts of the garden will be requiring plenty of water during the next few months, so be ready to practise deep watering wherever possible.

Feeding plants such as rhododendron, azalea, camellia, erica, pieris, daphne, hydrangea, Japanese maple and citrus trees, is very important at this time. They all seem to thrive best with pulverized animal manure, or blood and bone. If the ground around these fairly shallow-rooted plants is given a good watering first, the fertilizers applied and more water given immediately, the response will be seen within a week or so. Certain ornamental trees which tend to bleed when they are pruned during late winter or spring, can be safely treated now, if they have become too large. Silver birch, maple and even walnut trees have now started to pass the frenzied stages of growth, and bleeding from now onwards will be limited. However, any lopping which has to be carried out should be done by an expert. There are far too many badly mutilated trees around Australia and their repair can be expensive.

There is a host of plants which can go in now, including all container-grown plants. However, the best way of ensuring success at this stressful time, is to prepare the planting holes very carefully. Keep the plants well-watered while they are still in their pots awaiting planting. Dig a hole, wide and deep enough to hold the rootball, with plenty of room all the way around. Fill it to the brim with water and allow this to gradually soak away. Do this again, three or four times. Then plant the tree or shrub and, if possible, apply a generous mulch of old straw, or even sawdust, directly over the roots. This will effectively prevent evaporation and seal in the moisture.

In the fruit garden, the need for large quantities of water is fairly urgent. Trees carrying heavy crops of peaches, nectarines, plums, apples, pears and nuts should be watered so consistently and evenly that there is little danger of any further drying out. If drying out does occur and the trees are then watered, the fruit will often split, and will be open to disease and insect pests.

This common error of letting plants dry out, then watering them when they are clearly suffering, can have some adverse effects, particularly upon tomatoes. The fruit on bushes so mistreated will show symptoms of a condition known as Blossom-end Rot. In this case, the end of each tomato will go black and begin to decay. The fluctuating supply of moisture prevents the plant from taking up calcium and these wasted fruits are the result. This is another reason why heavy mulching, especially around tomato stems, is of such benefit. It means that one good watering every week will be enough to guarantee a good, healthy yield.

Planting this week in the flower garden will extend the period of bright colours well into the winter. Sow or plant the following: ageratum, alyssum, calendula, linaria, lupin, African marigold, pansy, Iceland poppy, stock, sweetpea, primula, viola, forget-me-not and wallflower.

Build an Outside Living Area

The place where the barbecue and outdoor furniture are situated is in many ways the most important part of a garden.

Unfortunately, bad design and overuse, especially at this time of the year, can create a scruffy, messy and smelly outdoor living section of the garden – guaranteed to blunt even the most robust appetite. In addition, if the area has been badly located, it can be an uncomfortable place in which to relax.

A simple solution is to use one or two light portable barbecues, which can be folded up and stored away after they have been used. They can be used in any part

> When using plastic margarine containers for growing seedlings, put the drainage holes low down at the sides, rather than underneath where they become blocked by the weight of the container.

of the garden according to weather conditions and there is no problem with ash blowing around later.

A permanent outdoor living area should be sited where there is plenty of privacy, usually out of sight from the street. One of the worst places is the slot between the side of the house and the dividing fence. Even on a slightly breezy day, such locations become miserable wind-tunnels.

Ideally, the best place for the barbecue and furniture is as close to the kitchen as possible, because so much of the food is prepared there before being carried outside.

As for the barbecue itself, there are some amazing and elaborate designs. Some bear a frightening resemblance to a sacrificial altar, where snags sizzle and squirm in a kind of agony while a drooling queue watches appreciatively. Other designs involve all sorts of cavities, cupboards and ledges, mainly for wood, kindling and paper, and while these are necessary, they can be a bit of an eyesore, especially when topped by a massive chimney.

Here are some guidelines for outdoor living areas.

1. Pick a place which gets plenty of shade during summer, but allows the sun through in winter. Near a big deciduous tree is excellent but make sure that the foliage can't become scorched. Good, dappled shade can be created by a simple pergola, built over the eating and drinking area. One or two climbers such as wisteria or ornamental vine will soon cover the bare structure.

2. Grass is not suitable in the immediate vicinity of tables and chairs, because it is difficult to maintain and under conditions of heavy use it soon degenerates into bare, untidy patches of compacted soil.

A hard surface can look good, especially if it has been made from pavers or bricks on their edges, laid on a thick layer of coarse sand with more dry sand swept into the crevices. If a small amount of cement is also added, very few weeds will establish themselves. Concrete pavers are easily laid and come in various earthy colours. If they have been rumbled to take off their sharp edges, they can look as though they have been down for years.

3. The barbecue itself need not be a massive affair, but there is a need for plenty of flat surfaces near where the food is cooked. This is an essential safety feature, and reduces the risk of people, especially children, getting burnt or scalded.

4. When siting the fireplace, think about the effects prevailing winds may have on the smoke. There is nothing worse than the sight of people, their eyes streaming with smoke-induced tears, trying to look as though they are enjoying themselves.

5. Children love a barbecue, but rarely seem to be provided for when it comes to outdoor furniture. Most of it is designed for adults, so give some thought to including small tables, preferably with attached seats.

6. Some people cannot resist the temptation of throwing their food scraps on the fire. When bits of plastic wrapping are included, the resulting fumes not only stink the place out, but are quite toxic. So, make sure a plastic-lined rubbish container with a secure lid is always handy. Then, even the flies might leave you in peace.

An Early Morning Stroll in the Garden

It's hard to imagine that although summer arrived only a few days ago, in about three weeks every day will become progressively shorter. We will hardly notice the change for a couple of months, but the plants will respond immediately. Some will bolt to seed, as soon as their leaves have detected the minute changes in the day length. Other plants will respond in a different way. Long-keeping onions will start to bulb out and their eventual size will be determined by how long they have been forming new scales.

This is the time of maximum growth in most plants. The long days, with the almost constant warmth, mean that an enormous amount of energy is pouring into leaves everywhere. The most urgent task of all in the garden is trying to keep up with the ceaseless demand for water. Some shallow-rooted shrubs, such as azaleas, rhododendrons, camellias, ericas, pieris and citrus trees, are now at their most vulnerable. Once the soil around their roots dries out, it is very hard to get it wet again. This is a major reason why these tight-rooted plants falter or even die, often months after the damage has been done.

I always celebrate the coming of summer by taking extra-special care with my plants. Usually, after waking very early, I sneak out into the garden and trudge quietly around in the dewy grass. They say that walking barefoot through wet, cold grass is some kind of natural tonic. All I know is, it's a lovely way to become fully awake. The birds make a bit of a din and even before the sun appears I find myself being constantly diverted from one job to the next, without finishing any of them.

Dead-heading is a gentle way to start and finish a day. Roses which have now bloomed benefit greatly by having the withered remains of the flowers snapped off. It means they will flower again, if they are allowed, sometime during January, but the speed with which they flower and then blow during that hot time seems almost a waste. Pruning them lightly, back to the next fat bud, will postpone the flowering until cooler times.

Next I examine the tub plants. These are the ones at risk from now on, because we can be tricked into thinking they have been watered, when they haven't. When any water pouring into the top, begins to leak out from the bottom immediately, we've got problems. It means the rootball has shrunk through drying out and the water is being deflected from where it is needed most, in the core. One solution is slow trickle watering, with the end of the hose next to the stems, until the rootball swells again.

Dahlias are thrusting up their tender shoots now, so their first decent watering can take place. But their enemies are skulking around, waiting to feast. I see the tell-tale, silvery trail, leading away from the oozing blob which was once the growing tip of my favourite dahlia. There should be enough spare 'eyes' on the tuber down below to make up the loss. Just the same, I follow the trail and find the culprit, clinging to the lower bark of a broom. That's when I peel it off, in order to crunch and squash it, smearing the remains around the scene of the crime. *The simple pleasures of the poor.*

There is a trend, these days, to use minced-up caterpillars or other pests as a protective spray over their target plants. I tried it, cynically at first, but it worked. However, even I can't bring myself to use the kitchen blender, as the dedicated do, to obtain a smoother mix. It's enough to put anyone off milkshakes for life.

The sun is well up now and I notice the seedling carnations, planted a few weeks ago. Each one is already sending up its first pipe. Sorry mates, not allowed. It takes only a few seconds to pinch off each one. This will force the plants to send out three or four sturdy side-shoots from their bases. When these start to form flowering pipes, they too will be cut off in their prime. Preventing carnations from flowering for a couple of months means tight, compact silver-grey domes which, when liberated, burst into a superb flowering, with at least twenty blooms per bun. How much better-looking and more managable than the usual floppy, straggly sprawl, so common with unpruned carnations.

There is an area I have been avoiding for months. Infested with masses of rope twitch-grass and spreading rapidly too. Preparations have been made. I have bought four punnets of African marigolds, the big, vigorous ones called Crackerjack.

After grunting and digging my way through the root-ridden soil and forking out as much of the twitch as possible, I squirt holes with the hose jet, leaving them filled with water – the easiest way I know of excavating planting holes and watering at the same time. A few minutes later, when the water has soaked away, in go the marigold seedlings, the great twitch destroyer, five to the square metre. I could swear I hear the twitch roots which still remain, squeaking with fear.

What a lovely way to start the summer.

DECEMBER: SECOND WEEK

Easy-care Gardens

Whether you are starting a new garden or have an established one, you can make things much easier for yourself with all sorts of tools and tricks. Here are some simple ways of reducing the more boring aspects of gardening – the unnecessary hard labour side.

1. If parts of the vegetable garden are becoming badly infested with weeds and they are about to form their seeds before you can pull them out, get stuck into them with your lawn mower. It won't kill them, but it will retard them dramatically, and if you use a grass catcher attached to the mower, you will have some lovely mulching materials which will not become slimy in the way grass cuttings do.

2. Construct mowing strips around your lawn area to eliminate the unsightly fringe of long grass and to save the effort of handcutting after the lawns have been cut. Alternatively, use a wiper wick, or even an old paint brush to apply a total weed killer to the lawn edges. This is a simple, easy job which need only be carried out three or four times per year. Trees or shrubs which are situated in grassed areas tend to develop tufts of coarse grass around their bases, and here again the paintbrush method can save a lot of work. But make sure that the green bark of young trees is out of reach of the weedkiller, whether it be on the brush or on the grass swaying around the trunk, or the plants you wish to spare will be poisoned too.

3. Wherever possible, construct sloping, shallow ramps rather than steps. This will allow you to move your wheelbarrow to most parts of the garden with little effort.

4. Use either a good thick mulch or dense groundcovering plants to protect the soil and suppress weeds. In the case of ground covering plants, some regular weeding is esssential, in order to enable these plants to spread and fully establish themselves.

5. Try to design the garden so that most of the trees, shrubs and other plants are together in the form of a general perimeter around the lawn area. Don't make the common error of dotting trees and shrubs all over the lawn. They are tedious to mow and tend to look spotty and boring.

Foliar Feeding

The most effective, and in some ways gentle, method of feeding many plants, is by spraying the leaves with heavily diluted minerals. Seaweed concentrate is particularly good, especially from now onwards.

Some people mistakenly refer to this dark brown liquid as a fertilizer. It isn't really, it is basically a soil conditioner. However, when it is applied to the foliage of plants, on a monthly basis, the response is so significant, that under these circumstances the term 'foliar feed' is quite accurate.

Some plants seem to like this form of feeding better than others. For example, citrus trees thrive with regular seaweed sprays, and plants such as camellias, rhododendrons, azaleas, viburnums, hydrangeas and roses all respond by producing better coloured leaves and more persistent flowers.

Most of these plants, and this also includes the majority of the broadleaved deciduous trees, can absorb certain minerals directly into their systems, through the pores in the leaf surface. The main thing to watch for when applying any kind of foliar feed is to make sure it is well diluted with water. Otherwise it is not only a waste of materials, but can sometimes damage a sensitive plant.

Early morning is always a good time to spray the leaves of plants, because there is less danger of diseases taking hold during the day, when the foliage dries off.

Other forms of easily made foliar feed include compost 'tea'. See page 153. Sometimes, with the addition of a little seaweed concentrate, this mixture can have a revitalizing effect on houseplants which seem to have lost their vigour.

The real benefit from such liquid treasures is with seeds and very young seedlings. Trace elements are essential, but only the most minute amount is necessary. If these can be absorbed into the freshly sown seed at the beginning of growth, the effect can last the life of the plant. For example, cauliflowers in many parts of Australia show a serious problem of molybdenum deficiency, usually in the form of 'whiptail'. The leaves become grossly twisted and elongated. While spraying with diluted sodium molybdate may help a little, it is often too late to correct the problem. I have found that watering the seed with weak compost tea, containing a tiny amount of seaweed concentrate and sodium molybdate, allows the swelling seed to take in the necessary minerals right from the start, and these mineral deficiency problems virtually cease to exist.

How the foliar feed or weak liquid fertilizer is mixed, depends to some extent on the special needs of some plants. Rhodendrons and similar acid soil loving plants are not very good at obtaining their iron needs. This is why, when lime is present in the soil near them, they will show a distinct paling of their leaves. The iron in the soil becomes unavailable and must be supplied in another form, which can overcome the lime. Chelated iron is easy to obtain and applied to the leaves after being well-mixed with water, will usually produce quick changes in the leaf-colour.

Some people's daft habit of throwing their woodfire ashes around their azaleas

---

In the vegetable garden this week almost every important vegetable can be planted or sown, and these include: beetroot, beans, broccoli, Brussels sprouts, cabbage, capsicum, cucumber, carrot, cauliflower, celery, Chinese cabbage, eggplant, leeks, lettuce, marrow, spring onion, parsnip, potatoes, pumpkin, radish, rhubarb (seed), salsify, shallot (seed), silverbeet, sweetcorn, tomatoes and winter squash.

and rhododendrons can produce shocking examples of this iron deficiency. I have seen azalea leaves which are almost white, while directly over the roots is a neat pile of highly alkaline wood ash. Yet an application or two of chelated iron, preferably with compost 'tea', has worked wonders within a few weeks. So here is one little job this week; wander around your garden and closely examine the foliage of the vulnerable plants, and be ready to make some 'tea' if necessary.

Greenhouses

There is a place in almost every garden for a greenhouse. They are worth their weight in gold in cooler districts because the relatively short growing season can be extended at both ends.

Greenhouses come in all shapes and sizes, from the traditional span-roofed type to lean-to designs which fit neatly against the house wall.

There are even circular greenhouses, and these have considerable ornamental value if they are carefully located in the garden.

Plastic tunnels are much cheaper than the conventional glassed structures, but need very good ventilation, preferably with fans, otherwise disease can be a problem.

Whichever type you decide to purchase or build, the siting of it will make all the difference to its effectiveness. The most important consideration is to take full advantage of light, especially winter light. A greenhouse in a shady spot is virtually worthless, but if you have difficulty locating an evenly, well-lit place in the garden, try to find somewhere which is certain to receive plenty of morning sun. This ensures that an early warming will take place every day, and the plants will benefit.

Some people still puzzle over the question of the orientation of a greenhouse. These days, modern designs allow in plenty of light from almost any angle, so whether the structure lies on an east-west axis, or a north-south one, is not so important. Sometimes the strength and direction of prevailing winds help you to make the final decision. There is nothing worse than a blast of cold air through a greenhouse, every time the door is opened.

It is surprising the number of keen gardeners who believe that the soil enclosed by the greenhouse is the place to plant things. For the first year this soil is all right to use, but from then on all plants are grown in containers on benches. This is because the sheltered conditions plus the warmth within the greenhouse will encourage a massive build-up of soil-borne diseases, which don't occur in the open garden. That's why, after the first year of using a greenhouse, all the plants are grown in containers, unless the owners are willing to carefully dig out and replace the soil regularly.

Even with containers, many people become discouraged by poor results, if they mistakenly use ordinary garden soil to fill the pots.

You must use potting soil, which is easily mixed, for the containers, otherwise there will be serious problems such as inability to hold water, and caking.

Potting soil basically consists of one part garden soil, one part granulated peat, and one part sand, to which the appropriate fertilizer is added. If your soil is very sandy, forget about adding more sand, but if yours is a clay soil, be prepared to counter this with extra sand. Every time your potted plants come to the end of their lives, chuck them on the compost heap with the potting soil and mix a fresh batch.

The real key to success with a greenhouse lies with correct ventilation.

Ventilators are opened on most days,

summer and winter. On warm, sunny days, the door is opened as well. The closing-down process takes place late in the afternoon, just before things start to cool down. This will retain the heat for hours, but if you leave it too late on a cool afternoon, most of the warmth will be lost, and the plants will be checked. Leaving the ventilators closed during a warm day could be a disaster, causing many plants to be cooked in their pots. Within a well-organized greenhouse, the atmosphere should be moving, or even a little bouncy. Stagnant air encourages disease to flourish.

In Australia we have the special problem of extremely high light intensity. It is the despair of many paint manufacturers, and is a major cause of excessive silvering of some timbers, such as western red cedar. Greenhouses must be covered with shadecloth, or the glass painted with a lime and water mixture all the year round.

The strength of our solar radiation is such, that many of the more sensitive plants will just shrivel up in a greenhouse.

The majority of these useful structures are without heating, but they still prove to be adequate for most plants. For winter and spring cropping of tender vegetables such as tomatoes, capsicums and cucumbers, or for growing certain kinds of tropical plants, artificial heating is necessary.

There is a whole range of equipment available these days which can not only provide consistent heat, but will automatically switch on or off according to the temperature required. To install a domestic fanheater can be both expensive and destructive unless there are good controls. However, many people content themselves with a cool (unheated) greenhouse, but with an additional small, propagating case. These are relatively cheap, and are a great asset when taking cuttings, or for the germination of difficult seeds. Carefully and wisely used, a propagator will pay for itself within a couple of seasons.

Watch Those Houseplants

Most normal, healthy houseplants are demanding fertilizers right now, while they are growing strongly.

It is of little value adding blood and bone or manure to the surface of the soil, because it can attract flies and even be smelt from inside the house. This is why fertilizers in liquid form are always best for houseplants. They must be well diluted with water before applying. The potting soil too must be well moistened, otherwise serious damage can be done by the fertilizers.

Slow-release granules or tablets are good value because the plant foods are made available to the plants very slowly over several months. Foliar feeding is another way of feeding houseplants gently. Seaweed concentrate, used exactly as indicated on the container, and no stronger, can produce, hardy and healthy plants, showing few problems of mineral deficiency.

Perhaps the greatest tonic for almost all houseplants is being rained upon. Almost anytime from now onwards is safe to carry the plants outside and leave them in the rain for as long as possible. They must be shielded from the wind of course and always taken back inside as soon as the sun reappears or they will be badly scorched. Rain will wash away all the accumulated dust and debris from the surface of the leaves, in a way we can never do.

So next time it rains, take full advantage of it and give your houseplants a treat.

DECEMBER: THIRD WEEK

Growing a Windbreak

Some of the most spectacular and beautiful gardens in the world have been created under the most difficult climatic conditions, especially exposure to constant winds.

So if this is your problem, don't lose heart. There are plenty of ways of overcoming even the most destructive winds. Planting special, wind-resistant trees and shrubs as windbreaks is one of them.

Growing a windbreak is an attractive proposition, because so many wind-resistant plants are lovely to look at and so play a dual role in the landscape plan.

There are two ways to plant a windbreak. The traditional way is to grow a belt of dense trees and shrubs to form a kind of hedge, on the side of the property from which the wind usually blows.

This can be both beautiful and effective, depending upon how much room there is in the garden. A typical twenty metre wide by forty metre long homesite will need plants which will grow to five metres in height in order to protect the rest of the garden. This means a windbreak at least three metres deep, which is taking away a large piece of the garden permanently. If the wind is really bad, however, this screening effect is worth the loss of space.

There are many types of plant, mostly natives, which are suitable for a standard sized block. Among the best for southern Australian conditions is the Ovens wattle (*Acacia pravissima*) because it withstands cold, wind, wet winter and dry summer conditions and heavy clay. It also produces branches which go right down to the ground, thus avoiding the icy winds which can cut sharply under bare-trunk trees. The real bonus of the Ovens wattle is the extraordinary beauty of this plant, either in flower during late winter or in full, weeping foliage during the summer. The tree will grow to a height of five metres, and a width of three. Planted four metres apart, this wattle will form a superb protective screen in any garden.

The other way of planting a windbreak is to place the trees or shrubs so that they form a series of copses which overlap. This method is particularly suitable for gardens on the side of a hill, with the house at the top. The orthodox type of fenceline screen is not very effective in such places because only the lower parts of the garden can be protected from the wind. The system of ornamental and practical tree groups, dotted up the slope, and so placed that there are no gaps in direct line with the direction from which the wind flows, leaves large parts of the garden open, but well screened. The landscaping itself gives a park-like effect to the homesite and can look quite beautiful.

So, don't allow yourself to be intimidated by the wind. You don't have to put up with it, and by controlling it you can also develop a very attractive garden.

Here are some small trees and strubs which are suitable for growing as windbreaks.

Acacia fimbriata (Sticky wattle). Grows to a height of four metres. Soft semi-weeping habit, masses of yellow flowers during late winter.

Acacia baileyana (Cootamundra wattle). An outstanding, popular small tree. Purple leaf form is particularly beautiful.

Eucalyptus alpina (Alpine gum). Furnished to the ground with its shining roundish leaves. White flowers.

E. viridis. Small, bright green, attractive mallee gum. Grows to three metres. Excellent ornamental value with long narrow leaves.

E. forrestiana (Fuchsia gum). Another small, tough tree growing to about two metres. Bright red, pendant fruit.

Leptospermum lanigerum (Woolly tea-tree). This is one shrub which can withstand both wind and heavy clay. When occasionally lopped, will produce masses of low-growing new branches and white flowers.

Banksia spinulosa (Hairpin banksia). Beautiful golden spikes with black glistening stamens. Grows a little more than a metre, but hugs the ground. Brings the birds in flocks. Excellent as a supplement to a larger windbreak to eliminate underdraughts.

B. ericifolia (Heath banksia). Growing up to four metres, this is an absolute gem. Flowers profusely, producing plenty of big, cylindrical, soft orange flowers that seem to glow. Perfect as an addition to any windbreak. Trim every other year to keep compact and dense.

Callistemon pallidus (Pallid bottlebrush). Masses of pale yellow brushes at this time every year, grows to four metres or more, but regular lopping after blooming will produce a more compact plant. Ideal for almost any situation from heavy cold clay to sandy loam.

Grevilleas. Most of these shrubs make good windbreak material. A wide choice is available, with enormous variation in flower and foliage.

Plants Make Unforgettable Gifts

This is the time of the last, frantic dash to buy Christmas presents but there is a way to avoid the crowds and, at the same time, select something beautiful, useful and long-lasting. Plants of all kinds make perfect presents, because they not only continue to improve in size or beauty but also are a constant reminder to the recipient of the giver. Even young children will appreciate a lovely tree or shrub, especially as it grows with them, providing a wonderful source of pleasure for many years. If children are allowed to take part in any planting operations, they will usually take a personal interest in 'their' plant, especially if it occupies a special place in the garden.

Nurseries are mavellous places to shop during the Christmas rush, because there is such a wide range of useful things available. Parking is not such a great problem and the atmosphere of a nursery is very tranquil indeed, compared to the hectic bustle of busy shopping centres. Naturally, the best types of plants to select are those which can never become a problem, either as drain-blockers, or by growing too large.

Here are some useful small plants which require the minimum care and attention, look good most of the time and are easily placed in a garden.

Camellias. These have lovely, shining leaves at this time and make ideal gifts. Most types can withstand a little shade, tolerate a wide range of soils, take up little room, can occasionally be cut back without problems and produce a magnificent bonus when they flower in late winter.

Azaleas. These look good now, especially the small-leaved kurume varieties, the foliage of which assumes a bronzegreen colour. They will grow in full sun, are rarely more than half-a-metre high, can be tucked-in anywhere and, apart from normal feeding and watering, require no maintenance.

Daphnes. A winner at this time, because this is when the best specimens are available. They will fill a garden with their fragrance throughout the winter and are always received gratefully.

Hypericums. Varieties such as 'Rowallane hybrid' and *H. henryii* are already flowering strongly and with a bit of luck can be bought in bloom. The flowers are like enormous, bright-yellow buttercups and will cover the one-and-a-half metre high shrubs for at least six months.

Incidentally, all these plants will grow to perfection in tubs, provided they are watered daily during summer. So if you feel like including an attractive terracotta or concrete container with your gift, it won't be wasted.

Houseplants are always popular presents, whether for their attractive foliage or their flowers. However, be sure to give the easily looked-after kind to people who are not familiar with more sophisticated methods of plant care. Cacti and succulents are excellent because they can be virtually neglected if they are in a sunny window. The main cause of failure with these tough plants is overwatering and fertilizing. They seem to thrive in the homes of those people who occasionally remember to water them after the potting medium has just about dried out.

The best fruit trees for presents at this time are the citruses. A lemon, grapefruit or cumquat will never look back if planted out now and given a good watering. They rapidly become established over the next five months and are bearing within a couple of years. The hardiest of the lemons is the smallest-growing, Meyer. It forms a dark-green, dome-shaped plant, bearing large numbers of bright-yellow, sweetly-juicy fruit, mainly in winter. The larger-growing Eureka and Lisbon will bear their large, lemony fruit for most of the year. Cumquats carry tiny, loose-skinned, attractive orange-like fruit with easily separated segments. They make an ideal tub plant for a sunny patio.

High quality, strongly-made garden tools will last a lifetime and seem to improve with age. Stainless steel forks, spades and trowels make gardening a pleasure, even when digging or cultivating. The advantages of the highly-polished surface go beyond mere rust-resistance. They are easily cleaned and slip easily into the soil.

Pruning implements are always received with grateful surprise by anyone with a garden, even if they don't do much

> This week in the flower garden plant or sow: ageratum, alyssum, bedding begonia, calceolaria, carnation, campanula, celosia, China asters, chrysanthemum, coleus, cosmos, dahlia, gazania, gerbera, gypsophila, helichrysum, kochia, marigolds, nasturtium, petunia, phlox, rudbeckia, salvia, snapdragon, sunflower, verbena, viscaria and zinnia.

in it. Pruning saws are always handy, while secateurs, especially good-quality ones, will give many years of useful service.

There are specially-designed secateurs for men and women, usually with brightly-coloured handles so they can be easily seen. Long-handled secateurs or branch-cutters are more expensive but there are few gardens where they cannot be used several times a year.

Even a wheelbarrow can be an unusual but greatly appreciated Christmas present, as long as a good-quality product is chosen. There must be countless thousands of old, worn-out and rusted barrows lying around in gardens everywhere. A pneumatic-tyred, lightweight barrow, with a good capacity tray will cost quite a lot but will last for decades. Double-wheeled barrows with a bar-type handle are excellent for easy gardening because they can be wheeled around comfortably with one hand. Elderly people in particular will cherish such a gift – it can be used for many purposes, including bringing in firewood during winter.

Finally, gardening books are among the most used of all literature. Many nurseries stock a small range of books and journals.

One more thought. When sending cards to friends and relations, why not include a packet of flower or vegetable seed? It makes a nice gesture – a creative one too.

DECEMBER: LAST WEEK

Seaside Gardening

This is the time of the year when the annual migration to the seaside gains momentum and every weekend the sounds of lawn mowers and brushcutters echo around seaside shacks which have been virtually deserted for months.

It is also the time of the year when some of those who live by the sea look wistfully at the shrivelled remains of failed plantings and dream of the day when they might successfully create a lovely, seaside garden.

Well, I have good news.

Wonderful gardens can be made in places where harsh, salt-laden winds and hungry, sandy soils are the norm. The secret lies in the choice of correct plants, those which will thrive in these situations, and a special way of dealing with the soil. Hedges protect seaside gardens from wind, see pages 40 and 193 for more information about them.

The best plants to use – trees, shrubs and smaller perennials – can easily be identified and it is not really necessary to know very much about different species. The tell-tale signs of those plants suitable for seaside conditions are in the leaves. Plants which have silvery foliage such as lavender, leucadendron, leucospermum, podalyria, senecio, and westringia not only do particularly well by the sea, but grow much better there than inland. The silver appearance of the leaves is actually produced by thousands of tiny hairs. Their job is to stop the plants being seared by the salty wind.

There are other plants too of course, with a different type of resistant leaf. Narrow, waxy foliage such as that of Norfolk Island pines, bottlebrushes, cordyline, cyprusses, genista, rosemary, tamarix, and casuarina, overcome the harsh environment by their flexibility and ability to prevent moisture loss.

Some of the toughest seaside plants have leaves which are shiny as well as waxy. This puts them into the front line against salt spray. The New Zealand mirror-leaf shrub (*Coprosma repens*) is one of the great ones but there are also the Mexican orange blossom (*Choisya ternata*), escallonia, Japanese laurel (*Euonymmus japonica*), privet, pyracantha and Holm oak (*Quercus ilex*).

There are dozens of other species which delight in a seaside environment, including some of our most beautiful native plants. These include banksia, Oyster Bay pine, correa, eucalypts (especially *Eucalyptus lehmannii* with huge green flowers), hakea, helichrysum, kunzea, Coastal tea-tree, melaleuca, myoporum, olearia, and the extraordinary *Acacia longifolia* var *sophorae*, which will actually grow on a beach within a few yards of the surf.

What about the soil at the seaside? In spite of the fact that it usually consists of sand and is deficient in just about every essential major element, this easily worked soil can be made enormously productive. The method is the easiest kind of gardening, the no-digging method.

After the initial surface clearing and light cultivation, sandy soil should never be dug again. This is where mulching really comes into its own. The best of all mulching materials is that found by the sea. Seaweed, seagrass, shredded brackenfern, sheoke and tea-tree leaves, all make an outstanding soil conditioner, provided they are spread on to the surface and never dug in. If you can also bring in straw, spoilt hay, even sawdust, and add this to the local ingredients, the enriching effects have to be seen to be believed.

Once this mulch has been spread at

least a hundred millimetres deep, and the area given a good watering, planting can take place. The mulch is simply pushed aside at the planting point, and seeds or seedlings placed into the moist soil, adding a little complete fertilizer to the base of the planting hole. Vegetables of all kinds will thrive with the extra benefit of a soil which is always improving in quality. Other plants can be mulched with this mixture, and the problems of watering and weeding around them are sharply reduced. The plants will be less vulnerable in your absence.

So, if you want an easily maintained, attractive, productive seaside garden, don't be discouraged by the harshness of the environment. It can be done, provided you go about it in the right way.

Raising Annual Seedlings

One of the advantages of flowering annual plants is the speed with which they can provide a colourful display. In fact it is now possible to purchase them as well-formed, good-sized plants in containers, and in full bloom. This is the type of instant garden which is perfect for borders, pots, troughs, tubs and window boxes. Naturally, the bigger the individual plant, the greater the cost, but if the area to be planted is fairly small, or is in a tub, these well developed 'bloomers' are excellent value.

Most people with larger areas to cover will either sow seed, or plant small seedlings. Direct sowing, even at this perfect time for growing these colourful annuals, can be risky, because very little control can be exercised during the crucial germination period. Sowing the seed into containers, using soil which has been pasteurized or treated in some other way to eliminate harmful organisms or weed seeds, can be very successful, and extraordinarily cheap. A special seed-sowing mixture can be obtained from most nurseries, and, failing this, it is possible to mix one's own. However, ordinary garden soil should be avoided, unless sowing the more vigorous type of seed. Soil from home gardens accumulates all sorts of diseases over the years, as well as many insect pests. I have always gone to the trouble of using bush soil, usually obtained from land which has never been cultivated. See page 96 for detailed advice on growing from seed.

The range of annual plants available as seed or plants is enormous. A magnificent summer display can be obtained from a planting during this month, when the warm soil and long days virtually ensure success. Here are some of the easiest to grow.

Zinnia. These lovely upright plants are excellent for cutting. One variety, Showman, bears large, dahlia-like blooms, while Happy Talk has an amazing range of colours in the large, quilled flowers.

Petunia. These are understandably among the most popular of annuals. My own preference is for single colour types such as Red Petticoat, White or Red Satin, or any of the remarkable range of colours from pale pink and rose to purple, blue or salmon.

African Marigolds. These are the ones for planting in areas with twitch-grass problems (often near and under a fence). However, full sun is essential for them to be able to control such grass weeds fully and some assistance during the early weeks of growth, to keep the twitch at bay, will make all the difference. Big, strong varieties such as Jubilee, Crackerjack or African Queen rapidly produce a superb blaze of colour which lasts for months.

Celosia. This is one annual which ought to be grown more in our gardens. The unusual, brightly coloured plumes make an arresting display in any sunny garden.

Phlox. Here is another bright annual which thrives during the summer, and is an essential part of any display. Like most of the other annuals, once established they require little attention.

There are too many annuals available now to be detailed, but here are some of the most flamboyant, all of which can be planted out now for non-stop colour for the next four months: ageratum, alyssum, aster, bedding begonia, nasturtium, salvia, sunflower, verbena, rudbeckia, foxglove, hollyhock, helichrysum, and lobelia.

Time to Lift Bulbs

The foliage of most of the spring flowering bulbs has now died back or, at least, turned yellow. This means that they have become dormant and may be safely moved. For many people, especially those who are growing daffodils in grassed areas, it is a great relief to at last be able to mow over them, without the danger of retarding their development. Daffodils may be left in the ground, often for many years, without any problems. They appear to be able to withstand the cold, saturated conditions so typical of southern winters, without any real problems. However, there are certain conditions from which daffodils and jonquils should be lifted.

If these bulbs have become badly overhung by dense trees or shrubs over the years and are in a situation in which they receive very little sun during their growing period, they will gradually cease to produce flowers. Leaves will emerge each winter, but no blooms.

Once such bulbs are dug out of the ground and examined, it will be easy to spot why this failure occurs. Bulbs which are grown in highly competitive situations with little sun become starved. Such bulbs will be smaller than normal and some will be tiny.

Once these bulbs are replanted in a new, open and sunny area, they will have a chance to regain their natural size and then begin to bloom again. They will need the first season to develop to this full size, so there will be few if any blooms for the first year in the new situation. Afterwards, they will flower as they used to when they were first planted many years ago.

Another occasion for lifting daffodil and jonquil bulbs at this time, is when a large increase in numbers is required. Not many people realize that even under the best growing conditions the closely grown bulbs compete with each other after a year or so, and the increase in the number of bulbs is fairly limited. However, should they be lifted and divided up to be planted separately, the increase will be quite staggering. In other words, if you have the time, lifting and dividing these bulbs every year will mean a huge increase in your stock.

Other bulbs such as hyacinths and tulips must be lifted every year and replanted in March or April. If this lifting is not carried out, the chances are that you will eventually lose your bulbs. In mountainous, better drained parts of Australia, the lives of these plants will certainly be much longer, but lifting and replanting is still more beneficial and results in healthier, more productive plants.

Many liliums are now either flowering strongly or have just finished blooming. In most cases, if they are obviously happy in their present situation, they may be left to quietly multiply. The seed may be taken when it is ripe, and if sown

> Carry out deep watering in all parts of the garden, at least once weekly. Avoid shallow watering, which is quite harmful.
>
> Foliar feed as many plants, shrubs, trees and vegetables as possible with well-diluted seaweed concentrate, to help strengthen them and to supply essential trace elements.

immediately into clean, peaty soil, in a container or seed tray, and kept moist and out of the sun, it will germinate quite readily. You will find that although the young plants may not produce flowers for two or even three years, they will have a vigour much greater than the mother bulbs.

Dahlia tubers which were planted during the previous weeks will be showing plenty of foliage now and actually producing the first flowers in some cases. The main needs of these beautiful but fragile plants right now are strong supports. Don't hesitate to use several stakes per clump if there is more than one main shoot. Once they start to add substantial amounts of topgrowth, dahlias are particularly subject to wind damage.

The other major needs of dahlias from now onwards are plenty of water and regular applications of fertilizers. Pulverized cow manure is just about perfect, especially when carefully applied around the main stems and gently worked into the top few centimetres of soil. Always water the plants both before and after applying any kind of fertilizer.

APPENDIX

Bordeaux Mixture

This is a reliable, well-tested fungicide. It is useful for controlling leafcurl in peach and nectarine trees. It is sprayed over most parts of the trees as soon as the leaves are cast in autumn and again just before the leafbuds break in late winter. This last spray is most important and is best applied as the flower buds are starting to swell, just before they open. If the spray is applied after the leaves emerge, it will be too late to prevent leafcurl developing in wet-spring districts. Bordeaux mixture is also effective when sprayed at the same time, against brown-rot of stone fruit and American gooseberry mildew.

It is particularly effective when mixed and used fresh. It is best used on its own and never on plants with sensitive leaves.

Dissolve 100 grams of copper sulphate in three litres of hot water, using a non-metal (plastic) bucket. Leave overnight to thoroughly mix. In a separate bucket mix 100 grams of hydrated lime in three litres of cold water. Then, carefully pour the 'milk of lime' into the copper sulphate solution and stir. Finally, add enough cold water to make up the total liquid to ten litres. This is an effective, strong mixture. Check for excessive acidity by dipping a bright steel nail into the mix. If it emerges dulled, add more milk of lime until it remains bright after dipping.

Burgundy Mixture

This is an even stronger fungicide. It is made in the same way as Bordeaux mixture, except that washing soda is used instead of hydrated lime. Very effective against American gooseberry mildew or leafcurl. Must not be used on plants while in leaf.

Lawn Sand

This is an old, safe way of destroying flatweeds in lawns, while stimulating the growth of grasses. Plantain, cat's ear and dandelion are among many of the broad-leaved lawn weeds which can be destroyed by this simple mixture of sulphate of ammonia and sand.

Mix two parts of dry sand (not sea sand), with one part of sulphate of ammonia. Broadcast over the weed-infested parts of the lawn, or drop a good pinch on to each flatweed. Within a few days most of the weeds begin to bolt out of the ground then, within a week or so, shrivel and go black. Persistent weeds may require a second or third dose before they succumb. If unsightly moss is also a problem, the inclusion of a half-part of sulphate of iron to the mixture will quickly destroy this weed too.

Sulphate of ammonia should not be used unless it has been bulked-out with sand, otherwise the grass may be burned.

Clover in lawns can be a problem when the flowers attract bees. Children in particular are likely to be stung, because they often run around barefooted over the lawn. The lawn sand mixture will gradually restrict the growth of clover so that it may be easily removed by hand.

Cross-pollination of Fruit Trees for Full Crops

Some fruit trees will not set fruit, or will carry only small crops if they are not cross-pollinated with another variety of the same fruit. Here are some commonly-grown fruit trees and their cross-pollinators:

Japanese Plums: Burbank (Wickson, Narrabeen). Santa Rosa (Mariposa, Narrabeen). Satsuma (Santa Rosa, Narrabeen).

European Plums: Angelina (King Billy, President, Grand Duke). Coe's Golden Drop (Greengage, Prune D'Agen). Jefferson (President, Grand Duke).

Sweet Cherries: Ron's Seedling (Moss Early, Early Rivers). Williams Favourite (Blackboy, Lambert, Napoleon).

Pears: Williams Bon Chrétien (Beurre Bosc, Doyenne du Comice). Packham's Triumph (Winter Nelis, Williams Bon Chrétien). Winter Cole (Clapp's Favourite, Beurre Bosc).

Apples (cross-pollination not essential, but will improve yield): Gravenstein (Jonathan, Granny Smith). Sturmer Pippin (Delicious). Cox's Orange Pippin (Tydeman's Early).

Hazel Nuts: Wandil's Pride (American White).

Almonds: Chellaston (Johnston's Prolific, Non Pareil). IXL (Johnston's Prolific).

Peaches and Nectarines: These, with the exception of J.H. Hale, are self-pollinating. The exception is pollinated by others which flower at the same time.

Apricots: most common varieties are self-pollinating. However, some newer, Canadian varieties need a pollinator.

This list covers a relatively small number of fruit and nut trees, but they are typical of varieties grown in home gardens. Most nurseries keep a detailed list, as do State agricultural departments.

INDEX

References to more substantial coverage in the text are indicated in **bold**.
An asterisk* beside a plant name indicates that it has become a weed in some areas.

Acacia 99, 117
   *baileyana (Cootamundra wattle) 193
   fimbriata (sticky wattle) 106, 193
   longifolia **96**
   pravissima (Ovens wattle) 90, 106, 193
   pruning 167
   replanting 109
   for windbreak 193
   vestita 90
achillea 3, 15, 27, 45, 48, 61, 167, 183
   dividing 91, 120
acidic soil 19, 37, 46, 49, 111
   acid-lovers **104–5**
acrolinium 3, 183
African daisy (*Arctotis*) 3, 5, 15, 27, 45, 61, 79, 93, 113, 167, **173**, 184
African marigold 3, 5, 15, 131, 147, 150, 168, 176, 184, 186, **197**
African violet (*Saintpaulia*) 4, **25–6**, **66**, 137, 151, **169**
Agapanthus orientalis (Nile lily) **163**
ageratum 3, 5, 15, 27, 131, 141, 147, 150, 167, 176, 183, 186, 195, 198
alder 135, 144
Algerian oats 40, 74, 145
alkaline soil 24
Allium schoenoprasum (chives) 36, 103
allspice 95, 110
almond tree 56, **57**, 202
   ornamental 57
   pests 4, 11
Alnus glutinosa (common alder) 135
alpine gum (*Eucalyptus alpina*) 193

alpine plants 69, **72**, **76**, 101, 102, 119, 146, **181**
Alyssum 3, 5, 15, 27, 45, 61, 79, 93, 113, 131, 141, 147, 150, 160, 167, 176, 183, 186, 195, 198
   saxatile – now *Aurinia saxatilis*
amaranthus 5, 131, 150, 160, 167, 176, 184
Amaryllis belladonna (belladonna lily) 55, 61, 82, 110, **163**
American dogwood (*Cornus florida*) 63, 126
American gooseberry mildew 114, 132, **140**
American mountain laurel (*Kalmia latifolia*) 24, 51, 87
ammobium 167
anaphalis 184
anchusa 131, 150, 167, 184
androsace 23, 102
anemone 15, 27, 45, 55, 61
angel's trumpet (previously *Datura*, now *Brugmansia* x *candida*) 163–4
animal manure 37, 58, 75, 84, 102, **111**, **112**, 114, **125**, 131, 141, 157
   nitrogen source 66, 67, 147
   on vegetables 111, 120, 122, 124, 133, 150, 151, 153, 155, 161
annuals 61, 113, 141, 149, 167, 183
   seedlings **197–8**
   for summer **173–4**
antirrhinum 3, 15, 27, 45, 131, 141, 147, 150, 167, 176, 184
ants 10–11, 126
aphids **10–12**, 14, 36, 103, **164**, **174**
   black 38, 41, 150

black cherry 11–12
black citrus 8, 143, 150
   on fruit trees 132, **178–9**
   green peach 150
   peach 132
   on roses 10, 64, 131, 149
   woolly 11
apple tree 56, 103, **115**, 159, 186
   choosing **57**, **202**
   harvesting 21, 28, **32**, 121
   pests 4, **11**, 18, 46, 114, 158, 168, 182
   pruning **18**, **80**, 132, 140
apricot tree **83**, 111, 115, 104
   choosing 56, **86**, 202
   harvesting 21, 122
   pruning 18, 48, 80
aquatic plants **21**, 23
aquilegia 3, 5, 15, 27, 45, 61, 79, 93, 113, 131, 150, 167, 184
arabis 167, 184
Arctotis see African daisy
Artemisia 98
   dracunculus (tarragon) 36
artichoke
   globe 113, 132, 150
   Jerusalem 79, 94, 113
arum lily 163
asparagus **45**, 62, **68**, 79, 85, 94, 104, 106, 132, 150, 168
asparagus pea 168
aspidistra 111
aster 3, 5, 15, 48, 131, 150, 167, 176, 184, 198
   alpine 102
   dividing 49, 91, 120, 121
astilbe 48, 91, 120
aubrieta 5, 167, 184
Aucuba japonica (Japanese laurel) 24, 87, 196
Aurinia saxatilis (previously *Alyssum saxatile*) 98, **180**

Australian plants **67**, **72–3**, **96**, 139, **116–18**
   fertilizing **37**, 46, 111
   for hedges **40–1**
   pruning **20–1**, 93, 94, 131, 147, 167
   seaside plants 196
   staking 20–1, 72, 117
   transplanting 72, 83, 109
   watering 96, **170**, **171**
   as windbreak 193–4
azalea 24, **44**, **65**, 69, 87, 113, **139**, **144**, **188**, **194**
   cuttings 16, 17
   fertilizing 37, 46, 124, 141, 186
   foliar feeding 190, 191
   transplanting 41, 51, **82**, **104–5**, 108
   watering 5, 167

baby's breath (Gypsophila) 3, 5, 15, 27, 45, 48, 49, 61, 79, 93, 113, 131, 147, 150, 168, 176, 184, 195
balm (*Melissa officinalis*) 36
balsam 3, 5, 167, 184
bamboo, Japanese sacred (*Nandina domestica*) 87
Banksia **72**, **96**, 109, 167
   ericifolia (heath banksia) 90, 96, 194
   spinulosa (hairpin banksia) 90, 136, 194
barbecues 186–7
barber's pole (*Oxalis rubra*) 119
basil (*Ocimum basilicum*) **36**, 104
beans 103, 134, 159, 160, **161**, 190
   fertilizing 68, 111
   harvesting 12
   see also specific beans
beetroot 3, 15, **19**, 96, **116**, **122**, 127, 132, 133, 141, 150, **155**, 168, 184, 185, 190
   companion planting **103**
   harvesting 53
Begonia 79, 167, 184, 195, 198
   rex 111
belladonna lily (*Amararyllis beladonna*) 55, 61, 82, 110, **163**
bellis 3, 5, 131, 150, 167, 184
Benlate **18**, 140
berberis 24

Bergenia cordifolia 95
berryfruits **18**, 85, 94, **168**, 182
   choosing **56**
   mulching 7, 16, 46, **54**, 58, 62, **71**, 132, **140**
   pruning 7, 46, 47, **53–5**, 62, 64–5
   transplanting 71
Betula pendula see silver birch
birds 65, **174–5**
   attracting 179
   deterring 92
   manure 65
'bitter pit' 46
black spot 3, **15**, 171, 183
blackcurrants **64–5**, 184
   pruning **7**, 46, 53
blazing star (*Liatris*) 49
Blechnum nudum (fishback fern) 24
blood and bone 37, 66, **67**, 73, 90, 112, 139, 142, 186
   for fruit trees 8, 16, 114, 143, 184
   for houseplants 111
   for lawns 6, 18, 34, 136–7
   on mulch 69, 75, 84, 147
   for ornamentals 26, 30, 62, 93, 113, 131, 149, 157, 167, 177
   in potting mix 87, 138
   for rock gardens 102
   for vegetables 3, 14, 39, 100, 113, 116, 120, 124, 125, 150, 152, 153, 161, 164–5, 166, 176, 180, 185
blossom-end rot 17, 154, 186
bluebell, Spanish 31
blue lupin 40
blueberries 56
bonemeal 67, **112**, 120
borax 10
Bordeaux mixture 18, 46, **50**, 62, 65 , 77, **114**, 143, 168, 201
border pinks (*Dianthus allwoodii*) 48, 55, **181**
borers 11, 64–5, 181
boronia 5, 105, 136, 167, 182
bottlebrush (*Callistemon*) **135**, 182, 196
box (*Buxus*) 110
boysenberries 54
bramble bushes, pruning 4, 46, 53–4, 56

branch cutter 70
brassicas 3, **20**, **38**, 45, **59–60**, 61, 79, 93, 94, **116**, **122**, 133, 134, 141, 160, **185**
   clubroot 178
   fertilizing 15, 150
   pests **184**
broad beans 27, **38–9**, **41–2**, 45, 59, 61, 71, 74, 79, 85, 94, 106, 113, 120, 132, 133, 141, 150
   fertilizing **39**, 47, **55**, 87, 110, 112
   supporting 168
broccoli 3, 15, **20**, 27, 38, 59, 71, 74, 87, 104, 113, 120, **122**, 132, 133, 150, **155**, 168, 184, 185, 190
   fertilizing **66**
   pests 116
broom 102, 110, **160**
   seed 161
   transplanting 83, 109
browallia 184
brown spot 66
brown-rot 16, **18**, 114, 132, 140–1, **179**
Brugmansia x *candida* (angel's trumpet) 163–4
Brussels sprouts 3, 15, **20**, 104, 133, 150, 168, **184**, 185
   harvesting 60, 79
Buddleja 16, 61, 79, 79
   salvifolia 96
bulbs 27, **31–2**, 45, 61, 79, 93, 113
   lifting 3, 15, **39**, 44, **55**, 132, **198–9**
Burgundy mixture 114, **201**
bush beans 133, 150, **164–6**, 181, 184
butter beans 12
Buxus (box) 110

cabbage 3, 15, 20, 27, 38, 42, 59, 71, 74, 87, 113, 122, 132, 133, 141, 150, 155, 168, 176, 190
   companion planting **103**, 104
   fertilizing 47, 111
   pests 116, 159, **181–2**
   summer 59, 132, 133
cabbage moth grub 116, 159, 184
cacti 4, 9, 25, 138, 169, 185, **195**

calceolaria 167, 195
calcium 38, **46–7**, 49, **68**, 135
calcium sulphate (gypsum) 135
calendula 3, 15, 27, 45, 61, 79, 93, 113, 131, 150, 160, 186
Californian iris (*Iris innominata*) 31
calla 184
Callistemon **135, 182,** 196
  pallidus (pallid bottlebrush) 96, 106, 194
  viminalis (weeping bottlebrush) 106
Calocephalus brownii (cushion bush) 41
calycanthus (*Chimonanthus praecox*) **95,** 110
camellia 24, **44,** 69, 87, 93, 96, 105, **139, 188, 194**
  cuttings 16
  defoliation **65**
  fertilizing 37, 46, 124, 141, 186, 190
  pests 126
  transplanting 41, **50–1,** 82, 108
  watering 5, 167, 170
campanula 5, 102, 147, 167, 184, 195
campsis 107
candytuft 15, 23, 27, 45, 61, 79, 93, 113, 131, 150
canna lily 49, 91, 120
canteloupe 184
Canterbury bells 3, 15, 27, 45, 48, 49, 61, 79, 93, 113, **158**
capsicum 3, 15, 115, 132, 133, 134, 140, 150, **153,** 168, 184, 185, 190, 192
Carbaryl 150
carnation 3, 5, 15, 27, 45, 48, 49, 55, 61, 79, 98, 147, **158,** 167, 184, **188–9,** 195
  pruning **20, 181**
carrots 3, 15, **19,** 27, 38, **39,** 96, 113, **115, 116, 120,** 127, 132, 133, 141, 150, **155,** 168, 181, 184, 185, 190
  companion planting 100, 103, 104
  harvesting 53
  improving **122–3**
  pests 178
castor oil plant 164
casuarina 117, 196

caterpillars **11**, 14, 45, 132, **159,** 179, 181–2, **188**
  of white cabbage butterfly 60, **63–4,** 79, 116, **159**
catmint 120
cats 91–2, 175
catsear 75
cauliflower 3, 15, **20,** 27, 38, **42,** 59, 60, 71, 74, 87, 93, 113, 120, **122,** 132, 133, 141, 150, **155, 168,** 184
  companion planting **103,** 104
  fertilizing 47, 190
Ceanothus 83
  impressus 90
celeriac 3, 185
celery 3, 15, 27, **68,** 132, 141, 150, **155,** 168, 184, 185, 190
  companion planting **103**
celosia 3, 5, 15, 131, 147, 150, 167, 176, 195, **197**
centaurea 168
cercis 109
Chaenomeles (Japanese flowering quince) 95–6
Chamaecyparis 51, 99
chamomile 103
chef's hat correa (*Correa baeuerlenii*) 41
chelated iron 190, 191
cherry tree 4, 11, 12, 79
  Japanese flowering (*Prunus*) **85**
  slugs 184
  sour 56
  see also sweet cherry tree
cherry-plum 11
chestnut tree 56, 57
chicory 132, 150, 168
Chimonanthus praecox (calycanthus; wintersweet) **95,** 110
China aster 175, 195
Chinese cabbage 3, 15, 27, 45, 61, 132, 150, 168, 184, 185, 190
Chinese gooseberry 56, 79, **80, 151**
Chinese greens 150, 168
chives (*Allium schoenoprasum*) 36, 103
Choisya ternata (Mexican orange blossom) 196
Christmas rose (*Helleborus*) 24
chrysanthemum 3, 5, 9, **20,** 102, 110, 131, 147, **149,** 150,

158, 168, 184, 195
  cuttings 113, 121
  dividing 91, 120, **141**
  fertilizing **67**
  pruning **181**
cineraria 3, 15, 27, 45, 184
cistus 83
citrus bud mites 18
citrus trees 56, 151, **188,** 195
  fertilizing 8, 16, 124, 186, 190
  mulching 143
  pests **18,** 28, **31,** 63, 114, **126–7,** 143
  planting **115**
  problems 65, **143–4**
  pruning 8, **127–8,** 132
  summer care **8**
  transplanting 41, 51, 108
  watering 5, 8, 16, 128, 143, 170
  see also lemon tree; orange tree; grapefruit
clarkia 131, 150, 168, 176, 184
clay soil **66,** 141, 143, 162
  turning into friable **134–6**
clematis 107
Clensel 4, 11, 12, 46, 105, 125, 126, 159, 179, 184
cleome 3, 5, 168, 176
clianthus 109
climbing beans 3, **12,** 103, 104, 112, 115, 121, 133, 150, **164–5, 168, 176**
climbing plants 5, 83, 106–7
clippings, lawn 146
clover 164
clubroot 93, 178
coastal tea-tree 196
cockchafer grub 64
codlin moth 4, 16, 46, 132, **140, 150, 158–9,** 168, 182, 184
coleus 111, 131, 147, 150, 176, 184, 195
collar rot 143
comfrey (*Symphytum officinale*) 36
common alder (*Alnus glutinosa*) 135
companion planting 14, 100, **103–4,** 123, **133**
compost 26, **28–30,** 56, 57, 58, **66,** 75, 79, **97, 112,** 117, 122, 125, 142
  from seaweed 37
  sheet 147, 162

for vegetables **14**, 45, 93
compost bin 28, 29
compost 'tea' 151, **153**, 190, 191
conifers 51, 108
    dwarf 5, 82, 88, 101, 102
    golden 99
container plants 12, 59, 61, 73, 93, **97–8**, 105, 149, 171, 174, 191, 195
    caring for **8–10**
    fertilizing **9**, 87
    planting **86–8**
    watering 186, 188
Convolvulus maritima 173
Cootamundra wattle (*Acacia baileyana*) 193
*Coprosma repens (New Zealand mirror-leaf) 196
corbies (grass grub) 64
cordyline 88, 196
corn salad 132, 150, 168
cornflower 3, 15, 27, 45, 131, 150, 168
Cornus florida (American dogwood) 63, 126
Correa 136, 196
    baeuerlenii (chef's hat correa) 41
    decumbens 90
cosmos 3, 5, 15, 131, 147, 150, 168, 176, 184, 195
cotton lavender (*Santolina chamaecyparissus*) 98
couchgrass 75, 176
crab-apple (*Malus floribunda*) 85
creepers 72
cress 4, 132, 150, 168, 184
crop rotation **13–14**, 67, 122, **133–4**, 178
cross-pollination **56–7**, **201–2**
crotalaria 96
cucumber 4, 15, **18**, 132, **133**, 141, 150, 153, 168, **178**, 184, 190, 192
    companion planting **103**, 104, 133
    harvesting **33**
cumquat 127, 195
Cupressus lambertiana (Lambert's cypress) 40
currants 4, 56, 140
cushion bush (*Calocephalus brownii*) 41
cuttings **16–17**, 24, 26, 27, 61, 121, 141
    hardwood 87

houseplants 151, 185
    planting 131
Cyclamen 28, 74, 132
    hederifolium 23
cypress (*Cupressus*) 51, 196
    hedge 40
    Lambert's (*Cupressus lambertiana*) 40

daffodil 3, 18, 31, 105, 109, **163**
    lifting 198
dahlia 3, 5, **125**, 131, 147, **149**, 150, 168, 184, **188**, 195
    dividing **156–7**, 167
    lifting 56, 67, 91, 79
    pests 126
    staking 185, **199**
daisy of the veldt (*Dimorphotheca*) **173**, 184
dandelion 7, 75
Daphne 87, 102, 105, 110, 113, 126, **194**
    cuttings **16**
    defoliation **65**
    fertilizing 141, 186
    odora 95
    watering 5, 170
Datura – now *Brugmansia* x *candida*
dead-heading 9, 27, 113, 174, 177, 183
    roses 3, **20**, **169**, 182, **188**
deciduous plants 5, 61, 115
    choosing **73–5**
    cuttings 87
    fertilizing 88–9, 190
    nitrogen deficiency **66**
    planting 12, 79, **88–9**
    pruning 79, 80–1, 94, 106
    transplanting 51, 74–5, 82, 109
    trees **84–5**
deep watering 186, 198
defoliation **65**
delphinium 3, 5, 15, 27, 45, 48, 49, 61, 79, 93, 147, **158**, 168, 177, 184
    cuttings 113, 121, 149
    dividing 120, **141**
    staking **83**
derris **11**, 14, 60, **64**
deutzia 16, 87
Dianthus 3, 5, 15, 23, 27, 45, 61, 79, 93, 98, 113, 131, 147, 150, 168, 184

    allwoodii (border pinks) 48, 55, **181**
Dicksonia antarctica (soft treefern) 24
dieffenbachia **163**
dill 103
Dimorphotheca (daisy of the veldt) **173**, 184
Dipel **11**, 14, **60**, **64**, 159
disease control **17–18**
dock 7, 75, 121
dogs 91
dolomite 30, 35, **46–7**, **68**, 102, 177
    for fruit trees 62, 88
    in growing medium 26, 97
    for vegetables 25, 38, 42, 55, 120, 134, 164, 185
downy mildew 18
drainage 44, **52**, **58**, **68**, 79, 94, 144
drip irrigation 151, **170–1**, 183
drive-ways, making 128–9
dry weather planting **12–13**
dryandra 109
dusky bells 136
dusty miller (*Senecio cineraria*) 98
dwarf beans **103**, 185
dwarf conifers 5, 88, 101, 102
dwarf flowering peach 88
dwarf pomegranate 88
dwarf rhododendron 16, 87

earwigs 159
'easy-bleeders' 45, **47–8**
easy-care gardens **189**
eelworm 176
eggplant 4, 132, 133, 134, **150**, **153**, 168, 176, 184, 185, 190
elm leaves 84
endive 15, 27, 132, 150, 168
English ivy **164**
English spinach **19**, **38**, 71, **95**, 106
Epsom salts **68**
Erica 5, 82, 88, 93, 108, 139, 167, **188**
    caniculata **96**
    fertilizing 37, 46, 141, 186
Erigeron speciosus **180**
Eriostemon 96, 110, 136
    myoporoides (wax plant) **41**
erythrina 109
escallonia 196

Index

eschscholtzia 168
Eucalyptus **72**, 110, 117
  alpina 193
  caterpillars on **179**
  forrestiana (fuchsia gum) 193–4
  lehmannii 196
  transplanting 109
  viridis 193
  wind damage 83
Euonymus japonica (Japanese laurel) 24, 87, 196
Euphorbia pulcherrima (poinsettia) **163**
European gooseberry mildew 140
European plum tree 56, 80, **115**, **121**, **202**
evergreens
  scented 110
  transplanting 27, 41, **50–1**, 61, 113

fences 121
fennel 104, 185
fernery 24
ferns 23, **24**
  pests 126
  in pots 16, **69**, 87, 114, **137–8**
  watering 4, 16, 169, 185
fertilizer 9, 65, 66, 128, 132, 139, 141, 167, 177, 197, 199
  Australian plants **37**, 46, 111
  choosing **111–12**
  citrus trees 8, 16, 124, 128, 143, 186, 190
  container plants 9, 87
  deciduous plants 88–9, 190
  fruit trees 37, 46–7, 111, 139, 182, 184
  herbs 35
  houseplants 62, **67**, 111, 169, 185, 190, 192
  lawns 6, 34, 51, 111, 136
  vegetables 25, 37–8, 39, 46–7, 57, 66, 95, 100, 116, 155, 156, 161, 164–5, 184
  see also foliar feeding; liquid fertilizer; manure
fig (*Ficus*) 56, 111, 126
fish waste 37
fishback fern (*Blechnum nudum*) 24
fittonia 111

Florence fennel 185
floribunda roses 62, **77**, 110
flower garden *see* ornamental garden
flowering, failure of 66
foliage plants **98–9**, 196
foliar feeding 38, 42, 66, 143, 151, **190–1**, **198**
  container plants **9–10**
houseplants **151**, 185, **192**
forget-me-not 186
foxglove 3, 15, 27, 45, 48, 61, 79, 93, 113, 177, 198
Fraxinus excelsior (golden ash) 99
freesia 3, 15, 27, 45, 55, 61
French beans 3, 12, 112, 115, **122**, 168, 176
  companion planting **103**, 104
French marigold 131, 150, 184
French prune 121–2
French tarragon 36
fruit garden, care of 4, 16, 21, 28, 46, 62, 80, 94, 114, 132, 150–1, 168, 184
  see also berryfruits
fruit trees **100**, 175, 192
  blood and bone on 8, 16, 114, 143, 184
  brown rot 16, **18**, 114, 132, 140–1, **179**
  choosing **56–7**, 74, **85–6**, 121–2
  cross-pollinating 56–7, 201–2
  fertilizing 37, 46–7, 111, 139, 182, 184
  flowering 120
  pests **4**, **11**, 132, **140–1**, **150**, 168, **178–9**, 181, **184**
  planting **88–9**
  stone fruits 18, 21, 28, 32, 46, 62, 115, 124, 132, **140**, 141, 179, 184
  watering 16, 50, 151, 182, 186
  see also citrus trees; mulching; pruning; and individual varieties
fuchsia **24**, 87
fuchsia gum (*Eucalyptus forrestiana*) 193–4
fungicides *see* Bordeaux mixture; Burgundy mixture

gaillardia 5, 131, 147, 150, 168, 184

garden design **43–4**
  see also landscaping
garlic 33, **68**, 79, 93, **100–1**, 116, 133
  companion planting 104
Garrya elliptica (tassel bush) **96**
gazania 5, 168, 184, 195
*genista 196
geranium 5, 131, 150, 168, 184
gerbera 131, 150, 168, 184, 195
germination (seed) **96–8**, **140**, **160–1**
geum 3, 15, 27, 45, 61, 79, 93, 113, 131, 150, 168
gifts of plants **194–5**
gladioli 93, **121**, **125**, 131, 141
gleditsia 109
gloves 69
gloxinia **26**, 46, **66**, **74**, 132
godetia 131, 150, 168, 176, 184
golden ash (*Fraxinus excelsior*) 99
golden chain tree (*Laburnum anagyroides*) **164**
golden elm (*Ulmus procura*) 99
golden honeysuckle (*Lonicera japonica*) 106–7
golden juniper (*Juniperus communis*) 99
gooseberry 56
  pruning 4, **18**, 114, **132**
  mildew 114, 132, **140**
grafting **115**, 132, **141**
grape hyacinth 31
grapefruit 127, 195
grapes 16, 18, 32, 56, 126
  pruning **80–1**
grass **139–40**, 151
  couch 75, 176
  for outdoor living area 187
grass grub (corbies) 64
grass-weed 5
green cherry tree (*Prunus serulata*) **84**
green manure crops **39–40**, 57, 79, 93, 117, **133–4**
greenfly *see* aphids
greenhouse 4, **191–2**
Grevillea **72**, 136, **181**, 194
  flowering 96
  gaudi chaudii 90
  'Golden Sparkle' 41
  pruning 94, 147
  rosmarinifolia 90
  transplanting 109

ground-cover 24, 45, 98
  in sloping gardens 72
  for weed suppression **89–90**, 189
growth problems 65
Gypsophila see baby's breath
gypsum (calcium sulphate) 135

hairpin banksia (*Banksia spinulosa*) 90, 136, 194
Hakea **72**, 96, 167, 196
  laurina (pin-cushion plant) **41**
Hamamelis mollis (witch hazel) 110
hanging baskets 9, 114, 151, 171
hardenbergia 90, 109
harlequin bug **125–6**
harvesting **32–3**
  see also particular fruits and vegetables
hawthorn 4, 11, 96
hazelnut tree 56, 57, 202
heath banksia (*Banksia ericifolia*) 90, 96, 194
Hebe 88, 96
  hulkeana 90
Hedera canariensis (ivy) 107
hedges 164
  Australian plants **40–1**
  clippings 112
  as windbreak **193**, 196
Helianthemum (sun rose) **173**
Helichrysum; 3, 5, 15, 23, 98, 126, 131, 141, 147, 150, 168, 176, 184, 195, 196, 198
  retortum 173
heliotrope 131, 150, 168, 184
helipterum 168, 184
Helleborus (hellebore) 45
  Christmas rose 24
herbaceous borders 46–7, **48–9**, 61, 91, 171
herbaceous paeony 61, 66
herbicides 89, **90**, **137**
herbs **35–6**, 132, 168
hibiscus 126, 131, 150, 184
hippeastrum 25, 169
holly 126
hollyhock 3, 15, 27, 45, 131, 150, 168, 177, 184, 198
holm oak (*Quercus ilex*) 196
honeysuckle 110
hoof and horn meal 66
horse beans 74

hose, soaker 170
hot weather
  garden care **20–1**
  mulching for **146–7**
houseplants **25–6**, **69**, **137–9**
  in your absence **4–5**
  care of 16, 28, 46, 62, 74, 80, 94, 132
  cuttings 151, 185
  disorders in **65–6**
  nitrogen deficiency **67**
  putting outside **169**
  repotting **114**
  see also fertilizer; watering
hoya 151
hyacinth 39, 55, 61, 109, 198
hybrid tea roses 62, **77**, 110
hydrangea 90
  fertilizing 186, 190
  pests 63, **126**
  pruning 55, 61, **63**
Hypericum 16, 79, 87, **194**
  calycinum 90
  pruning **63**, 79
hyssop 104

iberis 176
Iceland poppy 3, 15, 27, 45, 61, 79, 93, 113, 186
impatiens 130, 131, 150, 168, 184
Indian hawthorn 96
insect control see pest control
ipomea 184
Iris **30–1**, 48
  innominata (Californian iris) 31
  lifting 23
  unguicularis **95**
iron 66, **104**, 190, 191
ivy (*Hedera*) 107
  English 164

Japanese flowering cherry (*Prunus*) **85**
Japanese flowering quince (*Chaenomeles*) 95–6
Japanese laurel (*Aucuba japonica*) 24, 87, 196
Japanese maple 24, 186
Japanese plum **56–7**, 80, 111, 115, **122**, **201**
Japanese sacred bamboo (*Nandina domestica*) 87

Japanese wind flower 48
Jasminium polyanthum 107
jonquil 3, 18, 31, 109, **163**
  lifting 141, 198
Juniperus 51, 88
  communis (golden juniper) 99
  prostrate 90, 99

kalanchoe 25, 169
kale 74, 184
  ornamental 3, 15, 27, 45, 61, 79, 93
Kalmia 108
  latifolia (American mountain laurel) 24, 51, 87
knitbone (comfrey) 36
kochia 131, 150, 168, 176, 184, 195
kohlrabi 4, 15, 103, 104, 113, 120, 132, 141, 150, 168, 184
kunzea 196

Laburnum 83, **85**, 109
  anagyroides (golden chain tree) **164**
ladybirds 10, 132, 150
Lamb's ears (*Stachys lanata*) 98
Lambert's cypress (*Cupressus lambertiana*) 40
Lamiastrum (variegated dead nettle) 24
landscaping
  before building house **107–8**
  easy-care garden 189
  hedges 40–1, 193, 196
  outside living area 186–7
  patios and paths **128–9**
  rock garden 23, 62, 101–2
  shady places **23–4**
  with stone walls 171–3, 179–81
  winter garden 81–3
larkspur 5, 131, 141, 150, 168, 176, 184
lathyrus 3
lattices 106, 165
Laurus nobilis (sweet bay) 87, 126
lavender 88, 110, 196
lawn 3, 45, 61, 68, 79, 91, 113, 119, 135, 149, 164, 167, 189
  blood and bone on 6, 18, 34, 136–7
  clippings 146

Index

fertilizing 6, 34, 51, 111, 136
landscaping 82
making **33–4**
mowing **64**, 120–1
replacing with flowers **177–8**
sowing 27, 34, 121
spring care **136–7**
watering 6, 18, 34, 51, **170**
weeds 7, 121, 137, 141, 146–7, 201
see also grass
lawn sand 201
leaf curl 46, 49, **50**, **65**, **114**, **179**
leaf die-back **65**
leaves
  defoliation **65**
  fallen **84**
  plants for foliage **98–9**, 196
  resistant 196
  scented 110
  spots on 65, 66
  wilting 66
leeks 4, **15**, 45, 61, 71, 113, 120, 132, 141, 150, 168, **184**, 190
  companion planting 103
legumes 13–14, 67, 109, **160**
lemon tree 3, 56, 86, 111, 114, **115**, 195
  choosing **142–3**
  pests 126, 150
  pruning **127–8**, 132, 150
  summer care **8**
lemon verbena 110
Leptospermum lanigerum (woolly tea-tree) 135, 194
lettuce 4, **19**, 27, **42**, **60**, 61, 71, 79, 87, **93**, 113, **116**, 120, 132, 134, 141, **156**, 178, 181, 184, 185, 190
  companion planting **103**, 104
  fertilizing 15, 111, 150, 168, **176**
  seedlings **160**, 176
leucadendron 99, 196
leucospermum 196
Liatris (blazing star) 49
lilac 3, **85**, **110**
  Persian 87
lilium 3, 56, 61, 79, **105**, 110, **198–9**
lily of the valley 24, 45, 51, 105, 109–10, **163**
lily pond 113, 120
lime 23, **46–7**, 49, 61, 73, 104, 141, 149, 179, 190
  on ornamentals 30, 131, 158
  on vegetables 19, 25, 27, 38, 41, 42, 45, 55, 68, 79, 93, 95, 100, 116, 119, 133, 134, 145, 155, 156, 164
linaria 3, 15, 27, 131, 150, 176, 184, 186
linum 176
liquid fertilizer 26, 66
  for houseplants 16, 62, 67, 74, 87, 94, 114, 132, 185, 192
  for ornamental garden 20, 183
  when transplanting 109
  for vegetables 3, 15, 29, 38, 45, 60, 79, 152, 153, 156, 168
Liquidambar 84, 144
  styraciflua 135
Lithospermum diffusum 181
liverwort 69
Livingstone daisy 5, 131, 150, 168, 184
lobelia 3, 5, 15, 27, 79, 131, 141, 150, 168, 176, 184, 198
loganberry 7, 53
Lonicera japonica (golden honeysuckle) 106–7
Luculia gratissima 96
lunaria 131, 150, 168, 176, 184
lupin 3, 5, 15, 27, 45, 48, 49, 61, 67, 79, 93, 110, 113, 131, 133, 150, **160**, 168, 184, 186
  dividing 91
  seed 161
lychnis 3

magnesium 46, 47, **66**, 67–8
Magnolia **141–2**
  evergreen **110**
  soulangiana 51
  stellata 96
  transplanting 51
mahonia 24, 110
Malus floribunda (crab-apple) 85
mammothberry 7
Mancozeb 3, 140–1
manure 14, 29, 42, 50, 62, **111**, 113, 123, 156, 199
  fish waste 37
  poultry litter 150, 151, 161
  see also animal manure
maple
  Japanese 24, 186

pruning 34, 45, **48**, **158**, 186
Marathane 18
marginal leaf scorch 28, 65, 67, **105**, 114
marguerite daisy 79
marigold 195
  African 3, 5, 15, 131, 147, 150, 168, 176, 184, 186, **197**
  French 131, 150, 184
marjoram (*Origanum majorana*) **36**
marrow 4, **18**, 132, 141, 150, **156**, 159, 168, 184, 190
marshmallow weed 126
mealy bug 28, 132, 169, 185
Melaleuca 144, 196
  diosmifolia **40–1**
  spathulata 135–6
  thymifolia 110, 137
Melissa officinalis (balm) 36
melon 4, **18**, 126, 132, 140, 184
Mentha (mint) **36**
Mexican orange blossom (*Choisya ternata*) 196
Michelia figo (portwine magnolia) **110**
mignonette
  flower 79, 131, 150, 168, 176, 184
  lettuce 19, 39, 176
mildew **18**, 28, 114, 140, 178
mimulus 131, 150, 168, 184
mineral deficiency in soil *see* soil
miniature rose **62**, 88
mint (*Mentha*) 35, **36**, 167
mint-bush 167
mites 18, 46, **105**
mock orange (*Philadelphus coronarius*) 110
moluccella 131, 150, 168, 184
molybdenum 190
monstera 111, 138–9
moss **68–9**
mothballs 158
mother shield fern (*Polystichum proliferum*) 24
mulberry 56
mulching 5, 13, **39**, 69, 72, 92, **118**, 151, 186, 189
  berryfruit 7, 16, 46, **54**, 58, 62, **71**, 132, **140**
  citrus trees 143
  fruit trees 46, 50, 84, 94, 124, 132, 139–40, 150
  herbaceous borders 61

for hot summer **146–7**
ornamentals 84, 131, 157, 167, 183
to protect soil **75–6**
rock garden 102
seaside garden 196–7
seaweed 37
soil improvement 135, 162–3
vegetables 3, **14**, 17–18, 62, 76, 79, 113, 122, 124, 132, 150, 152, 153, 154, 155, 161, 168, 180, 184
for weed control **75**, 76, 89, 94, 119, 175
mustard 104, 132
myoporum 196
myosotis 3, 5, 15, 27, 45, 61, 79, 93, 113, 131, 150, 168, 184

Nandina domestica (Japanese sacred bamboo) 87
naphthalene 158
nasturtium 3, 5, 15, 27, 131, 147, 150, 160, 168, 176, 184, 195, 198
native plants *see* Australian plants
nectarine 32, 74, 115, 150, 186, **202**
choosing **56, 86**
fertilizing 11, 184
leaf curl 46, 62, 65, **114**, 179
pests 11, 49, 50, 150, 182
planting **14**
pruning 80
seedlings 86
nemesia 3, 15, 27, 45, 55, 131, 150
nemophila 131, 150, 168, 176, 184
nerine 55, 61, 82
nerium 83
New Zealand mirror-leaf (*Coprosma repens*) 196
New Zealand spinach 168
nigella 131, 150, 168, 176, 184
Nile lily (*Agapanthus orientalis*) 163
nitrogen, animal manure for 66, 67, 147
Norfolk Island pine 196
nurseries 73–5, 194
nut trees **56, 57**, 186
see also almond; hazelnut; walnut

oak leaves 84
Ocimum basilicum (basil) 36, 104
oka (*Oxalis tuberosa*) 119
okra 132, 150, 168, 184
oleander 126, **164**
olearia 196
olive 126
onion maggot 116
onions 18, **42**, 45, 55, **68**, 71, 79, 87, 93, 94, **99–101**, 106, 113, **116**, 120, **122**, 132, 133, 141, 150, **156**, 168, 188
companion planting **103**, 104, 123
fertilizing 47, 112
harvesting 33
lifting 15, 27
mulching 76
orange tree 126, 127
organic growing **13–14**
oriental poppy 3, 15, 27, 45, 61, 79, 93, 113, 131, 141, 150, 168, 184
Origanum majorana (marjoram) **36**
ornamental garden
planting 3, 5, 15, 27, 39, 61, 79, 93, 113, 120, 131–2, 141, 147, 149–50, 167–8, 183–4, 195
weeds 47, 62, 131, 149, 167
see also blood and bone; lime; mulching; watering
ornamental kale 3, 15, 27, 45 , 61, 79, 93
ornamental trees **84–5**
almond 57
pests 181
pruning 158, 186
ornamental vegetables **175–6**
outdoor living area 186–7
Ovens wattle (*Acacia pravissima*) 90, 106, 193
overfeeding 66
ovicide 4
Oxalis 117, **118–19**, 141
corniculata (yellow wood sorrel) 119
rubra (barber's pole) 119
tuberosa (oka) 119
Oyster Bay pine 196

Paeonia suffruticosa (tree peony) 161
paeony 47, 48, 49, 79

paeony rose 47, 93
painted daisy 126
pallid bottlebrush (*Callistemon pallidus*) 96, 106, 194
palm 4, 169, 185
pansy 3, 15, 27, 61, 79, 93, 113, 131, 150, 168, 184, 186
paperbark (*Melaleuca spathulata*) 135–6
parsley (*Petroselinum crispum*) 4, 15, **36**, 39, 120, 132, 141, 150, 168, 184
as border 175–6
companion planting 103, 104
parsnip 4, 15, **18**, 96, 113, **115–16**, **122**, 127, 132, 133, 141, 150, **156**, 168, 184, 190
companion planting **103–4**
passionfruit 56, 107, 121, 151, 159
pruning 127, **128**
passionvine hopper 159
paths
location of 107–8
making 24, **128–9**
patio, making 128–9
peach tree 74, 186, **202**
choosing **56**, 86
dwarf flowering 88
fertilizing 50, 111, 184
grafting 115
harvesting 32
leafcurl 62, 65, **114**, 179
pests 4, 10, 11, 46, **49–50**, 150, 182
pruning 50, 80, 179
pear and cherry slug 4, **11**, 179, 184
pear tree 56, 86, **115**, 186, **202**
choosing **57**
harvesting 28, **32–3**, 121
pests 4, 11, 114, 132, 158, 159, 168
pruning 80, **140**
peas 15, **42**, 45, 61, 79, 93, 95, 106, 113, 121, 132, 133, 134, 141, 150, **156**, 160, 181
companion planting 103, **104**
disease 178
fertilizing 47, **68**, 111, 112
harvesting **122**
improving yield **119–20**
supporting 168
pelargonium 25, 88, 169
penstemon 3, 5, 15, 27, 45, 61,

79, 93, 113, 168, 184
  dividing 120, 141
peppermint 36
perennial pea 15
perennials 47, **48–9**
  cuttings 141
  dividing 79, 91, 113, 131, 141
  planting 12, 158
  pruning 55
pergola 187
Persian lilac 87
persimmon 56
pest control 13–14, **174–5, 178–9**
  in autumn **63–5**
  herbs for 35
  oil *see* winter oil
  in spring **158–9**
  in summer **10–12**
  see also Clensel; Dipel; pyrethrum; white oil emulsion
pests *see* particular insects
Petroselinum crispum see parsley
petunia 3, 5, 15, 131, 147, 150, 168, 176, 184, 195, **197**
Philadelphus coronarius (mock orange) 110
philodendron 111
Phlox 3, 5, 15, 141, 147, 168, 176, 184, 195, **198**
  subulata 23
phosphorus 39, **66**, **67**, 73, **111–12**
  see also superphosphate
Photinia glabra rubens 88
Pieris 5, 87, 105, 108, 167, **188**
  feeding 141, 186
  forrestii 24
pin-cushion plant (*Hakea laurina*) **41**
pine needles 58
pinks 110
plant lice *see* aphids
plantain 7
planting
  citrus trees **115**
  for colour **95–6**
  in containers **86–8**
  cuttings 131
  deciduous trees and shrubs **88–9**
  dry weather **12–13**
  for foliage colour **98–9**, 196
  for privacy **40–1, 105–7**
  for a scented garden **109–10**

summer annuals **173–4**
  see also ornamental garden; vegetables
platycodon 131, 150, 168, 184
plum tree 18, **100**, 186
  choosing **56–7, 86**
  European **56**, 80, **115, 121, 202**
  flowering 85
  harvesting 32
  Japanese **56–7**, 80, 111, 115, **122, 201**
  pests 4, 11
  pruning 132
podalyria 83, 109, 196
poinciana 109
poinsettia (*Euphorbia pulcherrima*) 163
poisonous plants **163–4**
polyanthus 3, 15, 27, 45, 61, 79, 131, 150
  dividing 91
Polystichum proliferum (mother shield fern) 24
pools, creating **21–3**
poplar 7, 144
poppy *see* Iceland poppy; oriental poppy
portulaca 3, 147, 168, 176, 184
portwine magnolia (*Michelia figo*) 110
possums 90–1
potash *see* sulphate of potash
potassium 39, **67**, 112
potato 107, **115, 122**, 127, 132, 133, 150, 168, 190
  companion planting 103, 104
  diseases 145
  harvesting 27, 79
  no-dig gardening **123–5**
  planting **145–6**
potato onion 93, 99
potato scab 145
potato vine 107
potting mixture 9, 59, 67, 87, 137–8, 185, 191
'potting-on' 138
poultry litter 150, 151, 161
primula 3, 15, 27, 45, 186
privacy, planting for **105–7**
privet **164**, 196
problems, diagnosing 65–6
prostanthera 109
protea 96, 99
prune, French 121–2

pruning 3, 24, 45, 61, 63, 73, 76–7, **82**, 95, 96, 106, 114, 117, 126, 141, 150, 153–4, 169, 181, 182, 184, 186, 188–9
  Australian plants **20–1**, 93, 94, 131, 147, 167
  berryfruits 7, 46, 47, **53–5**, 62, 64–5
  citrus trees 8, **127–8**, 132
  deciduous plants 74, 89
  'easy-bleeders' **47–8**
  fruit trees 4, **18**, 28, 34, 46, 47, 48, 62, **80**, 94, 107, 132, 140, 158, 168, 179
  houseplants 16
  perennials 55
  shrubs **79**
  in spring **147**
pruning tools **69–70**
  as gifts 195
Prunus
  blireana **84**
  elvins **84**
  Japanese flowering cherry 85
  serrulata (green cherry tree) **84**
  'Shirofugen' 85
  'Shirotae' 85
*psoralia 109
pumpkin 4, **18**, 113, 115, **122**, 132, 140, 141, **151–2**, 153, **156**, **161**, 168, 184, 190
  companion planting 103, **104**, 133
  fertilizing 111
  germinating 150
  harvesting **52–3**, 61
  pests 159
purple beech 99
pyracantha 196
pyrethrum **4**, 8, **10**, 11, 12, 15, 46, 64, 65, 105, 123, 131, 132, 143, 149, 150, 159, 168, 179, 182, 184

Quercus ilex (holm oak) 196
quince 4, 56, **57**, 132, 158, 159
  Japanese flowering (*Chaenomeles*) **95–6**

radish 4, 15, **20**, 27, 39, **42**, 71, 74, 113, 120, 132, 141, 150, 160, 168, 181, 184, 185, 190

companion planting 103, **104**
rainbow chard 175
ranunculus 15, 27, 45, 55, 61
raspberry 56, **168**, **184**
   pruning 4, 7, 46, **54–5**
   transplanting **71**
raspberry leaf rust 168
redcurrant 53
red-spider (mites) 105
repotting 28, 46, **114**, **132**, **137**, **138–9**, **151**
retaining walls 171–3, 179–81
Rhododendron 3, 65, 69, 113, **139**, 169, **188**
   dwarf 16, 87
   fertilizing 37, 46, 124, 141, 186, 190, 191
   fragrantissimum 110
   pests **105**
   in pots **105**
   transplanting 41, **50–1**, 82, **104–5**, 108
   watering 5, 167, 170
rhubarb 10, **18**, 79, **85**, 150, **164**, 168, 190
river she-oak 144
rock garden **23**, 62
   blood and bone in 102
   creating **101–2**
   mulching 102
   plants for 72, 76, **101–2**, 146
Rogor 11, **65–6**, 105
roses 12, **18**, 24, 36, **44**, 79, 94, **107**, 120, 136, 147, 157, 173
   aphids 10, 64, 131, 149
   black spot 3, **15**, 171, 183
   choosing 61, **62**, 73, 74–5
   companion planting **30–1**, 103
   cuttings 45
   dead-heading 3, **20**, **169**, 182, **188**
   fertilizing 149, 190
   floribunda 62, **77**, 110
   hybrid tea **62**, **77**, 110
   miniature **62**, 88
   planting **74–5**, **88–9**
   pruning 3, **76–7**, 113, 127, 141, 188
   scented **110**
   staking 155
   transplanting 51, 83, 109
   watering **170–1**
   wind damage **83**
rosemary 110, 196
   prostrate 90

rosemary grevillea (*Grevillia rosmarinifolia*) 90
rowan 4, 11
rubber plant 138–9
rudbeckia 5, 131, 141, 150, 168, 184, 195 , 198
rust 19, 168
ryecorn 27, **40**, 74, 133, 145

sage (*Salvia officinalis*) **36**, 103, 110
Saintpaulia see African violet
salpiglossis 132, 150, 168, 176, 184
salsify 4, 113, 132, 133, 141, 150, 168, 184, 190
Salvia 3, 5, 132, 147, 150, 168, 176, 177, 184, 195, 198
   officinalis (sage) **36**, 103, 110
sandy soil 171
   improving **162–3**
Santolina chamaecyparissus (cotton lavender) 98
sanvitalia 168
saponaria 15
saw, pruning 70
sawfly 179
scabiosa 3, 5, 15, 27, 45, 132, 150, 168, 184
scale insects 10, 62, 114
   citrus 8, 28, 31, **115**, 132, **143**, 150
   hardwax **126–7**
   hydrangea 63, 126
scarlet runner beans 12, 176
scented plants **109–10**
schizanthus 132, 150, 168, 176, 184
scleranthus 69
scorzonera 168
sea sand 37
seaside garden **196–7**
seawater 38
seaweed 14, 58, 66, 87, 112, 198
   for foliar feeding **9–10**, 190, 192
   on houseplants 26, 185, 192
   as mulch **37**, 62, 161
   on vegetables 20, 42, 62, 120, 124, 161, **168**
secateurs **69**, 70, **195**
seed 9, 17, 184, 187, 190
   germination **140**, **160–1**
   sowing 59–60, 131

storing 21
seedlings
   annuals **197–8**
   containers for 187
   raising **96–8**
self-sufficiency **121–2**
Senecio 196
   cineraria (dusty miller) 98
shade-lovers **23–4**, 87
shallots 61, 93, **99**, 190
   companion planting 103, 104
shasta daisy 3, 15, 27, 45, 61, 79, 93, 113
   dividing 91
sheep's sorrel 75
sheet composting 147, 162
she-oak 72
silver birch (*Betula pendula*) **11**, 135, **160**
   pests 181
   pruning 34, 45, 48, **158**, 186
silver foliage 196
silverbeet 4, 13, **19**, 39, 42, 71, 87, 113, **116**, 120, 134, 141, **156**, 175, 181, 185, 190
   companion planting **104**
   fertilizing 15, 111, 150
slaters 158
sloping garden **71–2**, 75
   retaining walls **179–81**
   watering 170
   windbreak 193
slugs **11**, 58, **132**, 146, 149, 151, 174–5
snails **11**, **132**, 146, 149, 151, 174–5
snapdragon 126, 195
soaker hose 170
sodium molybdate 20, 42, 155, 190
soft treefern (*Dicksonia antarctica*) 24
soil
   acidic 19, 37, 46, 49, 111
   annuals 197
   Australian plants 73
   clay 135, 141, 143, 162
   draining **52**
   erosion 75, 76
   feeding **39–40**
   herb garden 35, 48
   improving 37, 39–40, 46–7, 65, 124, **134–6**
   mineral deficiencies in **66–8**, **162**, **190**

organic growing 13
ornamental garden 30
protecting with mulch **75–6**
rock garden 23, 101–2
sandy **162–3,** 171
at the seaside 196
seedlings 97, 161
spring bulbs 31
sweetening **46–7**
testing kit 46, 68
vegetable garden 14, 19, 20
solomon's seal 24, 105
sophora 109, 160, 161
sorrel 46
sour cherry 56
sow thistle 174
Spanish bluebell 31
spearmint 36
spinach **42**, 45, 79, 113, 132, 150
    English **19**, **38**, 71, **95**, 106
    fertilizing **68**, 111
    New Zealand 168
    seedlings **96**
spiraea 16, 79
spring onion 4, 15, **19**, 27, **42**, 45, **156**, 168, 181, 184, 185, 190
sprouts *see* Brussels sprouts
squash 113
    see also winter squash
Stachys lanata (lamb's ears) 98
stakes **83–4**, 155, 165, 185
    Australian plants 20–1, 72, 117
    dahlias 199
    deciduous plants 88
    magnolias 142
    tomatoes 153
statice 3, 5, 79, 132, 150, 168, 176, 184
steep banks *see* sloping garden
sticky wattle (*Acacia fimbriata*) 106, 193
stock 3, 15, 27, 45, 56, 61, 79, 93, 126, 147, 168, 176, 184, 186
stone fruit *see* fruit trees
strawberries **46**, 56, **58–9**, 79, **80**, 94, 103, 106, 132, 134, **151**
strelitzia 137
succulents 4, 9, 25, 138, 169, 185, **195**
sulphate of ammonia 7, 11, 67, **111**, 121, 136, 137, 167
sulphate of iron 7

sulphate of potash 26, 39, 41–2, 55, 61, **67**, 90, 97, 110, **112**, 113, 124, 136–7, 138, 139, 153, 167, 177, 185
    on herb garden 35
    on lawn 6, 34
    in potting mixture 87
sultanas 81
summer cabbage 59, 132, 133
summer savoury 103
sun rose (*Helianthemum*) **173**
sunflower 3, 147, 160, 168, 195, 198
sunlight 23, 31, 62, 66, 157
    container plants 87
    greenhouses 191, 192
    in herb gardens 35, 48
    for houseplants 25, 88, 169
    landscaping 23–4, 44
    in rock gardens 101
    seedlings 98
superphosphate 26, 39, 67, 87, 88, **111–12**, 120, 138, 156
    Australian plants 73
    herbs 35
    lawns 34
swede 4, 15, 19, 27, 113, **122**, 133, 141, 150, 168, **184**, 185
sweet bay (*Laurus nobilis*) 87, 126
sweet cherry tree **56**, **202**
    pests 10, 178–9, **181**, 182
    pruning 80
sweet chestnut tree 56, 57
sweet William 3, 15, 27, 45, 55, 61, 79, 93
sweetcorn 113, 115, **122**, 141, 150, 153, **156**, **161–2**, 168, 181, 184, 190
    companion planting **103**, 104, 133
    fertilizing 15, 43, 111
    mulching 4, 76, 147
sweetgum tree 135
sweetpea 3, 15, 27, 45, 79, 110, 132, 150, 160, 176, 186
sycamore leaves 84
Symphytum officinale (comfrey) 36

tagetes 141
tamarix 196
tampala 132, 150, 168, 184
tansy 163
taps, location of 108
tarragon (*Artemisia dracunculus*) 36

tassel bush (*Garrya elliptica*) **96**
tecoma 107
thrip 65–6, 125
thryptomene 96, 167
Thuja 51
    occidentalis 99
thunbergia 168, 184
thyme (*Thymus vulgaris*) 36, 110
tibouchina 79
ticbeans 27, 40, 67
tirenia 184
tomatoes 61, 79, 113, 115, **122**, 132, 133, 134, **137**, 141, 150, **156**, 168, 184, 185, 190, 192
    blossom-end rot 17, 154, 186
    companion planting 103, **104**
    fertilizing 15, **66**, 112
    germination 140
    harvesting **13**, **33**, 176
    improving yield **153–5**
    mulching 4, 76, 147, 180, 186
    as ornamentals 176
    pests 126, 159, 178
    staking 83
    watering 186
tools **69–70**
    as gifts 195
torenia 168, 184
toxic plants 163–4
trace elements 190–1
transplanting 65, 81, **82–3**, 104–5, **108–9**
    Australian plants 72, 83, 109
    berryfruits 71
    citrus trees 41, 51, 108
    deciduous plants 51, 74–5, 82, 109
    evergreens 27, 41, **50–1**, 61, 113
    shrubs 41
tree peony (*Paeonia suffruticosa*) 161
treefern, soft (*Dicksonia antarctica*) 24
trees
    killing of 7–8
    ornamental **84–5**, 158, 181, 186
    problem 7
    too big 144
    see also transplanting
trellises 106
tritonia 168
tropical plants 192
tub plants *see* container plants
tuberosa 49

tulip **39**, 45, 55, 61
  lifting 198
turnip 4, 15, **19**, 27, 39, 45, 61, 71, 113, 120, 132, 133, 141, 150, 168, 184, 185
  companion planting 104
twitch-grass 58, 177, 189
two-spotted mite 46

Ulmus procera (golden elm) 99
ursinia 176

variegated dead nettle (*Lamiastrum*) 24
vegetables 3–4, 15, 27, 55, 61, 67, 68, 71, 74, 94, 106, 141, 181, 189, 190
  companion planting **103–4**
  compost **14**, 45, 93
  crop rotation 133–4
  germinating seed **140**
  greenhouse 192
  harvesting **52–3**, 152
  late planting **38–9**
  ornamental **175–6**
  organic **13–14**
  protected sowing **59–60**
  in seaside garden 197
  seedlings 96
  for spring **41–2, 115–16**
  for summer eating **155–6**
  winter and spring **19–20**
  see also animal manure; blood and bone; lime; fertilizer; mulching; watering
verbena 3, 5, 15, 132, 141, 147, 150, 168, 176, 184, 195, 198
  lemon 110
vertical garden 179–81
Viburnum **16**, 96, 190
  bitchiuense **110**
  burkwoodii **110**
  carlesii 87, **110**
  tinus 24
viminaria 109, 117
vinca 5, 132, 150, 168, 184
viola 3, 15, 27, 45, 55, 132, 150, **177**, 184, 186
violet 45, 110, 184
virgilia 109
Virginia creeper 107
Virginian stock 3
viscaria 132, 150, 168, 176, 184, 195

wallflower 3, 5, 15, 27, 45, 55, 109, 132, 150, 186
walls, landscaping with 171–3, 179–81
walnut **57**
  pruning 34, 45, **48, 158**, 186
watering 20, 24, 66, 67, 76, 156, 159, 167, 198
  Australian plants 96, **170, 171**
  citrus 5, 8, 16, 128, 143, 170
  container plants 186, 188
  cuttings 17
  deep watering 186, 198
  drip irrigation 151, **171**, 183
  fruit trees 16, 50, 151, 182, 186
  hanging baskets 9
  houseplants 4–5, 9, 12, 28, 46, 62, 65, 79, 80, 87, 94, 114, 169, **185**, 192, 195
  lawns 6, 18, 34, 51, **170**
  and mulching 76
  ornamental garden 5, 15, 26, 28, 30, 67, 125, 157, **170–1**, 174, 183, 199
  vegetables 3, 17–18, 19, 152, 153, 154, 162, 166, 168, **170**
water-lily 23
  dividing 113, 120
wattle **72, 96**, 110, **160–1**
  pruning **94**, 131, **147**
wax plant (*Eriostemon myoporoides*) **41**
weedkillers, sea products 37, 38
weeds 17, 37, 38, 40, 84, 98, 134, 141, 174, 177, 189
  as compost **178**
  control by mulch **75**, 76, 89, 94, 119, 175
  fruit bushes 58, 151
  grass as **117–18**
  groundcover for **89–90**
  lawn 7, 121, 137, 141, 146–7, 201
  ornamental garden 47, 62, 131, 149, 167
  oxalis **118–19**
  vegetables 19, 94, 123, 124, 150, 155, 165, 168
weeping bottlebrush (*Callistemon viminalis*) 106
weigela 16
Westringia 72, 196
  fruiticosa 136
wheelbarrow 195
whiptail 20, 42, 155, **190**
white cabbage butterfly
  caterpillar 60, **63–4**, 79, 116, **159**
white oil emulsion 4, 8, 31, **50**, 62, **63**, 114, **115, 126**, 127, 132, 143, 150, **158–9**, 168, 184
white onion 71, 79, 150
whiteflies 159
willow **7**, 144
wilting 66
wind
  and Australian plants 117
  damage **83–4**, 85, 141, 199
  and fruit trees 143
  -resistant plants 99, 196
windbreak **44, 84, 193–4**
winter cabbage 133
winter lettuce 39, 45
winter oil spray (now called pest oil) **81**, 94, 114, **115**
winter squash 132, 133, 141, 150, **151–2, 156**, 168, 190
wintersweet (*Chimonanthus praecox*) **95,** 110
wisteria 83, 109, **164**, 187
witch hazel (*Hamamelis mollis*) 110
woodchips 146
woolly tea-tree (*Leptospermum lanigerum*) 135, 194
worms 14

yellow wood sorrel (*Oxalis corniculata*) 119
yew 88
youngberry 7, 54

Zineb 140, 168
zinnia 3, 5, 132, **149**, 150, 168, 176, 184, 195, **197**
zucchini 132, 133, 150, **156**, 168, 178, 184
  companion planting 103